To My Fellow Traveller,

Trusting this J evokes happy memories.

Ron.

June '91.

THREE RIVERS OF FRANCE

To the French Resistance of the River-Country
To those who died and are remembered
And to those who live and remember
I dedicate this book
F.W.

FREDA WHITE

THREE RIVERS OF FRANCE

Photographs and Commentary by
MICHAEL BUSSELLE

PAVILION
MICHAEL JOSEPH

First published in 1952 by
Faber and Faber Limited
This edition published in Great Britain in 1989 by
PAVILION BOOKS LIMITED
196 Shaftesbury Avenue, London WC2H 8JL
in association with Michael Joseph Limited
27 Wrights Lane, Kensington, London W8 5TZ

Designed by Bernard Higton

A CIP catalogue record for this book is available from
the British Library

ISBN: 1 85145 290 7

10   9   8   7   6   5   4   3   2   1

Typeset by Dorchester Typesetting Group Limited
Printed and bound in Italy by Arnoldo Mondadori

PUBLISHER'S NOTE 1989

Freda White's *Three Rivers of France*, first published in 1952, was quickly recognized as a travel classic. A new edition, revised by the author, was issued in 1962, but she died before she had time to prepare a third edition. This, which appeared in 1972, with a few small revisions by the late Henry Myhill, forms the text of the present edition.

Some of the information in Freda White's text as well as the practical advice she offered at the end of her book had inevitably become out of date. In this edition the former has been remedied where it was felt necessary by notes to the text. The latter has been replaced by a Guide for the Modern Traveller by Michael Busselle, who has also added an Introduction, and by a section of practical advice compiled by Barbara Mellor, who also prepared the notes.

The Publishers of this edition would like to express their thanks for permission to reproduce the text to Faber and Faber and the estate of Freda White.

Photographs. Half-title page: Summer sunshine on the River Lot, in the upper valley between Ste-Eulalie d'Olt and St-Geniez.
Title page: Looking eastwards at sunrise along the River Dordogne from the esplanade in the hilltop bastide of Domme.

CONTENTS

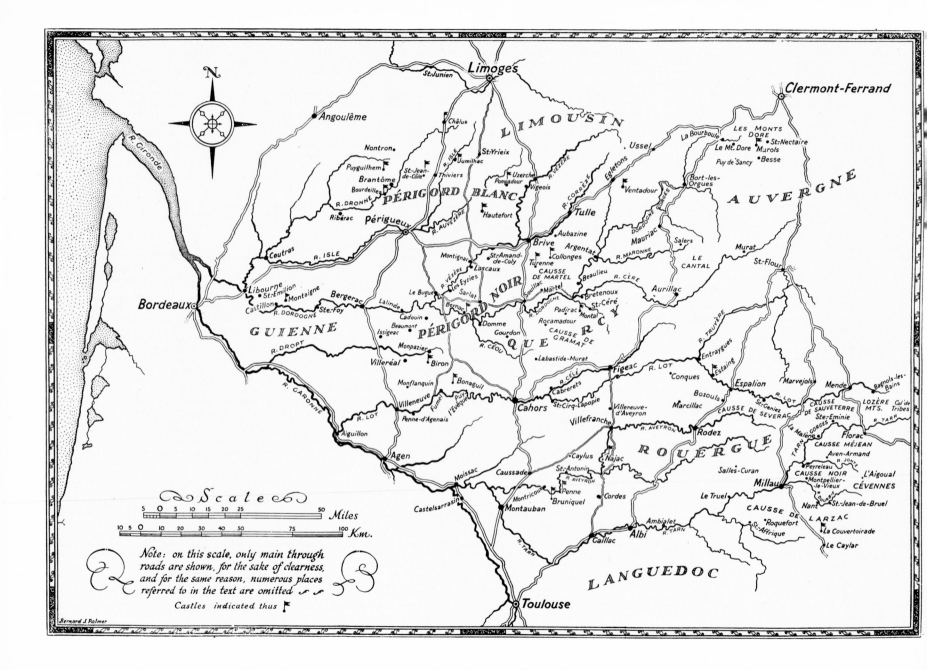

INTRODUCTION

Like almost everyone who has travelled in the south-west of France, I have been aware for many years that *Three Rivers of France* is the definitive book on the subject. Freda White's sure grasp of history and culture; her persistent and infectious curiosity and appetite for knowledge; the enviable lightness of touch with which she imparts it: these are the attributes of a first-class travel writer, and apparent in all her books.

Just how *useful* her masterpiece can still be to the traveller only fully came home to me in the summer of 1987 when I visited the Tarn, one of the few areas described in the book which was unfamiliar to me. Avidly read before setting off, and constantly referred to in the course of the holiday, *Three Rivers* turned out to be much more than a classic of armchair travel literature: it was an immensely helpful practical guide.

That this should still be so, 36 years after the book first appeared, seemed extraordinary; and it was during that Tarn holiday that an intriguing idea took root: how fascinating it would be to retrace Freda White's steps and to photograph the scenes she describes and to produce a new, fully illustrated edition of her classic book. The idea drew an enthusiastic response from my publisher, and in the summer of 1988 the project got under way. The three months of intensive travelling in Freda White's stimulating company turned out to be one of the most rewarding experiences of this photographer's working life, and at the end of it my admiration for the book was greater than ever.

On setting out, eager to visit the places which Freda White described, I was also curious to see how much they had changed. It occurred to me that it might be helpful to add some sort of brief commentary for the traveller who, like me, was using her book as a practical guide. Surprisingly, what struck one quite often was how *little* the places had changed; but there are indeed passages which are out of date, a few which could even mislead. However, rather than make unwanted intrusions into her flow, the best course of action seemed to be to keep comments to a minimum and, where necessary, add up-to-date information in the form of notes. We have therefore refrained from noting every occasion where her text seems mildly out of date. It goes without saying that many places have changed, some regrettably, in the intervening years. Readers will be able to judge for themselves which of her comments—usually those concerning the absence of tourists and cars—may be taken with a pinch of salt. A few passages, such as her vignettes of conversation with locals and notably the delightful idyll entitled 'The Spring of Beynac' in Chapter one, can now be read as period pieces, with no loss of charm. However, where for example a building which she describes as derelict, or privately owned and inaccessible, is now restored and open to the public, the fact has been noted.

Because the area covered by the book is extensive, more so in fact than it appears on the map, and most travellers have a limited amount of time, it is sensible to be selective. I have therefore taken the liberty of suggesting, in Chapter eighteen, how the areas covered in individual chapters can be combined to create a series of tours which can be comfortably explored in a couple of weeks or so. This is not always the order in which the book is written. Although it was planned to flow admirably in an editorial sense, some sequences work less conveniently as a tour. I have also added some notes about hotels, which I hope will be useful, and have tried to describe the cuisine and wines which are characteristic of each region.

As I followed in Freda White's footsteps, I sometimes almost began to feel her presence. I found myself wondering what she would have felt about the photographs I was taking. I hope she would have approved.

Michael Busselle

CHAPTER ONE

THE REGION

Introduction

The Dordogne, the Lot and the Tarn are sister rivers. They rise in the Massif Central, and run westwards towards the Atlantic. Their streams give life to a beautiful region of France.

Many nations have a word for their countries, to express what they believe them to be—perhaps what they wish they were. For the English, their land was for long 'merry England'. For the Scots, Scotland is still 'bonny'; and for the French, France is always 'la belle'. The Industrial Revolution killed much of the merriment of England, as it has killed much of the beauty of France. But France is a wide land, able to hold great stretches where the towns have hardly spread beyond the limits of their ancient walls, and the countryside is untarnished. This river region is one of these, so that the stranger, looking at it, will cry: 'Now I know why they say "la belle France"!'

Here, too, France is truly herself. Most foreigners visiting the continent of Europe make straight for Paris, and rightly. No country save France could have made Paris. Yet Paris is not France, any more than New York is the United States, and much less than London is England. The real life of France is elsewhere, especially in the farms and the little country towns. It is only by observing them that the traveller can understand the toughness, the vitality, the resilience of that manner of living and thinking which is called 'French civilization'. So if he is wise he will divide his time. He will spend half of it, and more than half his money, in seeing the sights of Paris, in storing his memory with the masterpieces packed into a city which is itself a masterpiece. He will bow himself out, as a courtier bows himself out of the presence of an old, indifferent queen. Then he will straighten his back, and go away and look at ordinary places and talk to ordinary people. And after dawdling for a short time in a country such as this of the south-western rivers, the wise traveller will know far more about France than if he had never left the capital.

Not only the present, but the past of the region is exciting to anyone who has a sense of history. Blake saw the world in a grain of sand, and eternity in an hour. But here between the rivers the stranger does not need the intuition of the mystic, but only the eyes in his head. Eternity, in any case, is a long word, too long for most of us, who are astonished if at rare intervals we can imagine the movement of time. Now the time of man's history, and of the history of the earth that is so much older than humanity, lie here revealed, layer upon layer, plain to the sight. The revelation is daunting at first, till dread turns to ravishment.

The riversides are little known outside of France. Indeed only a small part of them is commonly known to the French themselves. They are luckily unsuited to mass tourist traffic, for they have inadequate accommodation to offer to crowds, and no herd entertainments. The country is wrong for the innocent souls who want to build sand castles, and far more wrong for those who need promenades, casinos, and cinemas to stuff their empty skulls. But to lovers of beauty, to lovers of history, to those whom the French call people of cultivation, this land has everything to offer. Let them come here, and beauty and history will fill their minds as water fills a spring.

Land and Water

Once upon a time—that is how all the stories begin, even the story of the earth. But the earth was very old already, before this story, although it happened long ago, about two hundred million years, so the geologists think. Well, once upon a time, most of south-western France lay under the sea. The shore of that waste of waters was made of hill-ranges, the dark rocks of the Limousin, of Auvergne and of the Cévennes. The gulf that lay between them has been called by men of today 'the Basin of Aquitaine'. The tides washed to and fro within it, laying first a layer of sand and clay which hardened into a waterproof sea-bottom. Then slowly, slowly, for millions of years, the waves cast the shells and bones of sea-creatures on the beaches and ground them down till the ocean bed was covered far out to sea with a deep shelf of lime. All through these ages the mountains bordering it were wearing away. Pebble by pebble, grain by grain, their crests were washed down into the valleys. At the same time the earth was gradually rising, shouldering itself out of the sea where it found the least resistance. The waters ran down and out, as the sandstone and lime of the sea-bed worked nearly up to the level of the mainland hills. By that time the lime itself was three thousand feet deep where it met the inlet-heads of the old basin.

But the earth was far from having settled down. The terrific upheavals which made Europe as we know it were still to come. About fifty million years ago an age of volcanic eruption set in. The whole of the continent was wrenched and twisted into new shapes. The folding or wrinkling of the earth's crust threw up new mountain ranges; first the Pyrenees lifted skywards, and later the Alps. The older hills took the thrust, and themselves were changed. The Cévennes and the Auvergne

rose much higher. Between them and the hard plateaux of Rouergue and Limousin the softer rock of the old limestone layers was squeezed till it cracked every here and there. The scientific name for these cracks is 'faults', and indeed they are like the cracks in faulty china.

Nor were the great foldings the end of the story. In the ages that came after, long periods of intense cold were followed by warmer times when the ice-cap covering part of the mountains melted away, and the land became a boggy waste drained by enormous rivers. The waters of the sea sometimes came inland far beyond their present shores.

Yet gradually the mainland as we know it took form. The hardstone heights, the 'Massif Central', make a sort of capital C turned westwards. The Auvergne and Cantal volcanoes run north and south to form its back. The Limousin stretches westwards at the northern end, the tangle of the Lozère and the Cévennes at the south. Caught between these ridges are the limestone plateaux, the 'Causses', which continue far west of them, lessening in height between widening valleys till they level out near to the Atlantic coast. Seen from an aeroplane they ridge the land like reefs running out to sea, which is exactly what they once were.

It is the mountains and the causses that made the river-system of the south-west. The streams rise in the high hills, run through the faults of the causses, and find their way to the Atlantic.

The series of hills and valleys is tilted from north-east to south-west. The typical shape of a hill is a long slow slope westwards, a fairly gentle fall to the south, and an abrupt northern edge. As a result, the rivers have a long south-westerly course till they reach one of the sharp northern ridges which turns them westwards to seek the sea. Thus the Dordogne is the main stream of a system which rises in the Monts Dore and the Limousin plateau. The great river itself runs swiftly down from the heights through steep-sided gorges, till it meets the limestone of the Causse de Gramat. After that it follows the cliffs westwards to the plain of Bergerac, where a barely

Opposite: The Causse de Gramat in winter, from the road between Calès and Rocamadour.

10

A small roadside cascade on the Col de Redondet, below the summit of Puy Mary.

But the small streams which join it from the south, with the exception of the Cère, are all short-run.

The Lot and the Tarn are both tributaries of the Garonne. They rise in the Lozère and the Cévennes mountains, and with their various affluents run finally into the great river which is sometimes called the 'Gutter of Languedoc'. They, too, have long tributaries from the north, the Truyère and the Célé for the Lot, the Aveyron for the Tarn; though the Tarn takes a triplet of considerable streams from the Cévennes valleys to the south of it too.

It is perhaps sensible to explain at this point why this book pays no attention to the Garonne. Firstly it has an entirely different origin from the other three. It comes from the Pyrenees, curves north across Bas Languedoc, the flat wine-plain, collects the Tarn and much later the Lot, and proceeds on its businesslike way to the Gironde estuary, where only the promontory called Entre Deux Mers divides it from the mouth of the Dordogne. And then the Garonne is a useful working river, and like so many useful things, it lacks charm. It is large, it is dull, it waters Toulouse and Bordeaux. That is enough about it. These remarks would horrify a wine merchant.

This account of the formation of the region, absurdly simplified as it is, would horrify a geologist. But it is given like this partly because a book which has got to cover many questions of a technical kind will avoid, as far as possible, using technical language. All arts and sciences have their jargons. These are necessary to the scientists, and are quite natural to them. But they are often incomprehensible and nearly always boring to the lay mind. This is particularly true of modern science, which was born at a time when the old vivid names for things were used up, and fell back upon long muddling titles. So once for all, a book which is written for intelligent but unlearned readers will try to be clear rather than to be impressive.

The real reason for sketching the geology of the rivers is that it explains their curious course. In their early beginnings they are all mountain streams, such as drain the rainy hills

perceptible hollow guides it to the sea. A number of little streams and some sizeable rivers flow into it from the north. The Vézère, the Isle, and the Dronne are all long watercourses before they join the Dordogne to fill its wide Atlantic estuary.

everywhere. They tumble in waterfalls, ripple into pools. Their sides are steep, often narrow enough to be called gorges, of the v-shape eroded by water flowing with a strong head of power through ages too long to reckon. But as they reach the causses, the character of the rivers changes suddenly. There the long volcanic faults gave them their original beds. The faults are not slopes, however steep, but perpendicular cliffs where the rock has been split apart. Below the cliffs there is usually a tilted scree caused by stone falls; and below that again is the bed worn by the running river. Limestone is relatively soft, and the river-beds are worn down as straight walls, if they do not actually overhang, where the scour of water has hollowed them. And the rivers have worn the lime right down to the ancient hard sea-bed. Once they are in the limestone country, the streams do not fall very rapidly; they are fairly near sea-level all the way. Their gorges are called 'couloirs'— passages, or in the Tarn, 'canyons'.

The causses have other queer effects upon the rivers. Rain falling on the plateaux does not form streams; it just sinks into the porous rock as though it were blotting-paper. Then it works downwards, and collects in the caves and hollows with which the causses are riddled. Here and there it runs in underground rivers, at the level of the hard base, till it finds an outlet. The bottoms of the cliffs are pierced at intervals by strong springs. Many of these, in the Tarn especially, run into the beds of the rivers themselves. These springs, which are called 'resurgences', are very cold, pure, and clear. This has the surprising result that the lower reaches of the rivers are more limpid than the upper waters, which are dark-tinted with the soil and debris that colour all hill-streams. Where the cliffs are withdrawn from the river-beds, as they are towards the west, the springs furnish the drinking-water of the people. A good resurgence in this land of hot dry summers will make a city. Perhaps the best example is the Chartreuse, the fountain of Cahors. In the days of Gaul, and during the Roman Empire, it was worshipped as a goddess—as well it might be, running crystal-cold out of the scorching, chalky hill—and it is still

The Lot in the early morning, near the village of Calvignac.

carried under the Lot to supply the drinking-water of the town.

There is only one thing to be said against the causse springs. The water has been seeping slowly through lime, and it is hard, while the water of the upper streams is as soft as silk.

Even far west of the causses properly speaking, where the low hills are covered with woodland and fields, the ground has this porous, absorbent nature. So that between the water-courses it is singularly dry, and depends upon a rather untrustworthy rainfall for the ripening of the crops. Indeed the whole region makes the impression of a dry land threaded with rivers.

But the rivers give it a pattern of living waters like the veins in a leaf. Their head-springs are not far apart; they spread out to run in all the old valleys of what was once the Basin of

Aquitaine, and come together again at the Atlantic. No wonder the Romans, when they conquered this country of streams, and remembered their own precious, paltry, Tiber, gave it the name of Aquitania, the Land of Waters.

The Spring of Beynac

Above: The spring of Beynac by the road near the Hôtel Bonnet.

Opposite: A peaceful, shaded spot on the Dordogne near Beynac.

Only the road divides the cliff of Beynac from the Dordogne. The precipice starts up from the water in a series of pitches and overhangs. Houses are built on every narrow terrace. On the top, the castle juts out over 450 feet of space; with its great towers and battlements, it is the finest medieval fortalice on the river. The Hôtel Bonnet stands at the bottom beside the spring.[1]

Here is what French guide-books always call 'the centre of animation', when they describe a place. It is not a grand fountain, but merely an iron pipe sticking out of the cliff, from which a spout of water curves into an oblong stone basin on the roadside. A second basin takes the overflow, and then the water is led under the street into the Dordogne.

It took geological ages to make the spring of Beynac, but the spring made the little bourg about eight hundred years ago. Without it, the castle would never have been set upon that cliff, however madly the feudal barons were addicted to perching their forts upon rocks. The castle itself has cisterns upon its roofs, but the water they collect in winter would not last through a dry summer, let alone suffice for the needs of the people and beasts who fed the lord and his men-at-arms. Till a benevolent government tapped the rock farther up, and made three or four pumps for the upper houses, all the Beynac people came down night and morning to fill their buckets at this spring, and its companion down the road.

The spring drains the hillside behind the cliff. It runs pure and cold, strong and unfailing. Even in the terrible drought of 1949 its flow never diminished.

Today the spring has been the scene of great activity. From early morning, its second basin has been full of sheets in soak. The spout and the first basin, of course, are strictly reserved for the use of men and beasts; nobody would dream of rinsing their wash in water which the animals must drink. Two big black cauldrons have been simmering over wood fires on the ferry pier. Dozens of sheets have been boiled in them, soaked in the basin, and carried to walls from which they will be taken snowy and smelling of sunshine.

But after the silent moveless heat of the day, all Beynac wakes up in the evening. Then the guests of the Hôtel Bonnet, sitting under the Virginia creeper shade of the terrace, can observe the life of the village—or as much of its life as happens outside the old houses, outside the stone walls and the closed shutters. For its social activity concentrates in the few yards of space between the fountain and the hotel, where the road widens to a triangle, and below the road the pier runs down to make a landing for the ferry.

As the heat abates, bathers drift across the road, board the punts, the 'barques', which are the river-transport, and pole themselves to the far side, called with some exaggeration the beach. The river is shallow, with a fairly strong current. Later in the summer its level will be low; even in June it is barely cool. Still it is welcome to skins baked by the summer glare. Some of the bathers are Beynac men and boys; others hotel visitors who may include women too. But the older amphibians of Beynac tend not to bathe but to fish. The sportsmen stand in barques and use rod and line, as the fish begin to rise in the dusk. Those who are in need of larger quantities set nets sustained by floats, to be lifted in the morning. Fishing is the principal sport of the riverside people; it would be true to say that all of them can fish, and most of them do. But they fish for food as much as for sport.

The last pot-load of sheets is hardly cleared when the children gather for their nightly game. There are only about ten of them, even counting the Blonde Family of foreigners from Paris who have taken the house next to the inn for the season. They range from a lad of fifteen, who is already earning his living as a farm-hand, to a couple of two-year-old toddlers. In so small a company there can be little distinction of age, and

1 The hotel is closed in winter.

certainly none of class. They play catch, at which they are extremely adept, even with the babies running in and out among their legs and wailing for the ball. Then the game breaks up and the children take turns on the bicycle of the boy of the Blonde Family. He is thus able to exercise patronage and power (tempered by the strong sense of justice of the others), and even to curry favour with the farm-lad whom he worships. His small sister, who is the image of Alice in Wonderland, is hunting feverishly in the tiny vegetable garden by the pier, and Daniel, the hotel grandson, who has a tender heart, has gone off to help her. 'It is her tortoise,' says the waitress who has come to serve the watchers on the terrace; 'it preoccupies her.' But now maternal voices are heard calling the children, with that unmistakable evening note, on a rising tone of menace, which threatens 'No supper if you don't come at once!' In a moment the children have gone.

Then come the beasts. First a red cow is led out of her byre beneath a house, and watered. Then a horse, with a youth on its back. Then the farm-boy reappears, leading two oxen in a yoke. He does not let them drink; perhaps they cannot while they are still harnessed. Then a man from a workshop up the cliff; he strips to the waist and washes his head and arms; he must be a devotee of modern hygiene. At intervals, people come and fill their jugs at the cold source. There is running water in the inn, but it is warm with lying in a cistern, and all the visitors, last thing before going to bed, fill a wine-bottle apiece with spring water to drink in the night.

The fishers have all come home now. They stop for a few minutes to exchange news before dispersing. The river curves away, gleaming like polished steel under a jade-green sky, empty and still towards the distant railway-bridge. To the east, the red cliff where stands the rival castle, the ruin of Castelnaud, still catches a sunset reflection. Two or three young men sit on the wall still, but will anyone come out to join them? Perhaps not. Perhaps when their laughter dies away, there will be no noise except the spring plashing steadily into its basin.

CHAPTER TWO

NORTHERN APPROACHES

The Northern Marches

Hill-formation and village spring, these are the beginning and the end of the river-system. Now, the rivers themselves can be looked at one by one. British and American travellers will normally come from the north, so the Dordogne comes first, followed by the Lot and the Tarn.

It would seem the simplest method to follow the river straight from its mouth to its source. But this is not the best way of travelling it, either in description or in practice. The Dordogne is 300 miles long, and with its tributaries it covers a number of different regions, from the sea to the Monts Dore and Cantal mountains. The best thing for the motorist or walker to do is to choose a series of central points and to explore the country round them.

The account given here is not meant to replace an ordinary guide-book, for naturally the tourist will use the French guides which give place-to-place information. It attempts only to show the general nature of the country, and some things to look out for. Later it will give an idea of what lies behind the visible present, and the visible past.

The watershed of the Dordogne region is the height of land which runs westwards from the Monts Dore. The Puy de Sancy, where the Dordogne rises, is over 6,000 feet high. The stream rushes steeply down to la Bourboule, which is under 3,000. After that it has the slow fall to sea-level to make, beneath the round shoulder of the Limousin uplands. A main road runs

from Clermont-Ferrand in the Auvergne, along the plateau above the northern side of the Dordogne, by Ussel and Tulle. By then the river has turned south in its bed in the gorges, but the road follows the Corrèze to Brive, and then the Vézère till it, too, runs away south through a gap in the left-bank ridge. The road continues to stave on south-westwards through Périgueux to Bordeaux.

Now everything north of that road may be called the border-country of the river-basin. Several of the rivers have their sources north of it. The Corrèze runs its swift mountainy course by Tulle, to join the more sedate Vézère just below Brive. The Auvézère and the Isle rise in the wide plateau south of Limoges, the 'Bocage', and flow south-west to unite just above Périgueux. Near to them also the Dronne begins its parallel but more northerly course, to join the Isle near to the Dordogne estuary.

All those streams water varied country, sometimes cultivated and sometimes wild, with a general feeling of woodland. Where they are held in gorges, as the Vézère is below Uzerche, there is generally no road along their banks, and only a walker, and an energetic walker at that, can follow the streams. The country is pretty, in the east with forest, farther west in a pastoral way. For those who want to see the scatter of little towns and castles at the more westerly end, Périgueux is the best centre for motorists. It is a poor one for walkers, who

October sunshine in the valley of the River Vézère, near the village of Estivaux.

17

would do better to choose Brantôme, Nontron, or Thiviers. Up-stream the obvious centres are Uzerche or Brive. Ussel is the take-off for the Limousin 'Montagne'.

Motorists will tend to make either for Périgueux or Brive. To both of them there is a wide national road from Limoges. Those driving to Périgueux will be well advised to take the lesser but more beautiful route by St-Junien and Nontron, which crosses an unspoilt woodland shoulder. The historically-minded, however, will take the main road, for it traverses Châlus, with its hilltop castle. It was when he was besieging Châlus in 1199 that Richard Cœur de Lion was mortally wounded by an arrow shot from the castle walls. Nobody knows who was the killer, but tradition has it that it was one of the house of the lords of Gourdon, a turbulent clan three of whom Richard had executed in the rough justice of the time. Just south of the town the road crosses the young Dronne; the castle was one of the frontier-forts of the south-west.

This whole district, still sparsely peopled, and far from fertile, is spiked with castles which show how in the Middle Ages it was a frontier region between the France of the North and that of the South. The town of Thiviers is a good place from which to see some of them. It has a castle of its own, and a fine church, whose Gothic interior puzzlingly has Romanesque pillar-capitals. Then a blocked Romanesque arch comes into sight, and one realizes that the church is a medieval reconstruction, and that the builders were not going to waste perfectly good pillars. Among the castles near by are la Lambertie, and Jumilhac-le-Grand,[1] the most fantastically-roofed of all the castles of the region. It is as though the lord of the fourteenth century had said to his builder: 'Nobody in France shall have such roofs and gables, such turrets and weather-vanes as I,' and had deliberately made his castle like the scene of a fairy-tale. But perhaps the castle was only one of the many such which have vanished—if you believe the evidence of paintings such as the 'Très Riches Heures' of the Duc de Berry—and owes its survival to its lonely situation in the Isle gorges. Near to is the little china-town of St-Yrieix, with

Opposite: The main street and abbey church of St-Jean-de-Côle seen from the medieval stone bridge.

1 Part of Jumilhac-le-Grand is now open to the public. It can be visited morning and afternoon daily from 1 July to 15 September, and on Sunday and holiday afternoons out of season. From July to September it is illuminated at night.

a splendid church. This is all good walking country, for there is much pasture and wood, across which the walker can wander at will. In spring, the high meadows round Jumilhac-le-Grand are sheeted with scillas, coloured like wild hyacinths, so that the young green of the grass is shot with blue to make colour more tender than can be forgotten ever. But this can only be seen in early May.

It is about here that the traveller begins to notice village churches of the Périgourdin Romanesque style. They are plain enough and often small. But it is always worth while to stop and go into a church whose round-headed windows, set far up, whose square tower, or round east end, says 'Romanesque'. Inside there may be the characteristic domed roof of Périgord. Indeed it is here, in the north of the province, that such churches are most common, perhaps because the villages are remote and solitary, and have endured unchanged through the centuries.

Nontron is set on a ridge between two gorges, and has a wonderful view, and shops where they sell the wooden-handled knives made in the little town. But the things to see from Nontron lie in the upland country between it and Thiviers. They are the village of St-Jean-de-Côle, which has one of the most entrancing roofscapes of Périgord, a perspective of red rounded tiles; an unusual domed church; and the castle of la Marthonie, into which it is possible to penetrate since it is inhabited by a colony of families.[1] Near by is the castle of Puyguilhem, set on a hillside near Villars, with a green track where the grass has grown over the carriage-road, under huge old lime trees. It is the perfect Renaissance château, built with big towers to hold its staircases, yet a castle for pleasure, not for defence. Where in the older forts a battlemented *chemin-de-ronde* would have run round the tower for shooting at the besieger, Puyguilhem has an ornamental pretence of battlements under a string-course delicately carved with sprigs of oak. The Ministry of Beaux-Arts is repairing it, and skilled masons are rebuilding the fallen floors. It is covered with notices warning visitors not to go in as it is not safe. By luck, I

went alone and at lunch-hour, and the workmen looked the other way. Their work is as good as that of the first builders, but plain, for the Beaux-Arts does not believe any longer in imitating the ornament of places it restores. They told me that there is some idea of using the beautiful house as a home of rest for old and poor artists, and letting it be visited to defray the upkeep, which seems a pleasant scheme. In the withdrawing-room on the first storey, newly floored and with the broken casements restored, there is one new shaft elegantly carved with a palm-leaf capital, like the gables outside. 'Ah,' said the mason, 'that was M. ——. He stayed here to see our work, and he has been carving all his life.' Perhaps the sculptor was putting his mark on Puyguilhem, so that he could claim a room there, one day.[2]

The Dronne is a small river, gentle and clear, which like some women has the gift of perpetual grace. It is bordered by woods and meadows, and after it enters the limestone zone of Périgord, by cliffs coloured rose and dove-grey, in a manner giving it an air of amiable romance. There can be no pleasanter road in France than that which runs beside it from St-Pardoux to Lisle, or again from Riberac to Coutras, the latter if you avoid the main road and keep to the right side of the stream. But the place upon the river to rest is Brantôme.

Brantôme is an island-town set between two branches of the Dronne. It is a good example of an abbey-town, that has grown up round a religious house. The abbey was founded by Charlemagne, who gave it a relic of the bones of one of the Holy Innocents, St. Sicaire. That was for long a name of dread in the countryside, for how can a saint called after a hired assassin be anything but unfriendly? The abbey is still there, an Angevin church with a tall Romanesque belfry-tower, its glory and the finest in Périgord. The seventeenth-century monastic buildings now house the town hall.[3] A Renaissance abbot built a pavilion at one end of the dog-leg bridge, where he could sit on hot summer days and watch the reflection of the town in the water. There is a rose garden with frivolous little classical stone summer-houses. The town is full of old houses, many

1 La Marthonie now houses the Syndicat d'Initiative, which mounts arts and crafts exhibitions there in the summer months.

2 Puyguilhem is now fully restored and furnished, though sadly it does not house any old and poor artists. It can be visited daily, morning and afternoon, from 1 July to early September; and daily except Tuesdays from early February to July and October to mid-December.

3 The abbey buildings can be visited morning and afternoon daily, except Tuesdays, from Easter to the end of September. The belfry-tower is open in the afternoon from mid-June to mid-September. The abbot's rose garden, now a *jardin publique*, is the setting for classical music concerts in July and August.

of them with garden walls and gazebos overlooking the river.

Brantôme recalls the name of Pierre de Bourdeilles, who wrote his memoirs under the name of 'Brantôme'. He was a cadet of a great house, that of the lords of Bourdeilles, and like many a Gascon a soldier of fortune. He was given the commendation or lay abbacy of Brantôme as a reward for serving the Catholic cause at Jarnac, but felt it too small a bonus, and would have offered his sword to Philip of Spain but for a fall from his horse which crippled him. Broken and embittered, he set himself to write memoirs, which are of about the historic value of modern gossip-columns, though far better written. For the French, like the English, of the late sixteenth century was so fresh and strong a tongue that it seemed impossible to write it ill. Part of the memoirs which deal with the brawls and duels of the 'Grans Capitans' can only be read in libraries; but the part called 'Les Femmes Galantes' still sells as pornography. People often say to the visitor 'Et Brantôme?' with an upward lift of the eyebrow meant to inquire how the stranger will take it; for they are both proud and ashamed of his reputation. Scots will recall that he was sent as a guard with Mary Queen of Scots on her journey to Leith. It is difficult to imagine a less suitable escort for a young queen, even by the lax standards of her Guise kinsfolk; but he was, like the rest of the Valois court, subdued by her radiant dignity; and he was young then, too. At all events, she is one of the few women of whom he writes without fouling her with his scurrilous pen. It may incidentally be observed that the granting of church dignities to men as unfitted as Brantôme was a major cause of the contempt in which the church was held, and so of the Reformation. Yet in this case some good came out of evil; for when Coligny at the head of a Huguenot army was ravaging the country, in revenge for the Catholic massacres after the battle of Vergt, Brantôme appealed to him as an old comrade-in-arms, and saved the town from pillage.

Down-stream from Brantôme is Bourdeilles, the town of Brantôme's family, and one of the four baronies of Périgord. It is a castle-town, its main street running down to the river

under a crag topped by the great medieval keep. This is masked by a Renaissance gate-house, but at the crest there stand two castles. First there is a mass of medieval fortification; this was the castle taken by the English in 1369 and retaken by du Guesclin six years later. The octagonal donjon tower still stands, its arched chambers one above the other, with the stair spiralling up beside them, till it opens on the battlemented roof. If you go in spring, the jackdaws which nest in the embrasures will have covered the stair with the discarded sticks of last year's nests; they lie black on the white stone; white with a faint rosy reflection. It is hard to believe that the tower is six hundred years old. The eye plunges down to the river running under its old bridge far below, and then seeks the later château, set beside the old one on the rock. This is a plain square house, with a story attached to it. The Bourdeilles were Catholics at

The old mill house on the River Dronne in Bourdeilles.

Opposite: The domes of the cathedral of St-Front in Périgueux, seen from the bridge over the River Isle.

the time of the Wars of Religion, and the baron, Brantôme's elder brother, was the king's seneschal in Périgord too. When Catherine de Medici planned a propaganda tour in southern France, the lady of the castle, Jacquette de Montbron de Bourdeilles, invited the Queen to visit her, and designed a new house for the court to stay in. She had it made with large light rooms in the new style, and sent for the painter Ambroise Noble to decorate the walls. But Catherine de Medici had more to do than waste time on subjects whose loyalty was above question, and other employment for her train of light ladies, the 'Flying Squadron', than paying visits to virtuous matrons; and though she passed quite near to Bourdeilles, she did not come to stay. Jacquette de Bourdeilles was black affronted, and stopped the work on the new château; and it is still unfinished. Three finely decorated rooms are complete. Both castles belong to the state, and can be visited any day.[1]

The upland north of the Dronne between Bourdeilles and Riberac is worth exploring. Montagrier has an outstanding Romanesque church from which there is a wide view, and Brassac a fortified domed church.

Several good roads lead from the Dronne valley to Périgueux. As always in this country the rise from the river is steep, and is succeeded by a plateau. Here it is wooded, for Périgueux is surrounded on three sides by a forest belt. The road drops down into the Isle valley, and there is the town.

Périgueux

Périgueux is an ancient city that shows fewer signs of age than many French provincial capitals. This is partly because of a singularly troubled history. Time and again it was destroyed, only to rise again, because the fertile Isle valley needed a market and centre. It has always been rich, between wars, and it is rich today. Its wealth lies in the sale and export of luxury foodstuffs, such as *pâté de foie gras*, and in some minor industry.

There used to be two towns, each centred on a church. On the hill to the south overlooking the river was the abbey of

St-Front. Downhill was the cathedral, usually called 'la Cité'. Through the early Middle Ages the two were rivals. There was even a city wall between them where the boulevards run now, till they both accepted the position of royal towns and were induced by the French king to unite their councils. There was also periodic trouble with the Counts of Périgord. This family owed its name of Taillefer or Talleyrand to their founder, who clove a Viking with his broadsword. When the first Capet king, Hugues, asked him: 'Sir Count, who made thee count?' Adalbert Taillefer responded: 'Sir King, who made thee king?'—a repartee justified by the fishy way the Capets came by the crown. After this burst of brain the Taillefers sank into an unbroken course of greed and savagery so base that even the feudal system could not keep them secure in their places. They became, at the last, no more than robbers, like any free company chiefs, who lived by ravishing the country from their castle at Montignac. At length, the burden of the succession of Archambauts became intolerable, and the king sent his army to root them out of their castle in 1394, an early instance of the treatment which was later dealt out to many similar barons.

Périgueux was not disposed to submit meekly to these bandits, but it was scarcely ever secure. During the Wars of Religion the Huguenots took it and destroyed two bays of the cathedral in their siege of the bishop's palace; as a result St-Front became the cathedral when the city returned to Catholic hands. But the well-intentioned faithful were even more destructive than the Calvinists. The old church of St-Front, dating from the twelfth century, was dilapidated. The town gave over its restoration to an architect called Abadie. This deplorable builder wrought havoc far and wide through south-western France in the mid-nineteenth century. He knew, as he thought, just what a cathedral in the domed style ought to be; and he unpicked the old church completely and erected his fancy. The result is grandiose and dead. From a distance, it is fair to say, St-Front is not so bad; seen from the river-bank it piles up its five domes, its minarets, and its pillared tower in a fine bubbly mass. But near to it is unmistakably fake, and its

The ramparts of the château of Hautefort, rising above the village rooftops.

old streets round St-Front with Renaissance turrets and staircases. Down by the river there are three fine old houses. Two of them are lived in; the French are far too practical to turn habitable houses into museums, just because they happen to belong to the fifteenth century.[2] There is a shady public garden containing busts of Bertran de Born and Giraud de Bornheilh, the troubadours, and wide pleasant boulevards, set with good shops and cafés. There are some houses of the late eighteenth century, and an agreeable nineteenth-century quarter in the new town; for the conservatism of southern France preserved the decent simplicity and proportion of the eighteenth century long after it was over. Altogether, a pleasant city, and one to which its natives are devoted. They include a group of savants whose kindness to the inquiring foreigner is heart-warming. Eagerness to share learning is characteristic of the French tradition; and no doubt it is the generous giving of knowledge that has caused such a wealth of it to accumulate.

Motorists can visit all the north-west of Périgord, the region called 'Périgord blanc', from Périgueux. There are numerous old churches like the abbey of Chancelade quite close to, and castles like Lieu-Dieu, so called because the Sacrament from the cathedral of Périgueux was kept there while the town was in Huguenot hands. The pleasantest expedition, perhaps, is to Hautefort, the castle that dominates the valley of the Auvézère. The road runs near the river, set with old villages and towered manors, to the tiny town with its seventeenth-century castle in private ownership. Its towers are domed in the manner of the Baroque age. Its spirited chatelaine is restoring and refurnishing it after a dramatic and disastrous fire in 1968. The work will be completed by 1975, and visitors can already visit the chapel and a tower, and enjoy the fine ridgey views.[3] Hautefort, long before this castle was built, was the manor of Bertran de Born, the troubadour, who was the friend and enemy of kings. He used the light verse of the twelfth century to write political satire and propaganda, mostly in praise of war, and in mockery of his foes. He was probably the most effective political poet in history, next to Aristophanes. He

interior is vast, cold, and inexpressive of any religion. Outside it, facing the market-place, there is one wall of an early Romanesque church, called St-Front-Primitif, of great interest to architects. La Cité, or St-Etienne, the mutilated old cathedral, is far more impressive. It is a great block, small-windowed, with two domed bays remaining. It has the mystery of the Byzantine fanes from which, it is generally supposed, the Périgourdin domed churches were copied. What a pity that false economy has crammed its apse with an enormous Baroque reredos from an abandoned church! It could not be more inharmonious with the ancient building.[1]

Périgueux has considerable Gallo-Roman remains, ugly but interesting, a nice little eighteenth-century town hall, narrow

meddled in the empoisoned feuds of the Angevin family, making common cause with Henry II's heir, Henry Courtmantel, the 'Young King', who had been crowned king of England and duke of Normandy in his father's lifetime, but to whom the old lion would not give any real power. He justly thought the wastrel unfit for it. The Young Henry rebelled, and in company with Bertran de Born ravished the countryside, ending with the fearful sacrilege of sacking the shrine of Rocamadour. But he was wounded by its defenders, and was carried as far as Martel. There he died, lying on a bed of ashes, with a great cross heavy on his breast, in certain fear of damnation. Bertran de Born truly loved the bad prince, and shut himself in his castle of Hautefort, where Henry II, raging with affront and grief, came to besiege him. Bertran was far too old a soldier to offer vain resistance, and surrendered, to be condemned to death by the king. He asked first to sing a plaint, a 'planh', he had made for the Young Henry; and it was so moving that the king forgave him. So he rode away to make more mischief, in his manner, till age found him and he died a monk. Dante, in spite of his gratitude to the troubadours who were his forerunners, set Bertran in the darkest deeps of hell; for one who broke the law of loyalty, and incited a son against the authority of his father, offended the Italian's strongest principles. He says:

'I saw, and it seems that I see it still, a body go without its head, as went the rest of that sad flock. And it held the cut off head by the hair, lifting it in its hand as if it were a lantern, and looked at us with it, and said: "O me! . . . And since you seek news of me, know that I am Bertran de Born, he who gave ill counsel to the young king. I made father and son rebels the one against the other."'

It is possible, all the same, that his Creator agreed with Henry II, rather than with Dante, and forgave Bertran de Born at the last because of the excellence of his poetry.

The magnificent castle of today bears no trace of that turbulent genius. It is much more reminiscent of Marie de Hautefort, the lovely blue-eyed girl who went to the court of Louis XIII, and stirred that listless heart to almost its only

passion. But he bored her; he could only talk of hunting, she said, even when he was trying to make love; and she refused the post of king's mistress and married the Marshal de Schomberg.

Limousin

Those who seek the upper Dordogne will come by Uzerche and Brive. Even before they reach the meadow-upland south of Limoges, they may turn aside to look at the church of Solignac, a great abbey built in the domed Périgourdin style. The churches of the Bocage are apt to have a mixed character. Some are Périgourdin in shape, but most are Limousin. Hereabouts they are built of hard granitic stone, difficult to work. The masons seem to have taken vengeance on the recalcitrant material by carving capitals and the corbels under the roof into grotesque figures, as at Vigeois. The jongleur who offered his act to God before the altar is there sometimes, his heels doubled back behind his ears. The gem of the region is Uzerche. As you come to it from the hill-roads it lies below, on a ridge held in a horseshoe bend of the Vézère; a serration of towers dark against the wooded slope of the farther bank, like a city behind an enthroned Virgin in a picture. It is full of streets of the fifteenth and sixteenth centuries, in which each house has a staircase tower. They say: 'The man who has a house in Uzerche has a castle in Limousin,' and the saying is near enough to the truth. The town climbs up to a Romanesque church, long and shadowy, with a fine spire and a round tower as fortification at its west end.

West of Uzerche lies the castle of Pompadour, about which the guide-books make a great fuss. It is amusing to look at its stout towered gate-house, and to reflect that this was the castle whose fief and title was granted to the mistress of Louis XV. But two warnings must be uttered about it. Firstly Madame de Pompadour never lived in it; she would have thought it barbarous in the extreme. And secondly the gates and the towered outer wall are the only authentic part of the castle. The rest was destroyed in the Revolution. The main block is careful

1 St-Etienne is closed on Sunday afternoons.

2 The Syndicat d'Initiative organizes Gallo-Roman and Medieval-Renaissance tours on Tuesday and Friday afternoons in July and August.

3 The restoration work, which continued well into the 1980s, is now finished. The château is open morning and afternoon daily from Easter to the end of October, and on Sunday and holiday afternoons during the rest of the year (closed mid-December to mid-January).

reproduction. It is lived in by the officials of a state stud-farm,[1] as is the authentic castle of Lubersac, some miles north. From Uzerche south, the road runs through pastoral country, by the old town of Donzenac to Brive-la-Gaillarde. That gallant title still suits Brive, a prosperous and cheerful little city. It lives by the railway, partly as a junction, but mostly by using it to export early vegetables and fruits to Paris. The Basin of Brive owes its remarkable fertility to alluvial deposits and an outcrop of red sandstone, which always makes rich soil, whether in East Lothian or in Limousin.

The town runs downhill from the railway station to the Corrèze, pausing at the church of St-Martin. This has a soaring interior of high pillars; the structure has been restored with sober skill. The Saturday market round the church is a good place to find real lace.

Many of the places between Brive and Périgueux can be just as well visited from Brive, among them Hautefort and the queer perched abbey of St-Robert, in its little town which feels immemorially old; and a string of small places on the Vézère.

Turn up-stream beside the Corrèze, and you go through gorges beside the tumbling river, whose beauty is only partly spoilt by a series of quarries. On the southern side a road climbs the ridge to Aubazine. The village has a wonderful view and a great abbey-church. Aubazine is austerely plain, according to the Cistercian custom; all the same it has fine proportions. It includes a window of old 'grisaille', patterned grey glass, which has been copied all too much of late years,[2] a delightful set of choir-stalls carved in the eighteenth century with speaking likenesses of the village worthies—and unworth-ies—and the tomb of St-Etienne d'Aubazine. There is nothing austere about this tomb, shaped and carved like a reliquary with scenes of the reformer-abbot leading his monks to holiness in life and death. The abbey buildings now house an orphanage directed by nuns, who kindly show them to visitors.[3]

There is something sad about Tulle, perhaps because it is too shut in by the river-banks. It has an old quarter, with some fine

houses, but the best thing about it is the tall spire of the church. East of it the land slopes up to the Limousin 'Montagne'. This is no mountain, but a plateau some 2,000 feet high, partly forested, sown with small lakes, and bright with heather in August. Here and there a ridge carrying a road leads off southwards to the Dordogne gorges. The ruins of Ventadour stand on one of them. They look fine from a distance, but there is not much left of a castle whose history was as romantic as its name. Here, when it was the stronghold of the Vicomtes of Ventadour, a son Bernard was born to a castle serf. The Vicomte gave the engaging child a gentle education, and he became, of all the troubadours, the one who was most devoted to love-songs and love-making. Here, when the Hundred Years' War was interrupted by the Peace of Brétigny in 1363, Geoffroi Tête-Noire, a famous Breton leader of free-lances, established himself and held the land in terror. Froissart says:

'He considered the castle as his own inheritance, and had forced all the surrounding country to enter into composition with him to avoid being plundered, by which means he was able to keep up the state of a great baron.'

He died in his bed, too, though his inheritors lost the castle and were executed. Which just shows that the gangs of the United States were not original in organizing the demand for protection-money. Finally Richelieu, losing patience with the turbulent independence of the country nobles, called 'hobereaux'—clodhoppers—sent his army to destroy their castle-walls, and his artillery laid low the defences of Ventadour.

Just south of Ussel on the main road is St-Angel, a remarkable fortified abbey-church, which was used as a fortress by a Huguenot leader in the Wars of Religion. Ussel contains the town house of the later Dukes of Ventadour. It is the grandest of many turreted houses in the charming little town. There is a spider-web of old streets round the church, and good shops in the boulevards. When you inquire how it is that such shops find customers in a land of trees and pastures, you may be told:

1 The terraces may be visited morning and afternoon daily throughout the year, except on 15 August and race days. The stables are open on Sunday and holiday mornings, except from 1 March to the end of June.

2 Nearly all the windows at Aubazine are of grisaille glass, which is probably the oldest in France in such a good state of preservation. In July and August there are classical music concerts in the church.

3 The orphanage has moved, and the abbey buildings now house a lay spiritual community. The nuns continue to give guided tours, every afternoon at four.

4 Now locked in a glass cabinet behind the church door. Insert a franc piece to illuminate it.

'Look at that man over there, in patched blue dungarees and plimsolls. He has a flock of sheep. His land is his own; he has no expenses. He pastures his sheep twice a day, and for the rest, fishes and perhaps shoots for the pot. He sells the lambs, and makes at least £2,000 a year net.'

Take the road south from Ussel, past the Penitents' Chapel to the pilgrimage-church of Ste-Marie-de-Chabannes. There are the cones of the Monts Dore, floating above the horizon.

Lovers of old church ornaments will seek the churches of the region which hold reliquaries of Limoges enamel and beaten silver. These sometimes take the form of portrait-busts, life-size, with a glass panel in the breast to show the holy bones. The effect is startlingly macabre. One of them is renowned for its beauty; it is in the church of Ste-Fortunade, on the road from Tulle to Beaulieu. The artist, told to carve the bust of Ste-Fortunade, took copper and wrought the head of a dreaming child.[4]

Uzerche, early on a winter morning, from the bridge which spans the River Vézère.

THE LOWER DORDOGNE

The Dordogne valley divides naturally into three. The lower stretch from the sea to Lalinde is closed at that point by the hills on both sides of the river. The middle course from Lalinde to the junction with the Cère is the limestone country. Above Bretenoux the river flows in the Limousin and Auvergne gorges.

The Dordogne estuary is long and shallow. If it had been deeper, Bordeaux might have been built on it instead of on the Gironde. As it is, Bordeaux serves as the economic centre for both great rivers. Inland from the estuary lies the fertile Dordogne plain. This is country where history has come and gone, where armies and nations have passed and repassed, building cities and destroying them. Now there remain cattle and plough, the poplar-shaded roads, little towns standing where they have always stood by the river fords, castles besieged, now, by the ranks of the vine.

The lower Dordogne is strung with wine-towns. The richest owed their first prosperity to the export trade to England. For if Rome built the first Bordeaux, it was the English trade which raised it from the decay of the barbarian invasions. Libourne, the Dordogne wine-port, is called after its founder, the English seneschal Roger of Leyburn. It still has an arcaded square and a Renaissance town hall. The most interesting of the small towns is St-Emilion. It crowns a hill, and is enclosed by its medieval walls. There are many old things to see, a thirteenth-century castle, the Château du Roi; the queer monolithic abbey with its belfry-tower on the terrace above; a fine parish church; the well, in a school garden, where Madame Boquey hid her brother-in-law and six of his Girondin friends when Robespierre's terrorists were on their track.

But the life of St-Emilion, which still flows strong in the arteries of these ancient walls, is red wine. From the streets you can see the vineyards, meticulously cultivated, bearing labels, 'Cru;—' labels which thrill the heart of the connoisseur. The town is scented with the aroma of grape-blossom in spring, of grape-juice in autumn. Men are constantly at work in the wide gates of the stores cleaning the big barrels in readiness for the vintage; till in September the gathering begins and St-Emilion hums like a hive.

Down by the river is Castillon, where the English were defeated in 1453 in the last battle of the Hundred Years' War. There are two monuments, one to the battle, one to Talbot who fell so battered that his herald could only tell his corpse by its teeth.

The low hills which bound the plain of the north bank hold St-Michel-de-Montaigne. There is the tower of Michel de Montaigne, where he read and wrote his essays. It bears on its beams the mottoes he had painted to express his sense of the value of thought and peace:

'Michel de Montaigne, wearied long since of the slavery of courts and public pomps, has taken his entire refuge in the arms of the learned sisters. He wishes, free from care, to finish there the course of his age, already more than half run, and he has consecrated to repose and liberty this lovable and peaceful dwelling, the heritage of his ancestors.'

This he did in the midst of the Wars of Religion, for though he himself remained a Catholic, his brother was a Huguenot. He was the friend of leaders on both sides. Henry IV came to stay with him, and in the spirit of tolerance the two men were nearly allied. Montaigne is blamed by some controversialists for that same tolerance, which they think more undermining to the Catholic faith than open opposition; but to modern readers his essays seem the nonpareil of all that is most endearing in the French spirit. Unfortunately, the book-room tower is all that is left of the castle of Montaigne. The rest perished in a fire, and there is now a privately-owned modern château attached to it; but it can be seen on application.[1]

Ste-Foy-la-Grande and Bergerac were Protestant towns in the sixteenth century. In consequence, though they are old, they have few old things remaining. Ste-Foy still bears the regular plan of a 'bastide', a fortified town. Bergerac was called the 'Geneva of the West'. It was wholly Huguenot. It was taken and retaken, its bridge, its walls, its churches destroyed in the wars. And eighty years after, when the Revocation of the Edict of Nantes threatened all Protestants who did not abjure their faith with torture and death, the greater part of its population emigrated overseas, and the town fell into decay. But its rich farming country restored it, since corn and wine must be marketed, and it is now a prosperous city again, well kept and clean, with that unmistakable feeling of democracy and initiative that pervades southern towns with a Protestant tradition. Its red wine is largely made and marketed by a co-operative.

Bergerac wine is red. South-east of it lies Monbazillac, where famous white wine is grown. Throughout the Dordogne it is Monbazillac which people drink on ceremonial occasions; it is a wine for people who know wine, and like the sweet vintages of the generous south-west. The vineyard surrounds the castle, with its irregular towers, very like those of Bridoires, not far away.[2]

Above Lalinde there is a large power-station on the river, where the hills narrow it to rapids. Here is the lowest of the 'cingles'. Cingle means curve or bend; it is exactly translated by the word 'link' used by Scots to describe the windings, the Links of Forth below Stirling. From any height above the river valley one can see how the links happen. The hills or cliffs are set wide apart, leaving a flat valley bottom; and the water seeks the lowest point, and swings from side to side in an intricate meander. The low land contained in the curve is always sedulously cultivated. But the villages are often built on the steep side of the valley where the river flows close below it and provides both water and a narrow passage between stream and rock, easy to defend.

The Lalinde cingle has Trémolat in its curve with a fine domed church, and near by the charming castle of Laffinoux. The main roads divide and leave the river-banks aside, for this is difficult country, forming a natural barrier between the lower and middle Dordogne.

1 No special arrangements are now necessary to visit Montaigne's tower, which is open morning and afternoon, Wednesday to Sunday, from March to October.
2 In 1960 the Bergerac *coopérative*, the largest in the Dordogne, bought the château of Monbazillac. Now restored and refurbished as a museum of winemaking and a wine-tasting centre, it is open morning and afternoon daily.

CHAPTER FOUR

THE MIDDLE DORDOGNE

The Limestone Country. The Vézère and Sarlat

The Middle Dordogne runs through the country called Périgord noir, Black Périgord. The people also call the lower reaches the Sarladais, because they lie within the diocese of Sarlat. It is a land of delights. These can be summed up as beautiful form, colour and detail. The Dordogne itself is graceful. Here it is not a great river, but a wide and living stream. It is entirely natural, flowing along with varied current between banks that usually are tree-fringed, curving to meet cliffs or steep slopes from one side of its bed to the other. The river-plain looped by each link gives space and repose to the view. This is not Claude's Campagna, but there is an elegiac air about the Dordogne which often recalls the landscapes of Claude; the tree-framed water and atmosphere of diffused light may account for it. Two considerable rivers join it; the Vézère stealing deep and narrow within its cliff-held bed; and the Cère, coming down in haste from Cantal to quieten in the valley.

The land on either side is a complex folding of ridges. They are not tall; the crests are rarely above 1,000 feet. But the valleys between them are so sharp-cut that seen from below they seem higher than they are. When the road follows a ridge, the heights are often spaced to allow a perspective of shoulders one behind another till the eye sees the whole circle of the horizon.

It is coloured country. In spring the flowers succeed each other so fast that the hillsides change their tint daily; in autumn the woods hang orange and tawny against the blue distances. But the basic colour, revealed in cliffs, in the soil, and in buildings, is that of the rock. Limestone is naturally white; and here and there it keeps a marble whiteness as at Carennac, where it is quarried for fine building. The slopes behind St-Cyprien show white through the grass. More often, iron and other metals have dyed the stone with a multitude of colours. In some places it is amber, in others pink. Frequently the surface has weathered a dove's-breast grey that turns in certain lights to a pure purple of the depth of Parma violets. In the level rays of the setting sun a circle of cliffs will burn as though the rock were the transparent sheath of fire.

There is constantly varying detail. Every bend of the river, every turn of the road alters the view. The river holds its trees growing up and down in reflection, or divides over white pebbles round an island. A golden village pyramids up to the church tower in stepped red roofs. A castle shows its turrets coquettishly to the valley below, for it was carefully designed to do so. The shadow under the blanched market canvases conceals piles of apricots and tomatoes. Even the butcher's shop preserves a traditional seemliness, being marked by a pot of flowers in an empty window.

This is pre-eminently dawdler's country. The man who drives straight through it deserves what he will get, and that is a

A late spring afternoon on the Dordogne near St-Cyprien.

blurred impression of missing a great deal. He cannot drive quickly enough to escape noticing that he is missing things. The roads, which are as given to cingles as the rivers, will take care of that. But people who drive crazily across the Dordogne are no concern of ours. Happily there are lots of places from which to dawdle; from which to walk up the hills that may be only 800 feet high, but you would never believe it, so steep are they; to sit on a bank, or stand on an old bridge and watch the river currents till you are saturated with pleasure.

The prehistoric caves can be seen from les Eyzies or Montignac;[1] the former is within easy driving reach of le Bugue, the latter from St-Léon-sur-Vézère. For the country north of the Dordogne, Sarlat is a good centre for the lower, Martel for the middle, and St-Céré for the higher reaches. There is a succession of places to stay on the Dordogne itself: St-Cyprien, Beynac, la Roque-Gageac, Domme, Souillac, Bretenoux on the Cère. On the Causse de Gramat one may stay at Gramat or Rocamadour, and there are hotels in the bastides of Beaumont, Monpazier, and Monflanquin.

The traveller will make first for the prehistoric caves. There are two or three ways of reaching them from Périgueux, but the road signposted to direct motorists is the prettiest, skirting the forest of la Barade, and running down the little Manaurie past caves and overhanging rocks to les Eyzies. Coming from Brive the motorist must follow the Vézère all the way to Montignac. The caves are given a later chapter to themselves. But there are other things to see in this district, for the Vézère is strung with Renaissance castles from Condat to the pleasant waterside town of le Bugue. They are not all visible from the main road, though it passes near to the severe walls of Sauveboeuf and of la Fleunie near to Condat. Even there it is best to keep to the left bank; and below Montignac it is essential, travelling by the quiet unshaded road which runs to the carved fifteenth-century cross before Sergeac. But from it you see the two castles of Losse and Belcayre, perched on the right-bank cliff. Belcayre is an absurdly pretty castle, where you would never be surprised to hear that a little princess was guarded by a middle-aged

amiable dragon, stabled by day in the pigeon-tower. In fact, it is Losse that is lived in by an Annamese princess, who is deeply occupied in local good works.[2] Losse has a famous echo. Every visitor will be told how the seigneur of Belcayre, finding himself in a tight place, went to his neighbour to borrow money. Losse, a canny man, cried to the echo: 'Is Monsieur de Belcayre a good payer?' 'Moussur de Belcayre ei teu buon pagaire?' 'Gaire! Gaire!' 'Watch out!' answered his echo, and poor Belcayre did not get his loan.

Plazac, in the hills west of Thonac, is an ancient bourg with a magnificent donjon-tower on its Romanesque church; it was once a country castle of the bishops of Périgueux. Les Eyzies, too, has a fine fortified church, and so has Tursac, the impenetrable, whose door is always locked.[3]

The Sarlat road out of Montignac passes an inconspicuous lane. Take this and you come to the manor of la Grande Filolie, the perfect castle for a country squire. The road carries the tourist into a court before the great gate. There his affrighted eyes meet a stern notice: 'Order! A place for everything and everything in its place!' He is immediately overcome by the sensation that nothing could be more out of place than himself, and sneaks away. All the same it is worth the embarrassment.[4]

East of the Sarlat road, if you leave it at the crest of the hill, a stony lane leads to St-Amand-de-Coly. This tiny village has a tall abbey-church, its front formed by an immense fortress arch. In a simpler way, it has the effect of the west arches of Jumièges and Tewkesbury. Once there were 400 monks in this remote monastery. Why did they need that high defensive wall round the abbey? Well, there were the lords of all these castles; most of all the ferocious Talleyrands in Montignac. And besides, the monasteries kept their own men-at-arms to defend their own property.

Sarlat lies in a narrow glen. The town is cut from north to south by the Traverse. This street was made for the convenience of modern traffic, and turns its platitudinous shopfronts to the passer-by. But leave it on either hand and you will see why the whole of Sarlat is 'classé monument'.[5] The western side

1 Details of caves that can be visited are given on page 113.

2 She sold Losse to a Belgian lady, who has restored and refurbished it. It is open morning and afternoon daily from 1 July to 15 September.

3 In principle, the key is available from the house next door.

4 La Grande Filolie (4km from Montignac on the D704) is open daily in the summer months.

5 It is also now *un secteur à restaurer et à sauvegarder en priorité*. A wealth of information is available from the Syndicat d'Initiative.

clambers uphill in a series of wynds and courts lifting crooked gables against the sky. The heat of summer fails to strike the shadowy streets where old women sit shelling walnuts. There is a good Penitents' chapel. But it is the east side that holds Sarlat's treasure of old streets and houses. The churches are not of great importance, though the cathedral, formerly the abbey round which the town was built, keeps a Romanesque tower capped by a bulbous Counter-Reformation belfry. The town church has been turned into stores; its gargoyles hang out over the market-place. That must be one of the most decorative in the world, with its irregular shape and buildings of many dates pleasantly harmonized, even to a modern shop, like a party of women of all ages talking together. The turreted houses of the sixteenth and seventeenth centuries seem familiar to Scottish eyes, used to the Old Town of Edinburgh; and of course Scots architecture of that date was copied from the French; but it must be owned that Sarlat has more of them and better ones, especially the 'hôtel' in the Rue des Consuls, and another in a court off the market-place. It is in the little square behind that Henri II house that the citizens of Sarlat play a form of skittles which is, if not unique, at least rare. Three skittles are set in sand one behind the other; and the game consists of bowling them over from some fifteen feet away. And if anybody thinks it simple to hit three stumps in a vertical row, he had better go to Sarlat and insinuate himself into a game.

Sarlat affords a perfect example of the development of the *bourgeoisie*, the citizen class, in France. For long the abbey dominated the town—it would only be a monastery which would choose so indefensible a site. But when in course of time the abbey decayed, the citizens took over, under their consuls. That grand Roman title masks our modest town councillors. In the old days there were fewer of them, and they had more power. The citizens made up for the weak position of the town by surrounding it with walls and ditches. Sarlat was never taken in the Hundred Years' War. In the Wars of Religion it turned out its Protestants and remained Catholic. Coligny wasted a couple of days looking at it, and so was caught by the

Catholic army and defeated at Vergt. Turenne besieged it and breached its walls, but failed to take it by assault, for the resistance of the people was too tough. It was finally captured by Geoffroi de Vivant of Fayrac by a night escalade. He was Henry of Navarre's best captain in Gascony. He could take anything; he took Domme, too.

The town square of Sarlat has a statue of la Boétie. His birthplace was the beautiful Renaissance house opposite to the cathedral. His mind was typical of the learning and art that sprung out of the small cities of France at that time. Most people know of him as the friend whom Montaigne loved like a brother; the hero of the essay 'De l'Amitié', of whom he says, if he is asked why the two young men knew their hearts united as soon as they met, he could only answer 'Parce que c'était moi; parce que c'était lui.' 'Because it was I, because it was he.' La Boétie stands on his own feet, too. He wrote, as a schoolboy, the little pamphlet called *La Servitude Volontaire*, which was nicknamed 'Le Contr'un', because it upheld the rights of the people against tyranny. It appealed to Christian charity as the foundation of human equality; and it had the strange quality of moving the heart that a simple truth may have when it has been too long forgotten. La Boétie, who was a devout Catholic, became a source of inspiration for the Huguenots in their demand for justice and tolerance; and for that matter to the forerunners of the Revolution.

Castles on the Dordogne

From Siorac to Souillac, the Dordogne flows between castles. No doubt this is mainly because the river was the route of passage, in the days of bad roads over the uplands, or none. The cliffs that border the valley might have been created to please warriors who sought a high rock to build on and a wide view from their towers. Behind the castles stretch the upland forests and meadows; at their feet lie the alluvial fields. Beynac with the fertile river-plain to supply it, Castelnaud commanding the valley of the Céou, are great castles. Many are smaller, like the *gentilhommières* of Carsac. They vary in date from the

Opposite: A misty morning view westwards along the Dordogne from the esplanade at Domme.

37

The château of Beynac seen from the banks of the Dordogne.

1 In the 1960s the ruins of Fages, then being used as a breeding station for maggots, were bought by the present owner, who has since restored them. A sign announces that Fages is open 'exceptionellement' (and that the poor and young may pay their entrance fee in kind by doing an hour's work).

2 The cost of restoring les Milandes ruined her: in 1968 the château was sold at auction to pay off her debts. It is open to visitors daily, morning and afternoon, from Easter to mid-October.

3 There is now a good road to les Milandes and a bridge just up the river at Castelnaud. Ferries are a thing of the past, and it would be foolhardy and probably illegal to attempt to circulate on any of the railway bridges.

4 Beynac has been extensively restored and can be visited every morning and afternoon from March to mid-October.

5 Since 1969 Castelnaud has undergone major restoration work, and it now houses a museum of medieval siege warfare. It is open in Easter week and daily from May to the end of September, except on Mondays and Saturdays in May, June and September.

tenth to the eighteenth centuries. All that can be said of them generally is that as long as the gentry lived in castles, they built them on the banks of the Dordogne. Many are still lived in, fortunately, for this prevents them from falling into decay. They are not the palaces of the Loire, raised for princes to visit in the hunting season. But they are better situated, for the Dordogne is a lovelier river than the Loire. And they have a human air of habitation, and a pride of class which was haughty enough but subject to some natural limitations.

Coming up-stream, St-Cyprien runs up to its abbey-church, finely towered though much repaired. It commands a long view of the Dordogne. Above it the white chalky hills rise to a ridge topped by the castle of Fages, and the old tower of la Roque. Fages is a ruin, for the Germans burnt it.[1] Farther east, the other side of the river is decorated by the graceful Renaissance castle of les Milandes. Its history typifies the vicissitudes of such houses. The powerful family of the de Caumonts built it, to replace their grim castle of Castelnaud. It was a Protestant stronghold in the Wars of Religion, and stood a siege. Later it was lived in by Anne de Caumont, a great heiress. Poor child, she was abducted thrice, to be married for her money, the first time when she was only six. Miss Josephine Baker, the famous singer, owned it for several years, during which it was the home of her adopted family of children.[2]

Les Milandes is not easy to get at, except on foot. The Dordogne is somewhat poor in bridges. But there is a ferry at every village, and as the local Authority will tell you with a noble gesture: 'You may circulate freely on the railway bridge.' This is convenient for walkers, but not so good for a car.[3]

Beynac and the three cingles above it are the finest on the river, if land, water, and buildings are taken together. Beynac castle overhangs the climbing village, itself full of interesting houses. The fortress is a tall crenellated mass, composed of two towers connected by a spiral stair. It is in fairly complete repair; several rooms can be visited, especially a hall where the Estates of Périgord used to meet.[4] For Beynac was the senior of the four baronies of Périgord, the others being Biron, Bourdeilles, and Mareuil. The country behind the castle is untouched, and full of good walks.

Just across the river is the 'manoir' of Fayrac, patterning its turrets against the wooded hill. You can walk over the ridge above it, or along the stream, to Castelnaud, russet on its russet cliff. It is a huge ruin, still showing the strength with which Albigensian, English and Calvinist lords ruled the land for miles from its towers.[5]

The right-bank road runs by la Roque-Gageac, a strange village built up a perpendicular cliff, its houses clamped against the rock on a few terraces.[6] Its castle is tiny, and so is the fortified church. But the river vista is so entrancing that people like to retire to it. The de St. Aulaire family, whose former town house is one of the best in Sarlat, have a large imitation castle here. For France did not escape, any more than Scotland, from the nineteenth-century rage for building pseudo-baronial castles.

A mile from la Roque-Gageac, a road leads off to a bridge across which is the village of Cénac. There you may take a zig-zag road, or a remarkably steep lane, to Domme. Domme is the bastide of the Dordogne valley. It was built up in the thirteenth century, when fortress-towns were being set up all over this country. It was the custom to give the people privileges in order to induce them to build the places and inhabit them. But the luckless serfs who had to climb up that rock carrying stone for the walls complained bitterly that they were poor men who had to grow their food; why should they be forced to imitate goats? However, the walled village on its peak was finished at last; and Domme was reckoned impregnable, till de Vivant took it. It still has two gates, and a good deal of its walls; streets of honey-coloured houses, very old and strong, leading to the market-place and the Barre, the terrace overlooking the Dordogne far below and the waves of the hills receding to the Auvergne.

Domme stands so high that when you get up to it, you must just come down again. If you return to the north bank, you

A street leading down to one of Domme's fortified gateways.

soon pass the castle of Montfort, the third of the great medieval castles. It is inhabited, and has been altered a good deal in the Renaissance and later, but it has its original outer walls and gate, and is set on a needle's-eye cliff overhanging the river.[7] The road here is gouged out of the rocky bank, and gives wonderful views of the Dordogne and Montfort, till it turns away to Carsac. There the church is fine, part Romanesque and part late Gothic. The north-bank road runs on beneath the cliffs and impending slopes of the causse, till it reaches Souillac. It is not to be despised, but from Grolejac onwards the small road on the other side is more beautiful. It has some interesting country behind it. Gourdon is a hill-top town with one dominating church and several others set lower, including the fourteenth-century Cordeliers. The endearing castle of Lamothe-Fénélon is where the bishop-author of that name was

6 In 1956 part of the cliff collapsed, taking with it some of the houses. The scar can still be seen on the cliff face.

7 Montfort is privately owned and not open to the public. At Christmas it is illuminated at night.

Bastides

bred. Also the village of Prats-de-Périgord, which may not be haunted, but looks it; and Besse, with its church door carved with the signs of the Zodiac.

There are many bastides in the south-west. Their origin, as towns built as fortresses, and the character of their architecture, are explained in a later chapter. Most have lost their real aspect, for they have decayed into villages, or grown beyond their old bounds. But there is a group of them which seems to have been missed by change and chance. They lie south of the Dordogne, and can be reached either from Bergerac or from the middle river. They are among the most delightful things of the region, but are rather inaccessible except to people who have a car, for they are too far apart for convenient walking.

From the middle reaches the road crosses the Dordogne at Siorac or le Buisson, and runs through forest to Cadouin. There is a majestic austere abbey church, of the Cistercian Romanesque, its severity modified by a gaily decorated cloister in a flowery garden. The abbey used to be the bourne of a famous pilgrimage, to the Holy Winding-Sheet of Christ, which was housed in the church. It drew saints and sinners to the shrine of the relic, brought back in good faith from the Crusades. But a learned ninteenth-century monk insisted on deciphering the inscription woven into its margin, which proved to be a Moslem text, so the pilgrimage ceased to be. On the rise beyond Cadouin stands the fortified church of St-Avit-Sénieur, one of its watch-towers broken. Thence it is a good thing to take the road down the valley of the little violet-cliffed Couze, till the castle of Bannes shows its towers over the tree-tops. It looks exactly like the castle of the Sleeping Beauty, silent above the silent woods.[1]

Then the valley should be retraced till the road runs up to Beaumont, crowning a ridge, its four-towered church dominating the countryside. Beaumont is the first of the bastides. It has the typical central market-square, surrounded by the arcades called 'cornières'. The streets form a grid within the walls, of which a good deal remains, especially on the southern side. The little town was plainly built for defence. Once the gates were shut, the enemy would have to scale a double line of wall; and if he got through that, the people would take refuge in the church and defend it like a castle. Its towers are, in effect, donjons, still bearing traces of the battlement from which the defenders would shoot arrows at the invader, and the windows are set too high to be accessible without ladders.

How do the people live, in this medieval fortress? They could never have existed on its trade, though one of the 'franchises' of the free towns was always a regular market, and on fair-day[2] Beaumont hums with bargaining. But now, as in the old days, the people all own land outside the town. Perhaps their ancestors were serfs who gained their freedom by settling in it and, as they got land too, did well for themselves. Even now, with a prosperous agriculture, they do not do so badly.

The church of Beaumont is Gothic, of the style we call 'Early English' and the French call 'Angevin'; that is, tall, with pointed arches, slim lancet windows, and a flat apse. It is very fine and spacious, far too big for any population that can ever have lived in the town. But no doubt the kings of those times built partly for the glory of God and partly for their own. It is a noticeable thing that the English bastides have a boldness in their Gothic unusual in the south. Beaumont, Monpazier, and Villeréal were all Plantagenet foundations, and all have remarkable churches, possibly reflecting the northern connections of the Angevin line.

Beaumont is good, but Monpazier is better. It lies on its hilltop like a drowsy yellow cat, slumbering in the sun. The oaken market stalls, except on fair-day,[3] are filled only with shade, black against the white heat of the square. The shadow beneath the irregular Gothic arcades is black, too, and cool to sit in. Each arch has a shop behind it. Some sell food and clothes and kitchen pots, as they have always done; some photographs and radio sets, in the modern way. The merchant lives in the upper storey above the arch, as he has done since

[1] Bannes is not open to visitors.
[2] The second Tuesday of each month.
[3] The third Thursday of each month.

Above: An attractive window display in Beaumont.

Opposite: Monpazier's main square, seen from the covered market which still possesses its old grain measures.

1 In 1972 a violent hailstorm (with stones reputedly as big as pigeons' eggs) shattered Biron's roof. The buildings stood semi-derelict until 1979, when the *département* bought them and embarked on a massive restoration programme. They can be visited morning and afternoon daily from 1 July to 7 September, and daily except Tuesdays from early February to mid-December.

the town was made. The inn in the straight street leading from one towered gate to the other used to be the house of the Birons' seneschal. The town must have prospered in the Middle Ages, for the church has a Renaissance door, but it did not grow. All the amber-coloured houses with their arched doors are held within the lines of the old walls. There are a few more recent, naturally, but the newest, the doctor's house, is an admirable modernism of the traditional style.

From the gates, with their long prospect over the country, the sentries must have been able to see a band of men riding far away, to blow their horns to summon the workers from the fields, and to shut the doors. For the riders might be a troop of their own king's soldiers, moving from one station of Aquitaine to another; or they might be the French king's men, or worse, a company of freebooters bent on rapine.

Between wars, Monpazier must have lain then, as now, silent in the sun, till the evening cool. Then the old folk will come out to gossip in the doorways. The men will return from the fields that their families have tilled for seven centuries. The wives collect the little extras needed to cook the supper. The visitor tries to shake off the spell of the town, of its unhurrying, changeless life, and orders an aperitif before going to dine at the inn. But the memory of quietude and sun, of the black and gold of the arcades, will recur often to his eyes, afterwards, when the detail of more spectacular sights has blurred.

A few miles on is Biron, a tall castle, a famous name. From a distance the castle is etched against the sky. Near to, it is visibly damaged—it was partly destroyed in the Revolution—but it is still an imposing mass. You can ascend the ramp, ring a bell at the great gate, and enter the terraced courtyard. There is a view of the round horizon, and the outside of a delicately carved Renaissance chapel and gate-house. The castle is privately

owned now, not by the Birons, and the chapel is being repaired by the Beaux-Arts. Both are shut to visitors.[1] The chapel has lost its chief treasure, in any case. A 'Descent from the Cross' and a 'Deposition in the Tomb', both classed as historic monuments, were somehow declassed by a recent de Biron and sold to Pierpont Morgan. They are now in the Metropolitan Museum of New York, a fact the Périgourdins resent deeply. This sale is somehow reminiscent of the Biron history, for the men of that line, sitting in their castle that overbore the country as far as the eye could see, never admitted any limit to their needs or their desires. They were soldiers by heredity, but when the Renaissance touched them, they built their chapel actually on the roof of the old village church, which they no longer thought was good enough for them. Father and son, they were Marshals of France in the Wars of Religion, fighting against the Protestants, and later for Henry III and Henry of Navarre against the Catholic League. The younger, made duke and peer by Henry IV, thought he could get himself a kingdom by betraying France to Spain at the last, and was executed for treason.

The third bastide which retains its ancient shape is Monflanquin. Its *cornières* are the most complete of them all, running right round the square, and it is set defiantly on a peaked hill. Its fortified church, the knowledgeable will observe, has been a good deal restored, but it is fine all the same. This was a French bastide, for it was built by Alphonse de Poitiers, the brother of St. Louis, who was married to the heiress of Toulouse and left to keep the southern marches in order while the king went off on his ill-starred Crusades. From here the road runs down to Villeneuve-sur-Lot, itself a bastide once. The series of fortress towns that marks the frontiers between the Capet and Angevin spheres at the time of the English Henry III forms a chain across the height of land separating the Dordogne and the Lot. The traveller may choose this way of going from one river to the other. The country scenery is not perhaps so pretty as that farther east, but the towns are more interesting than those on the other roads.

Right: One of the carved stone panels which surround the old door in the church of Sainte-Marie in Souillac.

Opposite: A delightful stretch of the River Ouysse by the fortified mill of Cougnaguet near Rocamadour.

Souillac and Rocamadour

Souillac marks the mid-course of the Dordogne. It is an important crossroads, for here both road and rail from Paris to Cahors and Toulouse cut the river road. It is a good centre for touring the two causses, of Martel to the north and of Gramat to the south.

It may be because of this position that Souillac has lost the atmosphere of age. As the river towns go, it is commonplace. But it has a glory, the church of Sainte-Marie. This is, with the Cathedral of Cahors, the finest great church built in the Périgourdin Romanesque. Its domes, formerly roofed over, have been uncovered and repaired. From the east, they join with the round ends of the radiating chapels to make a delightful complex of circular lines and masses. Inside, the church is so proportioned that the domed nave and semi-domed transepts give an impression of mysterious space, of serenity and shelter.

At the west end there is a door removed from outside when the eighteenth-century clergy were ill-advised enough to add a classical west façade. The carvings are jumbled and, as it were, turned inside out, but they are important. The space above the

door is filled with scenes of the story of the Monk Théophile. He had a burning desire to build a church, but his superiors forbade it. The devil took advantage of his longing, and offered to see that he attained it, at the usual price, his soul. There they are, Théophile handing the signed deed to Satan, and then doing homage with his hands between Satan's hands. He built his church and dedicated it to the Virgin Mary. But the day of reckoning must come. Théophile, worn out with remorse and terror, fell asleep and dreamed. As you can see, the Virgin flew headlong down from heaven, snatched the fatal parchment from Satan's grip and gave it back to Théophile.

This tale was popular in the twelfth century. It seems to the modern mind to have singularly little connection with Christian morals, since the only person who emerges with some credit is the devil, who was at least a devil of his word. But it is a perfect example of the conquest of strength by cunning, of Brer Rabbit outwitting Brer Fox, the theme that runs through the legend of every clime—all that there is of the most *folklorique*, as the French say.

The Souillac carvings are, however, seriously interesting for the vivacity of the sculpture. Satan is a terrible figure, a skeleton consumed by evil, with the head of Pan, but of Pan with his merriment turned to cruel glee, the embodiment of panic fear. Here, far more than in the crude statues in the museums, is the legacy of the Romans, in a god who still perhaps was worshipped by the countrymen, and whom Christianity had turned into a fiend. One can look at this bas-relief and understand a good deal about the cult of witchcraft.

The carven pillar near by has two sides with the same play on fear. In front the Seven Deadly Sins are carved as animals, except for Pride, who is a man, with the strange Romanesque devil-beasts strangling and eating them. One side is devoted to Lust, chaining its victims together for ever. But the third is the theme of Redemption, with a tender Abraham hiding Isaac's eyes in his breast as he raises the knife to strike. On either side of the door are figures of two Messianic prophets. The Isaiah is

Opposite: Rocamadour seen from the road which leads up on to the Causse de Gramat from l'Hospitalet.

famous in sculpture. The figure with his scroll is alive, dancing with compassion. It is the Isaiah of 'Comfort ye!'

The best way from Souillac to Rocamadour is by the river to Pinsac, where the road crosses and follows the left bank to Meyronne between castles. The Castle of la Treyne, on the left bank over the bridge of Pinsac, contains the collection of M. Santiard. There are good pictures and carvings, and many antiques, among them the furniture of a state bedroom of that tragic potentate, the Emperor Charles V.[1] Then you mount the Causse de Gramat. It is a landscape of grass and stone walls, uneventful till suddenly the canyon of Rocamadour gapes beside the road.

The gorge forms the bed of the River Alzou. It drops four hundred feet sheer from the edge. At Rocamadour it actually overhangs the shrines built up the cliff on a series of narrow shelves. The oldest of them was destroyed by a rock-fall in the eighteenth century. A stair climbs the precipice from the sanctuaries to a rebuilt castle, which used to house the knights who guarded the shrine and now serves as presbytery for its priests.[2]

Seen from l'Hospitalet, the churches, the impending cliff, the straggling old village below, the gleam of the winding river, make a superb view. You feel that it must truly have been a holy place, for pilgrims to have come to this savage cleft.

Rocamadour was indeed one of the great pilgrimages of the Middle Ages. If it did not count with Jerusalem, Rome, and Compostella, it was as frequented as Canterbury. Yet no event of religious history sanctified it. It was a legendary shrine, in that paralleling that of St. James. In the eleventh century the body of a small man was found there. He may have been one of the early Christians who became hermits in solitary places. At all events the monks who found it declared it the body of Zacchaeus, the little friend of Christ. They averred that he had escorted the Marys to Provence, and afterwards come to this desert to devote a life of prayer to the memory of the Blessed Virgin. The faithful of the time believed the story, and a great pilgrimage to the relics of Zacchaeus, called Amadour, the

1 La Treyne is now a luxury hotel and no longer houses M. Santiard's collection.

2 There is now a lift from the village to the chapels, and a new lift service to the top of the cliff is due to open in the summer of 1989.

Lover of Mary, lasted for centuries. Its power was augmented by the presence in the upper shrine of a miraculous statue of the Virgin.

The lonely hamlet became a walled town—it still has six of its gates—much bigger than it is now. But with the decay of the habit of pilgrimage, Rocamadour became the scene of a small local fête, when the women of the neighbourhood mounted the stair to the chapel on their knees. In the nineteenth century an energetic *curé* determined to exploit the shrine, and revived it partly as a pilgrimage and partly as a tourist attraction, which is the character it bears today.

The way to the churches lies along the narrow street, till you reach the bottom of the Staircase of the King. At its top is a group of chapels built into the cliff. Some are modern, with eighteenth-century, and in one case Renaissance altars. The oldest is the Subterranean Chapel, containing the charred ashes of the bones of St. Amadour—for the Huguenots burned the relics in the Wars of Religion. 'These relics date from the time of Christ,' says the guardian, whose eloquent voice recalls the Comédie Française. 'And how do we know? Because, Mesdames et Messieurs, we have documents! And what proved that these bones, found uncorrupted after so many centuries after their interment, were those of Zacchaeus, was that they were the bones of a little man.' He leads the visitors upstairs to the upper church, Romanesque transitional in date, and much disfigured by vulgar and badly-painted frescoes depicting the Very Important Persons, such as kings and dukes, who visited the shrine long ago. It is hoped that the Beaux-Arts are going to remove these nasty nineteenth-century pictures.[1] Thence a terrace runs to the Virgin's Chapel, of which one side is the living rock. It replaces the shrine crushed by the fallen cliff. The rocky wall is black with the smoke of the candles that burn there always, lighted by pilgrims. A miraculous bell hangs in the roof; it used to ring of itself when the Virgin wrought a miraculous cure, but seems to have abandoned the habit of late. There on the altar is the Mother of Jesus. She is a Black Virgin, of time-darkened wood, small and very old. Unlike most Black Virgins, who are dressed in satin and lace robes like Korean dolls, she wears no robe beyond that carved by the original sculptor, save for a little tulle veil streaming behind her crown. This is because the bottom of the statue is worm-eaten, and the Beaux-Arts have ordained that she must be left in her pristine state to preserve the wood. It is notable that the style of her dress is that of the Middle Ages—much like that of the Belle Verrière of Chartres—not that of Roman times. But the guardian declares: 'You are seeing the statue of the Blessed Virgin which was revered by Zacchaeus. It dates therefore from the age of Christ; a veritable relic of the period of the Incarnation.'

Like most deeply venerated Black Virgins, it is not a work of art. This Mary might have been carved by the village carpenter, or by a monk unskilled in sculpture, for the creation of such a statue, to be announced as one thousand years old, must have been kept a secret. But such images are worshipped not for their beauty, but because of their emanation of supernatural influence. The Virgin of Rocamadour has that power. Her dark face wears a one-sided smile, proud and secret. Her eyes gaze straight in front of her. She regards neither the robed Babe between her hands, nor the pilgrim who, heedless of the giggling group of tourists in the church, has dropped to his knees before her altar. All round the church are votive offerings; thanks for her intervention; gratitude for cures inscribed on marble slabs in purple letters; fetters of criminals, so they say, whose punishment was to walk to the shrine in chains; models of ships she saved from wreck on the prayer of the sailors. But she smiles her strange, magic-working smile, as though she were amused at her own miracles.

Outside on the terrace are traces of medieval frescoes, and a replica of Roland's sword, Durandel, which he vowed to the Virgin of Rocamadour when he went to Roncesvalles (though the Virgin had not been discovered then). It is a tale among so many other tales which surround the shrine; some of them true. Even the list of pilgrim kings is not quite correct; St. Louis, the scholars say now, never came here. But the Angevin

---

1 They have.

King Henry II did, and at least two of his sons; lamentable John, to expiate his sins, and the wastrel Young King Henry, to cap all of his, by looting the shrine to pay his *routiers*.

At that time Rocamadour must have been immensely rich, and well worth the looting. You leave the shrines, with their queer mixture of the psychologically true and the palpably spurious, and descend the stair, where souvenir shops invade the very precincts, to the street lined with restaurants advertising expensive lunches for the greedy, and booths stacked with hideous medals and brass knick-knacks not even made here but in some northern factory. It is commercialized religion, profoundly disheartening and even shocking. Yet it is essential to make an imaginative effort and to see that in its great days the pilgrimage must have been the same in essence. Now there are charabancs in rows. Then there were Hospitallers of St. John to guide the pilgrims over the robber-infested causse. The too-eloquent guardian is the true successor of the monk who conducted the pilgrims of the thirteenth century. If you read the *Canterbury Tales*, you realize how strong the tourist and picnic element was in these pilgrimages. Nothing alters, in human history, about shrines. No doubt if a visitor wanted to change a large note, he could easily find a money-changer at Rocamadour. Yet there is still the real pilgrim on his knees, under the faint smile and level gaze of the Virgin.

Rudelle and Assier

The Causse de Gramat is poor country, but not so poor that it is incultivable. This may account for its abundance of old buildings. It has been possible for the people to make houses, castles, and churches, but with a great effort, out of their poverty. Once they are made, they have to last a long time. This being so, it is fortunate that the causse has one natural resource, stone of good quality and great beauty. This is the old province of Quercy, and there is a style in farm and village that can fairly be called 'Quercynois'. Red-tiled roofs, the older ones made of curved pantiles, turn up at the eaves, giving the houses

2 Assier is open morning and afternoon daily except Tuesdays.

a gay, Chinese air. Every farm has a pigeon-loft, rising above its roof like a tiny tower, so that it looks like a castle in miniature. Some villages are entirely composed of such houses.

Next to Rocamadour, the star turn of the causse is the cave of Padirac, of which an account is given later. The road from Padirac to St-Céré is well worth following to the turn marked 'Autoire'. This is a gulf that opens in the north edge of the causse. The stream in its bed has a high fall, greatly admired by the French who love waterfalls; and the road beside it drops to a gorge containing the picturesque village of Autoire.

The main road from Rocamadour to Figeac is not particularly pretty, but it leads to two interesting places. From any point, the traveller might suppose that Rudelle was built round a castle. And so it is, in a sense, for the church is neither more nor less than a donjon-tower. Its oblong mass is topped with battlements, and pierced with arrow-slots. Only the door, and the Virgin niched high above it, reveal that it is a church. Inside, like most fortress-churches, it is a Gothic building. At some point the demand must have been made for more light than the loopholes admitted. Unfortunately Romanesque windows were pierced in the walls, no doubt under the delusion that they were harmonious because they were the oldest form of window. There are two guard-room storeys before you arrive at the crenellated roof.

South of Rudelle lies Assier. Galiot de Genouillac lived here. He was the armourer of Francis I, and made a great fortune like many a munitions magnate before and since. He built himself a fine château in the new Renaissance style, and decorated it with carved pillars and scenes of the Labours of Hercules. But the Revolution left only one wing of it standing.[2] He rebuilt the church as well (Renaissance churches are rare in the south-west), and adorned it all round the outside with a frieze which must delight lovers of Walt Disney films. It shows cannon in all their uses. Huge guns protrude from the walls of tiny castles, or shoot great balls at the battlements. There is a complete campaign portrayed in strip-relief. Inside the church Galiot lies in his tomb; but his likeness stands over it in relief, leaning on a

Martel, Turenne, Collonges

gun-barrel, nonchalantly poised on one foot on a large cannon-ball, vaunting his success by his motto 'J'aime fort une', and by an epitaph saying that an honourable life survives death in good repute. It never seems to have occurred to him that there was anything odd about covering the walls of the shrine of a merciful God with the glorification of weapons of destruction. But this was the hubris of the French Renaissance, before the Wars of Religion came to shatter it.

Nine miles north-east of sophisticated Souillac, Martel crowns its causse. It is finely set, showing its seven towers, and the traveller says to himself that it cannot be as good as it looks from a distance. But it is quite as good. The little town lies within the wide street that marks its former walls. It is full of old houses, especially the 'Maison du Roi', a medieval house said to replace that in which the Young King Henry died in torment of body and soul. The market-place is delightful, apart from its old pillared stalls. The Raymondie, the town hall, is sixteenth century and must be one of the smallest and prettiest of France. It is so peaceful that the doorway is apt to be occupied by a hen educating a brood of ducklings.[1] The church is glorious. It is a fortress-church, whose towered east end is pierced by a Flamboyant window with some old glass. Under its great porch is a beautiful Romanesque door, surmounted by a 'Last Judgment'. It is less elaborate than most of the famous doors, but the figure of Christ is merciful and moving, between two flighty angels.

Martel distils lavender and a walnut-liqueur called 'noix'.[2] The prejudices of the author should have no weight in a traveller's book; but I cannot help stating here that of all the towns of the Dordogne basin, little Martel, old, dreaming, untouched by tourist maquillage, is my choice. It is also an excellent centre for the Bas Limousin and for the river road to St-Céré and Beaulieu.

All this country was part of the Viscounty of Turenne in old days. The title and land passed from one name to another, for

the Turennes were not accustomed to die in their beds, and their possessions sometimes went by distaff inheritance. But they were always important nobles. They held direct from the crown, paying homage to no lesser liege-lord; and within the county of Turenne they were independent sovereigns, running their own government, till the last of the line left his lands and title to the king in the eighteenth century.

Turenne, accordingly, is a capital city. It is on the small side, perhaps, with less than a thousand citizens. But it has all the marks of aged aristocracy. Few of its houses are later than the seventeenth century, many of them go back to the fifteenth. Their high-pitched roofs pile up to the castle walls. There are in fact two castles; one, the Tower of Caesar, is given rather too much seniority, since it dates not from the Romans but from the thirteenth century. The other is later and is still lived in. The visitor can climb the stair of Caesar's Tower and look at the view of hills and valleys all around;[3] for this begins to be the foothills of the Massif Central. Going down, it is worth while to go into the church. It has the air of the Counter-Reformation, but its interior is unusual, because it was built by the Protestant Vicomte de Turenne of the Wars of Religion, and its Protestant structure is still apparent, in spite of its conversion and a 'Spanish' gilded altar.

The Turennes had their own administration, but they did not keep it in their capital. It was situated some miles away, at a distance prolonged by difficult cross-country riding, at Collonges. Collonges-la-Rouge is rightly so called. It stands in the red sandstone outcrop of Limousin, and it is a red village. It is old, beautiful, and comic. The church has a fine Romanesque tower, and a doorway with a remarkable 'Ascension', in white stone, for the red sandstone is difficult to work, and the carvers brought their stone from elsewhere. The village consists almost entirely of castles. For the nobles who governed Turenne for the Vicomtes were by no means going to live in *bourgeois* houses. Each one of them must have a castle with a tower, or perhaps two towers. Two of them are still lived in as castles; the others have become farms, or in some cases shops. But they are

1 La Raymondie (which is now known to date back as far as the thirteenth century) houses the Syndicat d'Initiative and a small museum.

2 Lavender is no longer distilled, but *eau de noix* is still a thriving industry. Just outside Martel on the Bretenoux road is a working walnut oil mill which is open to visitors.

3 The château and Caesar's Tower are open morning and afternoon daily from early April to late September, and on Sunday and holiday afternoons the rest of the year.

unaltered in their air of solemn, ridiculous nobility; they are odd, they are delicious—they are Collonges, and there is nothing like it anywhere else.

'You find Collonges beautiful?' asked one of the two elderly ladies who had seated themselves in a strategic position at the door of their castle. On receiving an enthusiastic assent: 'Ah yes! But what is there to live for in Collonges? Nothing happens here. Only we old ones remain.' 'All the same, the land is particularly fertile; agriculture must be prosperous,' said the foreigner, looking at the rich red-soiled fields. 'Yes, prosperous enough, but there are no hands to do the work,' continued the lady. 'The young all go away. Why! Even Brive is thirteen miles distant! Now, my children are in Paris—' 'And mine in Bordeaux,' said the other. 'Naturally they return for holidays,' continued the spokeswoman. 'What becomes of the properties, then?' asked the foreigner. 'Big proprietors buy them as they become vacant,' said the dame. 'Only they can pay wages to the labourers. Collonges empties herself.'

Perhaps it is not so comic after all, the city of little castles.

Carennac and Montal

A road drops from Martel to a bridge at Gluges. The Dordogne is held here in a semicircle of high purple-pink cliffs called le Cirque de Montvalent, and on the way eastward the road runs between the river and the steep northern edge of the Causse de Gramat. Presently it reaches the red roofscape of the village of Carennac. The castle wall encloses the abbey, where Fénélon was Prior in the late seventeenth century, and whose surroundings inspired his novel of *Télémaque*. He was in small favour at Paris because he believed in persuasion rather than in violence in converting Huguenots to the Roman Catholic faith; yet his eloquence was so moving and successful that even the court junta of ecclesiastics could not ignore him. So it was only for a time that he held the dignity of this remote priory in his own countryside, living in the abbey-castle and watching the river flow over white pebbles round the islands he wove into his romance. Carennac was a backwater, no doubt,

for a priest of his talent; yet he was enviable enough. The abbey church built of the stone of the neighbouring quarry, is milk-white as when it was hewn eight hundred years ago. There is a fine Romanesque door with a 'Christ in Glory' on the lintel; inside the tall dim church a sixteenth-century 'Deposition in the Tomb', and beside it a small two-storeyed cloister.

Farther on, the northward curve of the Dordogne is dominated by the rose-red sandstone mass of Castelnau-Bretenoux. This is a great ruin, on the scale of its namesake down-river, crowning a conical hill. The donjon, the main walls and corner-towers still stand; the interior was burnt by a nineteenth-century owner for the insurance money. But M. Muliérat, a tenor of the 'Opéra Comique', bought it, restored it, and furnished some rooms, leaving it to the State when he died. So what was the keep of the second barony of France is shown to summer visitors, who find it worth the seeking out for the view from the tower alone.[1]

The main road passes the turn to Castelnau, and runs in a reedy glen till a sign says 'Au Château de Montal'. Here, perched on the hillside above a rough lane, is the most perfect Renaissance castle of the region. From below Montal is just another oblong, towered keep. But the courtyard, facing south, is carved like a jewel-casket with intricate gables, a frieze in bas-relief, and portrait-medallions.[2]

Montal has two stories, of the woman who built it and of the man who rebuilt it. In the sixteenth century, when France had drunk the gay wine of the Renaissance, Jehanne de Balzac, Baronne de Montal, raised a new house on the foundations of her castle for her adored son, Robert de Montal. But he was killed on the disastrous field of Pavia. His mother was heart-broken. She finished the wonderful manor, but on one of the gables, where a headless statue is said to symbolize Robert, she carved 'Plus d'Espoir—' 'No More Hope'. All round the court her initials and those of her son are intertwined in monogram among the delicate devices. A younger son, Dordé, was a priest in orders. Much against his mother's will he was dispensed from his vows to inherit the barony, and married

1 Castelnau-Bretenoux is open morning and afternoon daily except Tuesdays and public holidays.

2 Montal is open morning and afternoon daily except Saturdays. In July and August it is open on Saturdays too.

The interior of the castle equals the court; a series of noble rooms furnished in contemporary tables, chests and tapestries is shown. Its great beauty is the staircase, a superb transition between the spiral and the stair in flights, with the underside of each step carved in a different exquisite design. The delicacy of the carving in the white Carennac marble of which Montal is made has suffered neither stain nor flaw in the centuries.

Yet the château, not so long since, was only a shell sustained by that marvellous stair. It had passed from hand to hand, as such great houses do, and finally fell into the grasp of a villain who sold its treasury of carving at Paris. Museums and collectors, the Louvre, South Kensington, Berlin, rich Americans, sent their experts to buy, and the gables and friezes were dispersed about the world. But here comes the second story of Montal; how it found its rescuer. M. Maurice Fenaille, a petrol-millionaire with a finer sense of the uses of money than most wealthy men, saw the despoiled building and bought it. He spent many years and enormous sums of money in buying back the carvings, appealing alike to the cupidity and the artistic sympathy of boards of directors. He restored Montal, almost in its entirety, filled it with beautiful things true to its period, and left it (saving the lifetime of his children) to France. A plain plaque on a wall tells this tale in a few words:

MAURICE FENAILLE
1853–1937
Hanc Domum
Dilexit et Restituit

An old farmhouse in the red-stoned village of Collonges-la-Rouge.

into the Castelnau clan. Jehanne ruled Montal till she died and was buried, as she willed, in the presence of many priests. It is her head, Robert's and Dordé's, and those of their nearest kin, which are carved on the medallions in the court. They are brilliant portraits, with the exact and expressive life of the French miniaturists of the time. The best is that of Jehanne de Montal herself, the head of an ageing woman, her neck wrinkled beneath the strong chin, the eyes and mouth set in tragic lines.

St-Céré, at the end of this road, is set in a hollow at the foot of the rise over to Figeac, which can be traversed by one of two pleasant roads shaded by chestnut groves. The little town has not much interest in itself, but it has become the centre of an artist colony, and is frequented in summer by professors and students. It is surrounded by lovely country, for the Causse de Gramat here is seamed on to the hard rock of the Massif Central, and though some of the paths are rough, there is excellent walking on the slopes of the next lift to the uplands.

CHAPTER FIVE

THE UPPER DORDOGNE

Bretenoux, the Cère, Cantal

Any division of a river valley is bound to seem arbitrary, since the stream itself joins region to region and one town with another. None the less, the point where the Cère flows into the Dordogne does mark a real geographical change. The river-beds lie in a wide triangle of plain. Down-stream and to the west they are in the limestone causse-held valley. Up-stream they drain the crystalline hills of the Massif Central. Dark new colours show in the landscape. The cone of Castelnau-Bretenoux, with its huge red sandstone keep, is an outpost of the high hills.

Bretenoux town is a bastide on the Cère, and retains its grid-plan and some old houses. The Cère itself has a curious course. It is the most important river draining the Cantal, and yet it has never been usable as a water-route. This is because, a few miles above Bretenoux, it emerges from a narrow, rugged gorge, through which the railway runs to Aurillac, but which, in the lower part, has no road, nor even a path. So the only way to see the gorge is to take the train and get out at a wayside halt. Above the gorge lie the pastoral plateaux which are the pedestal of the Cantal. This is grazing country, covered in summer with dark red cattle, from whose milk the herds make an excellent soft cheese. There is an abundance of tall trees in the meadows, and at the top of every rise the view is edged by the Cantal itself. This range is perfectly formed—at least to eyes used to the ancient Scottish mountains. The Cantal was once a single

volcano, and its shattered crest cuts a diadem of cones and spires in terrible grace against the southern sky.

The district capital is Aurillac, a crowded noisy town, unexpectedly busy for this land of grassy heights. It lies in a small fertile plain, and owes its importance to the manufacture of umbrellas, but much more to the cattle-trade. It is the railhead for the region too, and distributes a summer population of visitors along the streams and among the villages; especially of hill-walkers and children sent to holiday camps. The roads and rivers lead round the hills; except for one road famed as the 'Route des Crêtes', which runs right over them. That to the north-east of Aurillac runs high above the Cère, with the rounded Plomb de Cantal across the valley, and the precipitous Puy Griou above it to the east. The Col de Lioran marks the watershed between the Cère and the strange volcano-studded plateau of the Auvergne. The roads north from Aurillac are beautiful. One is the Route des Crêtes, by which it is possible to go by Mandailles, almost to the top of the Puy Marie, or to Salers. That farther west leads to Mauriac, winding in and out of the ravines of the rivers draining the Cantal into the Dordogne. It is marked by ancient villages, most of them with dark Romanesque churches. St-Martin-Valmeroux, with its square surrounded by turreted houses, cannot have changed much for some centuries. Up the valley of the Maronne from it lies Salers, perhaps the prettiest little town

Looking down into the valley of the River Maronne by the light of a summer sunset.

of Auvergne. It was for long a judicial centre, and the towered houses round its tiny square belonged to lawyers, the 'nobility of the robe'. There is a painted stone Pieta in the church. From Salers a road with wonderful views of the Puy Marie and the Cirque de Falgoux runs to Murat, on the far side of the range.

Beaulieu, the Gorges, the Monts Dore

The Dordogne at Beaulieu runs wide and shallow over white gravel. The town used to bear a bad name as a dirty derelict place; but it certainly does not deserve it today. It is spick and span and welcoming. A modern street masks the Romanesque churches, the abbey and the Chapelle des Pénitents.

Beaulieu Abbey is a magnificent Limousin church, built with a nave and aisles, and chapels radiating from the passage behind the high round apse. Its effect is one of height and aspiration, an interesting contrast with the brooding mystery of the Périgourdin abbey of Souillac. From without, the east end circles up to a massive octagonal tower. The glory of the church is, however, the south door. This, if not the most beautiful, is the most complex of the carved portals of the south-west. It is a 'Last Judgment' dominated by the hands of God outstretched in blessing and repudiation. Below the ranks of the saved and the damned is a frieze of writhing apocalyptic beasts. The lintel is sustained by a strange figure flowing upward like a flame of prayer.

The river-road from Beaulieu to Argentat is fifteen lovely miles beside the river. Here it runs in the end of the upper gorges, no longer cliffs, as farther downstream, but steep forested banks some five hundred feet high. Argentat is an attractive old place lying on both sides of the river, in a last widening of the valley below forty miles of gorges.

The Dordogne gorges are beautiful. They were far more beautiful till the river was captured for electricity. But now the water is trapped at intervals and turned into artificial reservoirs, and the river-bed spanned by immense dams and power-stations. The lowest of these, le Chastang, is only a few miles above Argentat.

Right: One of the many old turreted houses and a fortified gateway in the walled village of Salers.

Left: An October landscape near St-Jacques-des-Blats.

The gorges were never accessible throughout their length to motorists, for the roads run zig-zagging down to them from the uplands on either side, and cross the river but do not follow it except for short stretches. But a rough path served the stout walker, or even the resolute bicyclist, and trains of canoes used to shoot the rapids in summer all the way down from Bort-les-Orgues. Now the Dordogne is useless to canoes above Argentat, and the walker finds his route far more difficult. The French are enthusiastically devoted to electricity, and hope that

Above: Old houses, some converted from tanneries, beside the Dordogne in Argentat.

Right: The tree-shaded banks of the Dordogne near Beaulieu in summer.

Opposite: The small château, or *gentilhommière*, near Sourniac.

the power may provide light industry in the riverside towns. Besides, the great works evoke their awed admiration. They have, indeed, the massive cubist effectiveness of all great engineering, as well as its defect of failing to satisfy the eye or the mind for longer than a brief interval. But the loss in natural beauty to France, and even to Europe, is vast and irreparable.

From Argentat one can ascend the Dordogne on the right side, by the Limousin heights, or on the left, by the Cantal uplands; the second is the more interesting. Near to Argentat itself the River Maronne runs in a deep and romantic gorge, with the Tours de Merle on an isthmus in the river-bed.[1] They are two castles where two lords lived till Richelieu's army levelled their walls as it did those of Ventadour on the other side of the Dordogne. To think what life must have been, for a couple of broods of these rustic nobles, cheek by jowl in that remote ravine, is a thing to make the hair rise on the head.

The road from Argentat to Mauriac is straightforward. Mauriac has a fine Romanesque church, Notre-Dame-des-Miracles, with a greatly venerated Black Virgin. It also has a magnificent cattle and horse fair on the 8th of June.[2]

Northwards the road lies over a tableland from which the Monts Dore can be seen from time to time growing nearer. The château of Sourniac is worth a detour. It is an endearingly perfect *gentilhommière*, its living-space cramped between four fat round towers. But its modern defence is a road as stony as a sea-beach.

Bort-les-Orgues, where the road touches the Dordogne once more, is an industrial town lying beneath a ridge of basalt columns to which it owes its name of 'organpipes'. From there the road lifts to the last shelf below the Monts Dore peaks, and the Puy de Sancy dominates the view.

The Monts Dore were once three volcanoes. Now they are a group of agreeable peaks and ridges, covered with grassy meadows and occasional fir-woods. They rise to 6,000 feet, but do not have the effect of anything like that height, because the uplands out of which they spring have already reached some 2,800 feet or more. The highest cone, the Puy de Sancy, is the source of the Dordogne. It is easily accessible on foot or by an electric railway, and has a table of orientation on its summit.

The Dore mountains as a whole are the water-tower of France. The Dordogne and its tributaries flow south-west from it, and many streams feeding the Loire run north-west and east. It has, too, several small lakes, caught in the craters of old volcanoes. France is poor in lakes, and such as exist are valued very highly. The Lac de Chambon on the east side of the range has a lovely view, and with Murols, is a fine walking-centre. Lac Pavin, a perfect circle, and the Lac de Chauvet, both near the road from Latour-d'Auvergne to Besse, are visited daily in summer by swarms of tourists.

The natural use of this high grassland is summer pasture; it is snow-bound for months in winter. But the herds, guarded by remarkably savage dogs, that graze in the summer season, are now secondary to the tourist trade. La Bourboule and le Mont-Dore on the Dordogne, and St-Nectaire on the far side of the ridges are spas where invalids are treated with water from mineral springs for various ailments, but they are also resorts for healthy holiday-makers. The towns are undistinguished, except for the famous Romanesque church of St-Nectaire, and are composed of hotels and boarding-houses. Their prices are high, as is inevitable in places living the year round on the takings of a short summer season. For those to whom urban character is more attractive than *pâtisseries*, Latour-d'Auvergne and Besse-en-Chandesse are preferable to the larger places. Besse is a dark old town. Its celebrated Virgin migrates each year to the sheilings of Vassivière for the summer grazing, amid an immense procession.[3] Latour-d'Auvergne has lost its tower. It was the stronghold of a family famous in French history, from which sprang Henri de Latour-d'Auvergne, the 'Great Turenne', who led the armies of Louis XIII and Louis XIV to victory.

Here in these peaks is the source of the Dordogne, the Dore Water. We have followed it from the sea, so far away; a river that, from its first beginnings as a waterfall in the Puy de Sancy to its majestic estuary, is lovely in all its length.

1 There are regular *son et lumière* presentations at the Tours de Merle during the summer months.

2 Also on 10 November every year.

3 This takes place every 2 July, and the Virgin makes the return journey every 21 September.

CHAPTER SIX

THE LOT

From the Garonne to Cahors

The perched village of St-Cirq-Lapopie
and the River Lot in winter.

The passage from the Dordogne to the Lot offers a wide choice of roads crossing the height of land. Along the height runs the frontier between the old provinces of Périgord and of Quercy and Guienne. For the borders were not, as you might suppose, the rivers themselves. On the contrary, in the days when boats on the stream were a safer and quicker means of transport than the tracks between villages, each province considered its navigable rivers as highways, and the people on either side were neighbours. But up on the barren or forested heights, where few men lived, the lands of the lords, and the grazing and woodcutting of the peasants faded out into areas nobody cared much about; and there ran the economic, as well as the political marches.

There is a main road from Bergerac to Villeneuve-sur-Lot. It passes near to the old town of Issigeac, with a good late Gothic church, and through Castillonès, a bastide which still has its *cornières*. But the rather longer way by Beaumont, Monpazier, and Monflanquin is far more choice. In the same way, the national road from Souillac to Cahors is rather dull, though a detour takes in Labastide Murat, the birthplace of Napoleon's Marshal, which has a wide view. But it does not compare with the chestnut-shaded slope from St-Céré to Figeac. The mountain roads from Aurillac to the Lot are beautiful, whether you choose that by Vieillevie, or that by the Truyère gorges to Entraygues.

The Lot itself, in its lowest reaches before it enters the Garonne at Aiguillon, is a composed and stately river giving no hint of its capricious upper course. It is not especially interesting below Villeneuve. This is a good example of a bastide which has expanded into a busy, and in this case a pleasant modern town. The heart of the city is old, with a thirteenth-century towered gate and an arcaded square. The bridge is old, too, and has a chapel at its north end where a venerated Virgin, almost invisible under her lace flounces, watches over the safety of its passengers. On the hill south of the river there is a little ancient fortified town, Pujols, from whose medieval walls the course of the Lot can be seen for a long way. It is so old, so dying of age, that one is surprised at the sight of a single child drawing water from the well in the tiny square.

Up-stream from Villeneuve, above the left bank, Penne is perched on a 500-foot height. It commands a long view, which no doubt accounted for its being chosen by Richard Cœur-de-Lion as his strong place on the Lot, when he was keeping order in the vast realm of his mother, Eleanor of Aquitaine. One of the fortress-gates is still called la Porte Ricarde, and the bourg is full of medieval houses.

Above Penne the Lot valley is slightly disfigured by industry, up to Fumel, though Monsempron is an interesting old place, and Lustrac with its old mill an enchanting one. From Fumel, however, a narrow valley leads north-east to Bonaguil. The castle stands on a beak of rock, where the valley divides into two, its great towers tall against the sky. A hamlet of old houses leans on the cliff, and at the Café des Ruines, where the castle fishpond is full of enormous carp, the visitor is given the key to the fortress.[1]

> Nine-and-twenty knights of fame
> Hung their shields in Branksome Hall
> Nine-and-twenty squires of name
> Brought them their steeds to bower from stall
> Nine-and-twenty yeoman tall
> Waited, duteous, on them all . . .

So says the 'Lay of the Last Minstrel'. Yet Walter Scott, or any of his countrymen, looking at Branksome, might be puzzled to know how a hundred soldiers could get inside it. But three times as many, with their grooms, armourers, cooks, scullions, and assorted womenkind, could live in Bonaguil without overcrowding. The puzzle here is why this enormous pile was ever raised in such a lonely glen, with neither rich land nor a strategic position to recommend it. Its history was odd enough. The thirteenth-century donjon, to whose roof one may climb, was built by a *seigneur* of Castelnaud, who took the huff at his neighbours on the Dordogne, and retired to the remotest corner of his lands. Later it passed by female inheritance to Jean de Roquefeuil, who rebuilt it from 1450 on. He and his son elaborated the fortress into a system of walls within walls, and towers guarding towers, the whole designed like the prow of a ship to offer as narrow a target as possible to guns firing from

the heights across the ravine. The castle itself had gun emplacements to enfilade attackers. This is a late example of deliberately military construction. But the day of the great medieval castles was over. Once the peace of the eighteenth century gained the interior of France, nobody wanted to live in a castle like this. Bonaguil went from hand to hand; one of its owners is said to have sold it for 100 francs and a bag of walnuts. After the Revolution the Commune of Fumel bought it; and when the visitor gives his fee to Madame the Proprietress of the Café des Ruines, he is helping to pay for its upkeep, and possibly contributing a few pence to the municipal funds. Back at the Lot, the road runs on the right bank. It would not be accurate to say on the north bank, for about here the Lot begins to reveal its true character, of the most winding river of France. The Dordogne is given to *cingles* in the limestone country, but it is nothing compared with the Lot. From its source to Fumel it turns and twists upon itself. Here in the lower reaches the curves may be two or three miles deep, with the neck of land at the top of the loop only a few hundred yards across. The steep hills, often enough cliffs, which limit the river are set fairly wide apart, and between them the stream links along at its capricious will, taking at least four times as long to find its eventual western way as though it ran straight. It is an idle, frivolous, time-wasting course, and it could not be more attractive. Beside the river, the scene changes with each meander; from commanding points on the hills the eye is fascinated by the ravelled thread of water.

The villages along this side of the river valley are ancient. Duravel has a church of the eleventh century, built on a crypt earlier still. It has a contemporary sarcophagus containing three 'Holy Bodies', brought back from Palestine, and no doubt sold to a simple Crusader in the same brisk traffic in bogus relics that endowed Cadouin with the Holy Winding-Sheet. Puy l'Evêque reflects its climbing streets of old houses, and the square towers of the castle of the Bishops of Cahors and of the church in the slow stream. Castelfranc is a bastide, facing the Château d'Anglars on the other bank. Luzech spans the neck of

a beautiful link with a canal carved through the hill. The Château de Mercuès, of which part is thirteenth century and part a modern hotel, dominates the hills from the north as the road runs into Cahors.

Cahors

Cahors is a natural stronghold. It lies in a loop of the Lot, surrounded by the river except for a narrow isthmus on the north. Part of its defensive ramparts still cross the neck. The only weakness of the peninsula was want of good drinking-water; but in peacetime that was supplied (as it is now) by the strong spring across the river called la Chartreuse. Once it was named Divona. There was an aqueduct, too, bringing the water of the Vers from the east. If these were cut off in wartime, the citizens could just drink the Lot and have dysentery.

The ancient city has been missed by modern industry. It is crossed by the main road from Paris to the eastern Pyrenees and by the railway to Toulouse. Apart from those and the suburbs built to house the modern overflow of population, Cahors is much as it was any time since its medieval wealth decayed.

The linen-export of Gallo-Roman times is gone. But red wine, 'Vieux Cahors', still sells to distant markets. The university established by Pope John XXII in 1331 in his birthplace was closed in the eighteenth century, though one of the students' colleges, the Collège Pélegri, keeps its fifteenth-century tower. The old town lying east of the main street is full of houses of any date from the thirteenth century onwards. They are put to modern uses, so that the sixteenth-century Hôtel de Roaldès is occupied by a bicycle shop. That is preferable, at least, to letting it fall down or turning it into an ineffective museum.[2]

Cahors has two monuments of its great days when its merchants were known all over the world—not flatteringly known since they were addicted to usury. The Cathedral of St-Etienne comes first. Its fortified façade on the market-place is grim enough. But inside is an early Périgourdin church

Opposite: The view of Puy-l'Evêque seen from the bridge over the Lot.

1 Sadly the Café des Ruines has gone, and the château entrance fee (which still goes to the *commune*) is collected at the gate. It is open morning and afternoon daily from Easter to September, and afternoons only from March to Easter.

2 It is now a private house, and may sometimes be visited in summer (details from the Syndicat d'Initiative).

formed of two great domes. The western dome preserves some fourteenth-century frescoes in the cupola; those in the eastern dome have been badly restored.[1] The round Romanesque apse was altered to Gothic in the late thirteenth century, but the builders managed to preserve the harmony of the original semicircle. So did not the canons of the eighteenth century, who clapped a graceless portico into the nave. There is a fine late Gothic cloister, unfortunately much damaged. The north door of the cathedral is its glory. It is of the same kind as those of Beaulieu and Moissac, but is the crown of them all. The subject is the Ascension. The figure of Christ is deeply moving; the still face expresses a godhead accepted, not desired.

The other pride of Cahors is the Pont Valentré. This fortified bridge is called the most beautiful in the world; and it well may be. Its three slim towers, its six great Gothic arches, and the diamond-shaped buttresses of its piles, are repeated in broken reflection in the rippling Lot.

City Fathers are an even more peculiar sort of men than Cathedral Canons. Cahors had three superb old bridges in 1850; another of the fourteenth century, and the third, the Pont-Vieux, even older and defended by five towers, no less. Anyone might suppose that the councillors, in the opening age of popular travel, would have cherished those bridges like their heart's blood, and then lived in prosperity for ever, upon the profits of admiring tourism. But no—cast-iron had been invented. So they pulled down the Pont-Vieux in 1868, and the other in 1907, and replaced them by the Pont Louis-Philippe and the Pont-Neuf, both hideous.

Cahors with its three bridges must have been one of the jewels among earth's cities. Even now, with streets of old houses and square towers, with the Pont Valentré and the cathedral door, it is an exciting place to wander in. As the capital of Quercy, it fairly sparks with history. Its bishops were great lords who treated the city as their appanage. They raised it against the English kings who owned Quercy from time to time. It gave birth to Clément Marot, whose verse translations

of the Psalms were the songs of the Reformation, and later the inspiration of the Camisards. But it was not a Protestant town; in 1562 the mob massacred the Calvinists at their meeting. Under its bishop, Cahors refused admission to its suzerain, Henry of Navarre; and after a hard-fought siege the king allowed his troops to sack it in 1580. The democratic leader Gambetta, who defied the Prussians in 1870, came from Cahors, and its main street is proudly named after him. There is also one called after Aristide Briand, which causes the tourist to wonder if the mind of Cahors is as old-world as its stones.

Cahors to Figeac

The Lot above Cahors and its tributary the Célé flow in faults in the limestone causses. The cliffs which hold them vary in brilliant colour from tones of yellow to shades of pink. Both rivers are dramatic; the little Célé perhaps the more charming of the two.

The road along the Lot follows the north side of the valley; every now and then it runs in a tunnel, for it is carved out of the cliffside. This valley does not have the rich alluvial plains of the Dordogne, and its castles, accordingly, are less grandiose. All the same, every gap in the cliffs, where a few fields afford life to a village, is surmounted by a tower. On the north side are Laroque, Conduché, and Larroque-Toirac, with its high medieval donjon. Here also lies Cajarc, where President Pompidou spends his holidays in a *résidence secondaire* he purchased from the uncle of Françoise Sagan, the novelist.[2] When General de Gaulle insisted that every one of his ministers must occupy some post in local government, to keep them in touch with the people, M. Pompidou presented himself as a candidate at Cajarc, and was duly elected to the town council.

On the other side of the river are Arcambal, the great castle of Cénevières built on a cliff overhanging the river, and Salvagnac. Few of them can be visited;[3] they are decorations of the landscape, as are the honey-coloured red-roofed villages. The best of these is Saint-Cirq-Lapopie, on the left bank. The

1 Nothing remains of those in the eastern dome. A restoration programme in 1981-2 removed the nineteenth-century work and found the original beyond repair. The western dome has been fully restored.
2 Mme Pompidou is still a regular visitor.
3 Larroque-Toirac is open morning and afternoon daily from 1 July to 1 September; Cénevières morning and afternoon daily from Easter to 1 November.

Opposite: The village of Calvignac, perched on a cliff overlooking the Lot.

village clambers up an escarpment so steep that the door of each house is about level with the roof of that below. A great Gothic church crowns the height; and the whole is encircled in a hollow hill. The entire village is 'classé monument', and indeed there is not a modern house in it. There are drawbacks about the position of a protected beauty spot. Nothing can be altered without the leave of the Ministry des Beaux-Arts. 'And the Ministère des Beaux-Arts', said a householder of Saint-Cirq-Lapopie, 'quite simply does not answer letters. We had a part of a roof damaged. You cannot leave a hole in your roof; you risk a serious dilapidation. We wrote to the Ministère explaining that we had to mend it and asking them to subscribe to the cost, since they dictate the use of old curved pantiles. For as you know they are hard to come by and very dear—and moreover they do not wear so well as the new ones. Well the Ministry did not reply for nine months and so we mended the roof. We used modern tiles, but we took great care, and they are not visible from anywhere. And then this individual from the Ministry came and told us that we should not have done it. And Mademoiselle, I ask you, how can we share in modern progress if we have to ask leave of the Ministry before we install so much as a window or a water closet?—and for the rest, if they will not answer communications? If they want to conserve us as a historic monument, they ought in equity to share the expense.'

The road passes below the village of St-Pierre-Toirac, which has a curious Romanesque church with fourteenth-century fortifications, and runs up the 1,000-foot ridge dividing the Lot from the Célé to Figeac.

Figeac is a prosperous town, with suburbs of horrible new villas round an old centre. It is always a surprise to find degraded modern architecture side by side with an excellent traditional idiom; one would suppose that the architects would revolt at the sight of their own blue-prints and the masons strike rather than build. But alas!—this does not happen. Incompetent men in some city such as Bordeaux have no shame in disfiguring fine places with roguey-poguey villas, just as if they were building societies running up bad work in a London suburb.

Figeac has some good old houses. The windows in this part of the country are characteristic, for it used to be common to leave one room of the upper storey open as a sort of veranda, locally called a 'soleilho'—a sun-room. There are a couple of old churches, both badly damaged in the Wars of Religion, when Figeac was captured by the Huguenots and held for some years. The finer, the Romanesque abbey of Saint-Sauveur, has been decently restored. The showpiece of the town is a thirteenth-century mint, a charming little building with a market-hall below and a galleried upper storey.[1]

The principal export of Figeac is M. Charles Boyer.

Figeac lies on the Célé, and the valley of that river to its junction with the Lot is one of the most romantic things of the region. At first it is a wide gentle vale, but soon it narrows between cliffs and steep hills, with the little river meandering to and fro between them. There is everything the heart could desire: old buildings, sometimes rather ruined, and small; tall poplars by the fishy stream, a Renaissance castle standing in the fields, a cave with Magdalenian sculpture at Ste-Eulalie, a former convent-church at Espagnac with an altar-piece by Vouet, terribly repainted, representing Anne of Austria unsuitably ascending to heaven as the Virgin of the Assumption.[2] Espagnac, among many others, might be chosen as the perfect example of a Quercynois village.

Brengues lies below a curious castle called the Château des Anglais which is really a refuge-fort built into the cliff. Marcilhac is entirely constructed within the remains of a tenth-century abbey burnt by the Protestants. Below this point the Célé runs in a menacing gorge, where the village of Sauliac claws on to the red rock, to Cabrerets where there is a museum of prehistory in the château. Near by is the cave of Pech-Merle, with animal paintings on the walls.[3]

The French, whose fortitude in sightseeing is astonishing, will advise the tourist to make a round of the Lot and Célé valleys, beginning from either Cahors or Figeac. But in fact

1 It now houses a small museum and the Syndicat d'Initiative.

2 The lady who looks after the key is usually to be found near by; otherwise ask at the Mairie.

3 The Amédée-Lemozi Museum has moved up the road to a building beside the entrance to Pech-Merle. Both are open morning and afternoon daily from Easter to 1 November.

there is far too much to see to attempt this in a single excursion; and members of less enduring races will do well to give at least a day to each of those valleys.

The Causse and the Valley

Old, unchanging beauty is too often purchased at the price of stagnation. It must be owned that much of the fascination of Quercy is attributable to poverty. If the fortress-mill of Coimbre on the Lot is fifteenth century, it is because the millers could not afford new buildings and machinery. The people of the valleys live a life which is hard enough; those on the causse one which is harder still. A wayside conversation illustrates the point. The tourist had parked her car at Causse de Brengues, above the cliff shadowing Brengues. She asked the way to the Château des Anglais, and picked her steps along a scree-path below the last pitch of the cliff, retreating respectfully before the wriggle of an adder. On her return—as commonly happens—she found people ensconced beside the car prepared for some polite converse. They were an elderly couple and a young girl. She was lovely, with the delicate small features of a Fragonard comtesse, lightly shadowed by the wide straw hat the countryfolk wear for field work.

Madame asked if the tourist had found the castle. Yes, replied the tourist, it was most interesting; could Madame tell her why it was called the Château des Anglais? 'Ah! Because it dates from le Temps des Anglais—the Time of the English.' 'You come from the valley?' said the girl. 'Yes, from Figeac.' 'It must be interesting at Figeac.' 'But here it is very beautiful, Mademoiselle.' 'Yes, but it is not interesting; it must be much more interesting in the valley'—she sighed, the pretty young thing, living there the tied, unending routine of a farm on the causse, with only the people of the other scattered farmhouses for neighbours. No doubt she might be already fiancée to some suitable proprietor's son. But the blood in her round cheeks, the blood drumming in her veins, longed for the pleasures, for the excitement, of life in the villages of the Célé valley.

Right: A winter view of a farm on the banks of the River Célé near Cabrerets.

CHAPTER SEVEN

THE UPPER LOT

Capdenac to Espalion

The Figeac–Albi road cuts across the Lot just at the border of the old provinces of Quercy and the Rouergue. It has to drop about a thousand feet to the river. This is the line, roughly speaking, where the limestone joins the hard stone of the Cantal, and the same formation continues south of the river, for the slaty hills thrust a salient south as far as Villefranche, and east of them is a red sandstone belt called 'le Rougier'. It is not till Espalion that the Lot marks the frontier of the causses, which from that point lie south and east of it, rising from the 1,500-foot Causse du Comtal to the Great Causses. The Lot has worn a narrow bed from Espalion to Capdenac through those old mountains.

Here the balance of attraction shifts. Lower down, the country, especially the cliffs bounding the streams, is often remarkable. But the special delight is human art, buildings of every sort. Up-stream from Capdenac there are villages, castles, and churches, too, some of them splendid and one, at least, supreme. But as a rule it is the natural landscape that holds the eye. As in all true hill-country, the mountains dwarf man and his works. But too much must not be made of this difference; the scales dip on either side only just perceptibly.

The road down to la Madeleine passes some of the last and the best of the Quercynois farmhouses, crosses the river, and turns east to Capdenac-Gare. Or you may take the shorter way by the village of Capdenac, standing on a promontory of the

Summer foliage reflected in the River Lot at the southern end of the gorges, near Estaing.

right bank, looking down at the railway-town across the stream. There could not be a greater contrast. Capdenac was built as a strong point. It has its old gates and ramparts, a donjon-tower, a castle in which Sully lived for a time after his fall from power. It is innocent of sanitation, no doubt, but how much better a place to live in than Capdenac-Gare, ready-made as a railway centre! This is the typical graceless product of the Industrial Revolution, without form or soul, made on the orders of the employers to whom men are hands, not human beings. There is not much modern industry in this part of France, but elsewhere, as here, it bears the Mark of the Beast. Decazeville, farther east, Carmaux, near Albi, have the same inhuman sluttishness. There are, it is fair to say, two kinds of enterprise which seem to remember that workers may care to live in pleasant surroundings. Some of the forestry camps have agreeable wooden houses; and the electric power companies supply their workers with small but decently built flats built in blocks of four.

East of Capdenac the road runs in a narrow valley, steep and wooded. The road is cut, for much of the way, out of the cliffside, in what the French call a 'corniche'—a cornice—and it winds with the stream. It has to be taken slowly. That is all to the good, for it is quite an effort to leave one curve, lest the next should not be so lovely; but it always is. High above the road, at this point is the 'Chataigneraie', the chestnut-country of the

73

Opposite: Estaing's medieval houses, stone bridge and château overlooking the Lot.

Cantal; this can be attained by three roads between this and Entraygues, but it is a stiff climb.

Almost at once the difference from the Causse de Gramat shows in the houses. They are built on the river-bank with the road running above them. They have the same high-pitched roofs as we are used to; and the same pigeon-cote rising above them. But they are made of dark grey or brown stone, and their roofs are covered with round grey slates, laid in a decorative fish-scale pattern. The road runs now on one side of the river, now on the other. At one point it climbs steeply to avoid an escarpment, leaving the village of Livinhac-le-Haut on the other side. There is a secret about that village; no tourist ever visits it, because the tarmac road draws traffic away up the south slope almost, but not quite, to Decazeville.[1] That mining town lies in a lateral valley; the hills here are dark, sharp, and slaty. It is the 'Black Country' of the region. Coal mines are allied with zinc foundries; and Decazeville exudes the whole-hearted gloom of small French industrial towns. But the Lot valley shows no sign of it, and presently the road seeks the river ravine again.

The glen narrows, and the hills grow higher, till in a gap the Truyère comes down from the north, and the road crosses it by a medieval bridge into Entraygues. This little old town is perhaps the best centre for exploring these reaches of the Lot, for it is conveniently placed for both rivers, and for Conques and Rodez to the south. It has a castle, some Renaissance houses, and another fine bridge, the Pont-Marie.

The Truyère is a larger river than the Lot. It has a famous gorge, somewhat spoilt by the dams farther up, which withhold much of the water, except when the sluices are opened and the bather finds himself fleeing up the bank with his clothes clasped to his wet bosom, pursued by a rising tide. To many people the Barrage de Sarrans, the vast electric power works, is itself a great attraction, though permission must be obtained to visit it.[2] The modern enterprise, and the settlements built to house its workers, contrast with small ancient towns and villages, like Orlhaguet, Mur-de-Barrez, and St-Flour.

St-Flour stands on the high pastures of Auvergne, almost on the north–south watershed of the Massif Central. It is a stern hill-town, so strongly placed and walled, in the past, that it resisted all attacks. The Huguenots, for instance, failed to take it. 'Only the wind has ever forced its way into St-Flour,' say its proud people. But the Revolution obliged it to raze its walls, and now it is interesting mainly for its haughty shape, and for its cathedral. This is a dark-coloured Gothic church, with two towers set too close for beauty, and a generally grim aspect, surprising when you learn that it was built to the designs of the master-of-works of Jean, Duc de Berry, that lavishly Flamboyant builder. It contains some interesting things, a Renaissance Christ, a Pieta, and a Black Christ. This Romanesque crucifix, unlike most 'Black' images, is an artistic masterpiece. The figure of Christ, carved with a restrained and simplified technique, is profoundly tragic.

The Lot gorges between Entraygues and Estaing were renowned. And rightly, they were the most beautiful river stretch of France. The spiring cones of the hilltops still overhang them, but the running rapids are gone, drowned beneath a hydro-electric reservoir. With atomic power on the way, the murder of beauty such as this is an unforgivable crime. Estaing is the most picturesque town of the upper river. From its bridge a statue of the Bienheureux François d'Estaing looks at the castle of his birth towering over the riverside houses, reflected in the stream. He was a saint of the Renaissance—a very rare phenomenon. Coming of a long line of soldiers and churchmen, he was the greatest of them all. It was he who built the great tower of Rodez Cathedral out of his revenues as its bishop. On the first Sunday in July the tiny town celebrates its fête; and then the people dressed in costume, as the Heavenly Host, pilgrims to St. James of Compostella, and the members of the line of d'Estaing, walk in procession to church and round the streets.[3] The girls of Estaing refuse to cut their hair short, for that would disqualify them from figuring as angels, let alone as the Blessed Virgin herself.

Above here the valley opens to a strath some 1,000 feet high.

1 Livinhac-le-Haut now boasts several campsites and a new bridge.

2 It is no longer possible to visit the Barrage de Sarrans, but a good view of it may be had from a viewpoint 1.5km from its westernmost point, on the D98 to Cantoin.

3 Known as the Procession de la Saint-Fleuret, this is still an annual event. During the summer months there are regular *son et lumière* presentations at Estaing.

To the north lie the slopes of the Monts d'Aubrac, round featureless hills sparsely dotted with big farmhouses devoted to summer dairying. To the south is the abrupt rise to the Causse du Comtal, a desolate plateau lifting to a ridge here and there. Espalion is a gay town decorated by a riverside castle and frequented by artists in summer. It is a good road-centre. Near by is the rude Romanesque church of Perse, with a queer 'Last Judgment' over the door. On the road to Rodez a turn leads to the village of Bozouls, built in a huge pot-hole of the River Dourdou. It, too, has an odd Romanesque church; for the builders tried to make it too tall for the round arches to carry the strain, and the pillars splay outwards.[1]

The Aubrac hills are too exposed for summer walking, except where the streams that drain their round sides are shaded by beech woods. But in spring, in this region of immemorial pasture, they are covered with flowers, narcissus, cowslips, and many variants of gorse and broom turning the slopes to white and gold.

The river changes its name here to the older, Celtic form of 'Olt'. The people stick to the title partly to show that they belong to the old pre-Roman stock, and as they aver, are undegraded by admixture with Teutonic barbarians. As the Olt, it links to St-Geniez. This is a secretive old town, with an air of decay except in the strawberry season, when it reaps a brief rich harvest. It has a Gothic Penitents' Chapel, and a parish church which, with the Black Penitents' at Villefranche, is the most elaborate example of Baroque decoration in the region.

The Lot runs here along the north side of the Great Causses, the Causse de Sévérac and the Causse de Sauveterre. These are high deserts, almost empty of population save in the grazing season. They are crossed by one main road, from St-Flour to Millau on the Tarn, which gives at one height a wide view of the Cévennes. But it is to be avoided by any who are susceptible to the overwhelming desolation of the country. North of the Lot, however, on this road lies the mountain bastide of Marvejols, with three fortified gates.

The river-road from Barjac on is beautiful, for the Gévaudan has the authentic savage mountainy aspect. Savage is the right word. This is the country which late in the eighteenth century was terrorized by wolves; where the Beast of the Gévaudan killed and ate scores of women and children. The king sent his best shot to destroy it, but when the body was taken to Versailles in 1765 it was only an ordinary-sized grey wolf. None the less, the whole countryside was deforested after that to rid it of the wolves. A few may have lingered on till not so long ago. Wolves were, on the whole, less brutal than the

Left: The ruined château of Tournel, near Bagnols-les-Bains in the upper valley of the Lot.

Right: The church and old riverside houses of St-Geniez d'Olt, seen from the bridge which crosses the Lot.

Mende and the Source

1 The roof, originally covered with *lauzes* (stone tiles) laid on a thick layer of earth, was also too heavy. It was replaced in the seventeenth century.

feudal lords of the Gévaudan, who had an evil name for cruelty, and had to be rooted out like wild beasts too. Even the city of Mende was held for years in the Wars of Religion by de Merle, a Huguenot captain renowned for cruelty. And in 1944 the Germans brought the survivors of the Bir Hakim Maquis, whom they had surrounded and slaughtered on the Causse Méjean, and shot them on the town square of Mende.

Mende, the centre of this wild land, shows little sign of its ferocious history. It lies atilt on the steep slope up from the Lot. With only 7,000 inhabitants it is the smallest *chef-lieu de département* in France. Yet it has the proud air of a capital city, self-sufficient, prosperous, and notably clean; quiet except on market-day, when the 'forains' spread their wares under the cathedral walls. It is an excellent take-off place for the Tarn, whose course lies parallel to the Lot here, with the Causse de Sauveterre and Mont Lozère dividing them.

The Lot at Mende is a smallish mountain stream, and it is pleasant to follow it to its source. The road is consistently agreeable, for it looks across the river to Mont Lozère, a long ridge whose northern side drops in cliffs and buttresses of dark slaty rock wrenched into slanting strata by ancient stresses. They overhang a high valley of small farms, orchards and pinewoods. Bagnols-les-Bains is a tiny modest spa where people have gone to drink the waters since the days of Rome. A mile or so farther on the road runs through a tunnel under Tournel, the perfect robber's castle, from which the medieval lord could see travellers coming either way and fall upon them as they struggled up to the col. Then comes le Bleymard, a hamlet, with the windows of its Romanesque chapel boarded up with planks; and the baby Lot turns away from the road into the northern hills. A path runs on the moor beside it, crosses it by a boulder where a birch tree is reflected in a round pool, and companies it into young fir plantations. There it rises in the Montagne du Goulet, at some 4,000 feet. The road climbs the Col des Tribes, and drops immediately beside the River Altier which runs into the Rhône. Here on this grassy col is the spine and watershed of France.

ROUERGUE UPLANDS

Villefranche and Rodez

The Rouergue uplands between the Lot and the Tarn can be approached from several points. The main road from Figeac to Albi passes near to many of the best things. Rodez and Conques lie nearer to the upper Lot villages. It is necessary to make an arbitrary division, and this is easiest where the Aveyron comes to Villefranche from the east and turns southwards. The astonishing group of castles north of Albi will be described in a later section.

The road climbs the steep rise from la Madeleine to the Ségala. The 'rye-land' is so called because its soil, unkind and sour, used to yield little but the poor man's corn. Recently it has been limed and produces good wheat. There is a noticeable contrast between aged and down-at-heels—though charming—villages and handsome new farmhouses, almost as comfortable as those of Britain. But the whole of upland Rouergue is queer deceptive country. The Aveyron is the only considerable river that drains it; and even it runs for most of its course in unroaded gorges. From almost any hilltop there is a wide view of what seems like unbroken plateau. But if you try to go to the village whose church tower shows a few miles away, you will find that you must travel far round, in order to wriggle down and up a ravine a thousand feet deep, at whose foot runs a little brook. Except for the ruins of a castle holding the path from one side to the other, these cracks do not as a rule have any houses or population. It is not the canyons, but

the manageable fields of the heights above them, which are desirable here. The main roads follow the ridges, and avoid the ravines as far as they can.

Villeneuve-d'Aveyron lies just off the road. The bastide-builders, if they were planting entirely new towns where no village existed, were uninventive in naming them. France is peppered with Villes neuves, Villes franches, and Sauveterres; the only thing that is pretty sure about these names is that any place bearing one of them is about seven hundred years old. Villeneuve-d'Aveyron is no exception. It still lies inside part of its ramparts. Perhaps it is possible to drive a car through its fortified gates, one of which is topped by a high tower. But it is strictly inadvisable. The church has partitions between its interior buttresses allocated to families, according to the rule of fortified churches, where every family knew its own place in case of danger.

Villefranche-de-Rouergue is a bastide too, but very different. It is on the Aveyron, where that reserved river makes a rare excursion from gorges and joins the Alzou. Round it are high hills, from any of which the town can be seen as a design of roofs crowned by an immense church tower. Nobody will be surprised to learn that it was founded by Alphonse de Poitiers, that indefatigable colonizer. Its purpose was strategic, no doubt. But it became a rich city, trading the wool of the high farms, and lead and silver from the nearby mines. The houses

The confluence of the Lot and Dourdou rivers near Conques.

Right: André Sulpice's choir stalls in the church of Notre-Dame at Villefranche-de-Rouergue.

within the walls were rebuilt as the hotels of opulent merchants, and they stand still crammed together in the grid-plan of narrow streets, showing here a fourteenth-century door, there a Renaissance window, and often elegant hand-wrought iron balconies. For the city had a school of metal craftsmen. Many village churches of the region have fine crucifixes and monstrances, made by the smiths of Ville-franche. The walls have gone, and there is a dull spread of modern suburbs outside the line they used to bound. But inside it the town is as perfect an example of a medieval trading centre as can be found.

The town square, slanting uphill, is completely surrounded by *cornières*, with the street running beneath the arches. But it is impossible to stop gazing at the church. It cuts the north-east corner of the square diagonally with an immense Gothic arch, on which is based nearly 200 feet of tower. It is built, as the whole town is, in pearly stone. They say it is unfinished, that there should have been a lantern above the roof. A carillon rings from it at midday and on fêtes and solemnities.

The interior of the church of Notre-Dame is as impressive as the tower. The lancet windows of the apse have some old glass. Unusually, for southern Gothic, there are transepts, though short ones. It has the most enjoyable woodcarving of the whole region. The choir stalls are the work of André Sulpice, a wood-carver who came from Marvejols. They are his master-piece, though his work can be seen in other churches, in the charterhouse of Villefranche too, and in Rodez Cathedral. He belonged to the last quarter of the fifteenth century, near to the end of the art of the Middle Ages; but his carving shows none of the decadence, of the liquescent over-elaboration, that renders Flamboyant disquieting. He used naturalistic forms in his designs, detailed and delicate, but carved with gusto, with a sort of innocence, as though in this hill-country the craftsman had attained absolute skill without losing his joy in work. André Sulpice signed his all over, as the great masters do, by his very use of the chisel. But he has favourite designs too; curly greens, a chestnut leaf, a plump, cheerful mermaid who

presumably swam up the Aveyron to serve as his model. His human figures are portraits, sometimes comic, sometimes sad, like the head of a young nun at Rodez. Here in Notre-Dame the entrance to the choir has wonderful gates, where in a screen of foliage, Isaiah, young and grave, looks across to an exquisite Virgin on her knees. The traveller has often to call up reserves of historic understanding to forgive the Huguenots for destroying statues they thought idolatrous. Perhaps other strangers besides myself find that tolerance harder to reach in Villefranche than almost anywhere else; for they sawed off many figures from this gay choir.

There are other churches to look at. The chapel of the Black Penitents is a pleasant seventeenth-century building, with a bulbous lantern-tower. Inside it is octagonal, and filled with an extraordinary profusion of ornament; especially a reredos covered with coloured and gilded figures surrounding the main subject of the Crucifixion. This is the culmination of the Counter-Reformation church carving that, throughout the south-west, derives from Spanish Baroque. Down in the valley near the river is a rarity, a charterhouse undamaged by the Revolution. It is a small fifteenth-century foundation, built by the widow of a merchant who died on pilgrimage to Rome. In the eighteenth century it had so few monks that they were withdrawn to another house, and the Chartreuse became the alms-house and hospital of the town, as it is still.[1] Thus it escaped mob vengeance on the church which the people believed was allied with their oppressors. It has two churches, one for strangers, to whom the monks gave shelter without allowing them to penetrate the house of their enclosed order; and the other with stalls by André Sulpice. The refectory has a fine pulpit. Of the two cloisters, one is a large plain oblong off which opened the apartments of the monks, each with his workroom and his oratory; and the other a small Flamboyant cloister, its buttresses capped with pinnacles. This enclosed the lodging of the Prior.

'Have you seen Moissac?' said the Secretary of the Syndicat d'Initiative, from whom the traveller was buying M. Jean Gazave's excellent book on the Rouergue. 'And la Merveille at Mont St. Michel?' and when the stranger said she had, 'And do you think either of them the equal of our Chartreuse?' The stanger said nervously, feeling her way: 'Well, Moissac is of a period so different, and damaged also; and la Merveille gains so much from its situation . . .' No good, of course, a steely light

glinted in the eye of the Secretary. She had given offence by failing to say instantly that the Chartreuse had the most beautiful cloister on earth. Cast down, she melted away, thinking that all the same, the passion of the French for cloisters is in inverse ratio to their number. They are ground-floor structures, easy for the speculative builder or the neighbouring peasant to break up and cart away in time of revolution. It would be nice, thought the stranger, to take the Secretary just one little walk round Oxford.

Rodez, like Jerusalem, is as a city built on a hill; it cannot be hid. From far away its tower shows over the causse. The nearer to, the more compact it seems. This impression is correct. The city is built on a 'mamelon', a breast-shaped hill, its top giving just room to the cathedral, the market-place and a few old streets. More run down its sides to the boulevard which marks the vacancy left by the destruction of the walls; and below that modern streets descend towards the plain and the River Aveyron. It is an ancient town, going back to pre-Roman Gaul. Yet it does not give a great impression of age, except for the cathedral and bishop's castle and a few medieval houses. This is perhaps because it has always had a considerable trade, being the centre for a wide stretch of country; and has therefore tended to be rebuilt from time to time.

The cathedral is surprising. Its west front is part of the city wall, and presents a cliff of red stone pierced by a rose-window. Above this rises an early Counter-Reformation façade, with a sort of baby Jesuit church on top. But the glory of the church is the great tower. This was built by François d'Estaing, bishop in the early sixteenth century. It is high, sumptuously carved, and perfectly proportioned. The play of light on its carvings of peony-red stone is bemusing. The interior of the cathedral is northern Gothic, of the thirteenth century, with a nave, aisles and side chapels. It is foreign to this meridional clime, and may represent the invasion of the south by the power and influence of the French kings. Its tall pillars are plain, and give the feeling of springing height of the northern style. It contains a number of fine things. The choir stalls are by André Sulpice, though

1 Entrance is through the main door of the hospital at any time. In July and August a fee is charged, which also gives entry to the chapel of the Black Penitents and the museum.

they are not quite so good as those of Villefranche. There is one beautiful Renaissance Noli Me Tangere, an earlier Pieta carved with deep emotion, a strange Entombment with its personages dressed in the extreme of fashion of 1530.

Rodez, to the foreigner, seems hard and barely lovable. But a lady of Entraygues says firmly: 'We love Rodez. It is our *chef-lieu départemental*, our county town. We think it very beautiful, and in any case we love it.' She is voicing a fidelity not to this rather bleak, severe city, still less to an administrative centre, but to the tribal capital of her ancestors, back through two thousand years.

Conques

From Rodez to the Lot a road runs first across the blistering Causse de Comtal, and then through a valley of le Rougier. This is a band of red sandstone hills, traversed by some little rivers which run into the Lot. Salles-les-Sources, at the beginning of the red gorge, has three churches, the lowest Romanesque; it is one of the most picturesque villages of the region. Farther north Marcillac is the centre of the culture of a delicious red wine, pressed from grapes of the kind grown in Burgundy. They can be coaxed into fruiting on the tiny vineyards of the slopes. Then the Dourdou runs into a wooded gorge, from which a road slants up a near-precipice, twists to gain height, and reveals Conques.

The three pyramidal roofs of the towers rise from their heavy bases over the high-pitched old houses of the village. All round the hills rise sharply to ridges. There is hardly a level foot of ground in Conques, save for the terraces cut to floor the houses and the larger one on which the abbey is set. This grand, haughty church is built in a wilderness. It is impossible to imagine how the villagers now, or ever, managed to grow their food in this ravine.

The overwhelming impression of the abbey church grows, instead of diminishing, the more you look at it. It is early Romanesque, for it was a century a-building and was finished about 1140. The purity of the style was probably due, in part,

to its remoteness. Go to the little terrace in the village street which overlooks the east end. The semicircles of the chapels, of the apse, of the lantern, sharpen to the cone of turret and the pyramid of tower. There is little ornament; the design is caused by the disposition of the church within, it is completely functional, in modern jargon. And it is completely satisfying to the mind and eye. Then go down to the small square before the west door; and if you can bear to, give its carvings the go-by till you have been inside.

The church gives the same feeling of strength inside as out; but here there is also height and illumination. The nave is long and uninterrupted, so that one looks straight to the altar, and to the circling chapels behind it. The roof is supported by piles which form the pillars of the side-aisles; their line continues across the transepts to run round behind the altar and leave a processional path between it and the chapels. The windows of the aisles are repeated by windows in the upper part of the nave where the wall is pierced by a clerestory, and the light shines directly on the carved capitals of its passage-pillars. No doubt the builder meant this, when he planned to ornament them with palms, birds, beasts, stories from the Bible, scenes of chivalry. On the blind wall of the north transept there is a great Annunciation; curiously, this is less delightful than the smaller sculptures, for the Virgin is strained and afraid, and the angel wears too menacing a smile. There is something exclusively male about the Conques carvings, as though the master-sculptor anticipated the spirit of Michelangelo, in the convention of his own time. His point of view dominates the hundreds of different subjects. He was not averse to imaginary creatures, such as a winged lion, Babylonian in appearance, but after all the symbol of St. Mark. But the nightmare monsters eating each other of the abbey of Souillac are not here. Of course the figures are stylized, with huge heads, hands and feet and dwarfed bodies, nevertheless they are realistic, lively, and humorous. In the garth outside there is a delicious capital of monks finishing a tower of the church. They bulge out of the top like a litter of puppies, arguing amicably about the work; you can fairly hear

The west front of the abbey church of
Ste-Foy at Conques.

them. It would take a month to see and appreciate the detail of the capitals alone. In a day's visit you can carry away only the memory of a few. Yet the abiding impression is not of detail, but of ornament contained in a space of measure and proportion, of strength and light.

When Conques was rediscovered a century ago, it had fallen into some degree of dilapidation. France owes thanks to the Beaux-Arts for the manner of its restoration. It is easy to see it, in roof and wall, but it has just been honestly repaired.[1] The roofs have been covered with the round slates used locally. They repeat the circular Romanesque pattern, and their purple-grey weds admirably with the warm yellow, tinted with red and rose, of the walls. The only regrettable part of the restoration is the windows. The glass is made by a Limoges works who have captured the custom of progressive restorers hereabouts. It is far less objectionable than the degraded stuff of the mass-produced religious 'art' of the north. But the design is unconvincing, being an attempt to regain twelfth-century figures; and the colours are a reaction against crimson lake and prussian blue into a series of reds and yellows somewhat false in tone.

This church, for all its masculine spirit, is dedicated to a girl, Sainte Foy. And thereby hangs one of the two epics of the abbey; for Conques unfairly has two good stories. The first is more than a thousand years old. In the ninth century, Conques, a colony from Cluny, was a struggling abbey, with a much smaller church. The pioneers had chosen a spot endowed with good spring water, but without bread to eat. They had to give hospitality to pilgrims to Compostella, but nobody gave them alms in return for the meagre fare they offered. So the Abbot Bégon made a plan. He summoned his faithful monk Aronisdus, and instructed him to carry it out. Aronisdus put off his habit, and went to Agen. The abbey there was rich, for it owned the relics of Sainte Foy, a girl who suffered martyrdom for her faith under Diocletian. Poor child, she was only eleven. But her bones wrought many miracles, and the abbey grew fat on the gratitude of the saved. Aronisdus

entered the abbey as a postulant; served its rule impeccably for ten years; and was finally promoted to the guard of trusted monks who kept watch over the sanctuary and the precious relics. At last, one night he was left alone with them. He stuffed them in a sack and fled for the hills. The Agen monks took the alarm and hunted him, but the relics (surprisingly fickle in their favour to their protectors) caused a miracle, and Aronisdus was cloaked by mist, and escaped to Conques. Once there Bégon would have stood a siege sooner than give them up; and there they have been ever since. As soon as they were set in a chapel of the abbey, the relics performed miracles for many supplicants. No longer did the pilgrims of St. James pass without giving gifts; at this altar, as well as at Compostella, their prayers might be answered. The abbey grew in riches and power. It called on the people to give treasure to make a fitting reliquary for the saint. The poor gave pence, and the great ransacked the jewels in their dower-chests. The monks made a golden statue to hold the bones, and covered it all over with jewels and ornaments; and a gilded chair for the statue to sit in. And afterwards, they built the wonderful church that we see today.

Centuries went by. The passion for pilgrimages died out. Sainte Foy kept a local fête, when the statue and the treasures of the abbey were shown to the people. And then the abbey decayed, and the monks left; and now there happened the second tale of Conques. For in the Revolution the officials of the Republic seized the treasures of the abbeys and cathedrals and melted them down to coin money for an empty treasury. They had ravished Rodez; and someone warned Conques that they were on their way. So the Mayor of Conques held a village meeting. 'We are about to have our Revolution,' he said, 'and we shall take the abbey treasures and share them among us; every man his piece, and I shall remember which family has which jewel.' Then the officials arrived, and called for the Mayor, and told him they were come for the abbey treasure, so that Conques should be privileged to celebrate the Revolution. 'But we have had the Revolution!' said the Mayor. 'Citizen-

1 The abbey is again in need of major repair work. The Service des Monuments Historiques is conducting a comprehensive survey to gauge the extent of structural decay. The Syndicat d'Initiative provides free guided tours on request.
2 The treasure (Trésor I) is still housed in the presbytery next to the abbey, and there is a museum (Trésor II) in the Syndicat d'Initiative. Both are open morning and afternoon daily except in January, when they are open by appointment only.

Comrades, we had it last week. And the citizens, filled with Revolutionary zeal, seized the treasure. And you know that it is not possible to recapture anything that may have been taken by a Rouergat peasant, particularly from one who is a good revolutionary, as we all are in Conques.' With these words, or words to this effect, the Mayor outfaced the officials. And they reflected on the centuries during which the people of this poor country had hidden their small possessions from *routiers*, and taxgatherers, and the abbey bailiffs at the tithing season. So they went away. But when the Terror was over, the people of Conques brought out the abbey treasures from holes in the walls of their houses, and holes under the trees in their orchards, and gave back every one. So that Conques has one of the very rare medieval treasures of the world.

It is kept in a house by the abbey.[2] Of late years, there have been monks again, a body of Premonstratensian fathers, who enjoy the use of the abbey on condition that it is open to visitors. A lay brother shows the treasure. It is a strange mixed collection, from early enamel work to seventeenth-century vestments. Some of the Romanesque work is beautiful, and the later monstrances are finely made. But the unique treasure is the statue of Sainte Foy. There it is, the Golden Majesty, just as it is carved on the west door, where the Hand of God is pulling the saint out of her chair and into heaven. It is made of pale gold studded all over with jewels, miscellaneously assembled to make a rough embroidery on its robe. There are even earrings in its ears. Many of the jewels are cameos and intaglios that must have been handed down from the time of Rome. The figure sits bolt upright, its elbows bent and its hands outstretched to hold flowers. Its throne is jewelled too, with its arms and back ending in round crystals.

The statue is hideous. The golden face is like that of a paralytic, stricken and staring with its black-and-white cat's-eyes. It is as horrifying as a Senegalese fetish. And as potent. Beyond question that image had magical power. Even now— even in this sunny room, behind this glass case—the stranger looks at it first in curiosity, and then with a cold chill. The

relics are in a casket behind the altar now. Yet after all, that sinister, bedizened idol was made to hold the bones of a little . girl.

There remains the west door. Here was where the lay folk came in. This was what they looked at every time they came to church; and they looked at Doom. The upper section of the round arch is filled with a Last Judgment, the culmination of all the abbey sculpture. It is early, as the great Dooms go; scholars date it by the technique of the eyes, which are pierced to give them a living look. The work is pervaded by the spirit of the Conques workshop. The Heaven of Last Judgments is usually dull; there is a tedium about beatitude. So the designer boldly endowed his resurrection of the dead with humour. The usual procession enters at the right hand of God; the founder, then an abbot and behind him a king. The king is sure he has no right to be there; he shrinks back behind the abbot's broad back. But the abbot leads him in with absolute assurance, announcing (as anyone can see), 'This gentleman is with me.' The left side, the side of the damned, is realistically brutal. Devils torture the lost souls with glee. The lost personify the Seven Deadly Sins. They were the gross sins of a gross age, when the poor decayed with slothful despair, and the rich spent their wealth in gluttony; when the great gave rein to pride and fury. It is deeply interesting to look at this door and to trace the sins of the mind, to which the religious, the intellectuals of that time, were addicted perhaps without knowing it; their intolerance, cold cruelty, and lust for domination over the souls of men. There they are, the totalitarian vices, over the door, for succeeding ages to see.

As you go away, stop where the road rounds the buttress of the hill and look back. The evening light lies level, edging each ridge with shadow. The round design of the Romanesque abbey is invisible from here. Instead the three pointed tops of the towers, the sharp-roofed houses, the sides of the ravine towering to narrow *arêtes*, make a pattern. The works of man repeat the design of nature in unity.

CHAPTER NINE

THE TARN

The Gorges

The Tarn gorges at dusk, from the road which climbs from the village of les Vignes to the Causse Méjean.

The Tarn rises at over 4,700 feet near Malpertus in the Lozère. This river is taken from its source downwards, because people coming to it directly from the north will probably travel by way of Auvergne; and because its head and that of the Lot are so near to each other that it is a good plan to travel up the Lot and down the Tarn.

In its higher reaches, and indeed to near Albi, the Tarn is a mountain and then a causse river. The country on either side of it is wild and lonely. But it has been much more organized for tourists than our other rivers. The state has made a number of remarkable roads, by means of which motors can climb the most unlikely precipices. There are good hotels at various strategic places. Mende is above the head of the gorges, Millau at their foot. Florac serves those who want to explore the Cévennes from the north, Meyrueis is not far from the Aigoual. Le Rozier is at the mouth of the Jonte gorges where they connect with the Tarn; St-Jean-du-Bruel commands the Dourbie gorges and the Causse du Larzac; and there are lesser places to stay.

The Tarn flows quietly from its source, collecting many burns on its way to le Pont-de-Montvert. That is the first town on its course. It is haunted by the memory of the outbreak of the Camisard revolt. The Arch-Priest du Chayla, Inspector of Missions in the Gévaudan, kept his private torture-chamber there, tormenting Protestants before handing them over to

death or the galleys at the hands of the secular law. In 1702 a group of peasants tried to rescue some of his prisoners. He refused to release them. The band burnt the house and killed him in the garden. It was the breaking-point after many years of merciless persecution. The Calvinists took to arms. Peasants led by peasants, they held their mountains for two years against the armies of France commanded by a batch of Marshals. Their defeat was inevitable, and Protestantism went into the 'Desert' still pursued by gaol and execution even for children, till Louis XVI, scrambling for popular support at the close of his reign, abolished the penal law in 1787. But hereabouts the majority of the people are Protestant still, in many places on both sides of the watershed. For instance, the training-college for ministers is at Montauban. And they are so conscious of their history that they talk about it often; it is impossible for any traveller to ignore it. So that while le Pont-de-Montvert is now a summer trout-fishing resort, the traveller who is not an angler feels it grim.

Soon after it the river runs into fine gorges with woods clawing up the slopes and streams falling down them; for this is granite country and the water still runs on the surface. But they end in a little fertile plain below Florac, where the Tarnon joins the Tarn, and the Great Causses begin with the Causse Méjean across the river. Here is the road-knot of the upper river. You can go north by a zig-zag road up to the Col de Montmirat.

A view from the road up to Mont Aigoual from the Col de Perjuret.

There is a splendid view of the Cévennes, and if you happen to be there at the right moment, the pasture is thick with the rare pulsatilla anemone, with dark purple slender petals, back-turned and covered with yellow down. From there the road runs to Mende. The other road from Mende to the gorges crosses the Causse de Sauveterre, and drops to Ste-Enimie. The view and the driving are sensational, but the one is as harmless as the other. It is perhaps at this point that it should be said that most of the roads which ascend the causses are hair-raising for passengers, but so well engineered that they are easy for drivers, even if they sometimes demand a back-and-turn at the corners. But it is not safe to take roads which are not tarred; for the 'routes blanches' are immemorial tracks traced, probably, by goats in the first case; and they make no concessions to frail automobile steering.

To the south of this junction, Florac lies high, under a cliff. Its steep fields feed cattle in summer, and its woods are laced with wild laburnum. From it you can take off for the Cévennes roads or the innumerable paths worn by the herds. The Cévennes are partly wooded, owing to the efforts of the Ministry of Waters and Forests. The older trees are the serviceable, glorious chestnuts that every sun-scorched walker will love with his whole heart.

The whole of the Cévennes are centred on the Aigoual, the highest point, which tops 4,700 feet. It dominates the lives of the people and dwells continually in their imagination; they speak of it every day. No wonder, for it is the cloud drawn down by the Aigoual that waters this country of denuded hills. Nobody can describe mountains. No painter has painted them successfully, unless it be Cézanne simplifying and embellishing a single cone. It is only possible to tell the facts about the Cévennes. They are complex, a tangle of ridges. They are scoured and peeled to the rock by the long rains of winter and the violent summer tempests, except where the uniform forest of the Eaux-et-Forêts has grown some soil upon their bones. Sheep manage to feed on their pastures in summer; and the people grow fruit and grain in pockets of earth terraced on the

hills, walled away from the river-bottoms. With all these hard things to say about them, the Cévennes are grand hills.

Below the Tarn–Tarnon junction the road runs through one of the fruitful small plains of the region, and then into the beginning of the lower gorges. A humped bridge crosses the river to Quézac; it was built by a pope to serve pilgrims to the Virgin's shrine there. Then on the left bank Castelbouc appears. It is named for a rude legend of a *seigneur* of Crusading times, who was left the only man in the village, and was the lover of all the women. He died in a great storm, and to the blast of thunder a huge goat was seen flying over the village as his soul departed in its sins. His successors were as disreputable. They held the valley to ransom and had to be rooted out. The defences of the castle were razed; it is a ruin against the cliff whence springs emerge.

At Ste-Enimie roads ascend the causses, but except for that to Mende, they are hardly to be recommended. The main road continues down the gorges on the right bank.

Now the river is running in a fault in the causses, Sauveterre above the right bank, Méjean over the left. This is a true canyon, 1,500 feet deep in places, and only a hundred yards across at its narrowest point. The sides are broken cliffs; in several places they form 'cirques', semicircular corries. Usually the crests are cliffs, with a slope below them where a few vines tilt against the tilted soil. At the bottom the Tarn runs clear as glass, for it is purified by the springs bursting in its bed. There is no road on the left bank, and few houses. The question is how the inhabitants of the few manage to live; and the answer that they exist like the people of the villages by the road, largely on the tourists.

It is important to go through the gorges on a sunny day, for it is under the sun that the rocks show their colours of red, red ochre, amber, blue, and grey. Without light they dim. But in too great heat they reverberate, and the traveller must fry; so he should, if possible, be choosy. The forms of the rocks are often fantastic; it is easy to see how the tale of Ste-Enimie's chase came to be told. She was the abbess of the tiny convent at the

village named after her; and she was much troubled by Satan. But she refused his temptations. More, she hunted him right down the gorges. With his long goat's legs he skipped from boulder to boulder, and he was just going to escape her, when she called on the rocks to help her. They rushed down the slope and fell upon the devil. He was almost trapped, but unluckily the huge slab upon him left a tiny crack, and through it he squeezed and got away to hell. And if you do not believe this story, it just shows that you do not understand the nature of evidence, for the Roque Sourde still lies there, blocking the river from sight, at the Pas de Souci.

At la Malène barques can be hired. The boatmen pole them down-stream, through the narrows called les Détroits, the Straits. The cliffs there are hollowed by the stream, and the current stills to a round pool. Beyond it the boat turns the passengers out at a pier below the road.[1]

Below le Rozier the gorge widens, and the dolomitic rocks stand apart buttressing the sides, till they edge the plain of Millau.

Two gorges run into the Tarn from the east. That of the River Jonte is less deep but more precipitous than that of the Tarn itself. The angle where the two join is crowned by the Rocher de Capluc, up which anyone can climb who has a steady head. It is not at all difficult, but is what climbers call 'exposed' in two or three pitches. Iron ladders are set against them to help the ascent. There is a fine view of the two gorges from the top. The Jonte itself disappears and runs under the rocks of its bed for part of the gorge in summer. Le Rozier is the centre of delightful walks on the path by the stream, and up the causses. It is above it that the most interesting caves of the region can be found; Dargilan, going up to the Causse Noir, and the Aven Armand on the Causse Méjean.[2] Farther up the Jonte is Meyrueis, from which a negotiable road runs nearly to the top of the Aigoual.

Millau is a busy modern town, occupied with the tourist traffic and the glove industry. Here the other gorge holds the Dourbie coming in from the south. A beautiful road follows the river through its gorge, which is less savage than the others, past some aged villages to the upland valley called the 'Garden of Aveyron'. The garden was the creation of the monks of Nant, who cultivated the valley long ago. Their abbey church is the parish church of the little town. It is Romanesque, but has been harshly treated with Gothic alterations. Scholars think that it was an outpost of Catholicism restarted by Pope Innocent II in his rivalry with the anti-Pope Anaclete, and may have been inspired by St. Bernard. If so it would explain the curious interior; for some of the pillar-capitals are 'storied'; and the rest show the bosses where carving should have been chiselled, but are left in the mass. St. Bernard, that towering character and reformer, was a sair saint for the church in matters of beauty. He hated art as much as he hated thought; both in his view undermined piety; it is an interesting reflection that had he lived three hundred years later he would almost certainly have founded a sect of reformers compared with which the Calvinists, who always fostered intelligence, would have seemed luxurious. St. Bernard especially abominated carvings in churches. They were forbidden in his own Cistercian order and his influence was such that they ceased in others too. If this church of Nant was really due to him, it offers a living example of his opinions. You can imagine the abbot coming to the carver and saying: 'No more of that, my son. Bernard says we mustn't.'

St-Jean-du-Bruel, at the other end of the vale, is a good place to stay, for it has walks up to the causses, both the Noir and the Larzac, along the ridges of the Cévennes, and by the upper Dourbie, which runs deep in ravines between slabs of black cliff. The air is cool here, when the Tarn gorges are already heating like a brazier; and the flowers linger late.

Below Millau, the Tarn adopts the linking habit of the Lot and Dordogne. But it still has a narrow valley, very beautiful as far down as Truel, where the road climbs the causses and leaves the village far below. At St-Hippolyte a road up to the causse climbs and divides. The right-hand branch leads to Castelnau-Pégayrols, an abbey-village which has not changed since the

Opposite: The Jonte gorges in autumn, seen from the road which descends from the Causse Méjean to Meyrueis.

1 The fare is expensive, but includes a taxi back to la Malène. In high season an early start is recommended.
2 Opening times for Dargilan and Aven Armand are given on page 117.

early eleventh century. It has two plain Romanesque churches. The houses are built in a tight group, there is no street to admit a car. The other road goes through Montjaux, with a domed Romanesque church. Its pillar-capitals are carved in high relief with brutal subjects. Farther on the road to Rodez is the little town of Salles-Curan, the country residence of the bishops of Rodez, whose church has a window of lovely glass and finely carved stalls, as well as a treasure of a silver crucifix and monstrances.

Below Truel the Tarn pursues its winding way sometimes without even a path beside its rocky bed, sometimes with a 'white road' impracticable for motors. The main road from Millau to Albi lies to the south, and keeps mostly high on the causses. But you can leave it at Alban and drive down a wriggling descent to the river valley, or farther on at Villefranche-d'Albigeois. The latter will take you to the link of Ambialet, where an old bourg lies in an almost closed meander.

When it reaches Albi, the Tarn is a stately river. It runs beneath the walls of the bishop's palace, as majestic as a ripe actress at a reception. Its sensational youth is behind it—except in flood-time when it can produce a devastating scene in the plain that shows how well it remembers its wild beginnings.

The Great Causses. La Couvertoirade

There are four Great Causses. The Causse de Sauveterre lies north of the Tarn; Méjean, Noir, and Larzac south of it. Towards their junction with the Lozère and Cévennes, the top of the causses is often higher than 3,000 feet. They diminish gradually in height as they sink westwards to the plain of Albi and Toulouse; but the southern edge above Bas Languedoc is a series of high cliffs. They are really a huge plateau, divided by the rifts of the river canyons. In winter the wind blasts their unsheltered expanses. In summer they are scorched by the sun. Here and there a hole gapes in the ground, an 'aven', a roofless cavern. In some parts the rains have split the rocky heights into a 'chaos' of dolomites and boulders. The vegetation is thin grass and a few scrubby bushes of lavender and other aromatics.

Here and there a depression can collect some moisture, and forms a tiny cultivable field. But the farms subsist on the summer grazing of sheep which are watered at dewponds; the houses have no water but cisterns.

All this goes to make a terrifying monotony. Yet there are people who are causse-addicts; who love them as hillmen love their hills. The average Frenchman is genuinely shocked at the sight of so much land that only feeds flocks of sheep from May to September—it has been my lot to drive across the causses with a dismayed British farmer, and also with a Frenchman who kept up a sort of keen of horror. But the lovers of the wilderness feel very differently. For them, the enemy is the Department of Waters and Forests which has an eye on the depopulating causses for plantation.[1] They will have little to say to the comparatively mild and habitable causses of Gramat and Martel; less to the small causses from which green fields and villages can be seen in the distance. Nothing will do for them but the Great Causses with their silence, their solitude, their thin, high air and long empty vistas. For they are spiritual children of the desert; and the causses are desert country.

They are not quite empty. There are the occasional farms, and the huts where the shepherds spend their nights. Roads cross them. For instance it is an exciting drive from le Rozier to Meyrueis, thence up the Causse Méjean, across it, stopping to see the Aven Armand, and down to la Malène on the Tarn. The view of the Tarn from the zig-zags is splendid. Both the ascent and the descent are *corniches*, but the roads are good, only needing care in driving.

The top of Causse Noir has the chaos called Montpellier-le-Vieux. Good walkers can reach it from le Rozier; drivers better from Millau by la Roque-Sainte-Marguérite on the Dourbie. This strange chaos is formed by rocks which have broken and worn away perpendicularly, down the grain of the rock, so that they look like a ruined, nightmare city. That is why the people, half in mockery, half in fear, call it Montpellier-le-Vieux.

The Causse du Larzac is the largest, though not the highest of them all. It carries the old pilgrim-road from Millau to

1 A more recent threat came from the army, which wanted greatly to enlarge its base on the Causse du Larzac. So great was the outcry that the plan was abandoned.

94

Lodève, on the route to Compostella; and a series of ancient villages mark the stages of the slow convoys of horses, mules and pilgrims on foot. The causse was infested by brigands, robbers of pilgrims, who had no protection of towns on that bare expanse, and who carried with them their offerings to the shrine. The Templars set up a hospital for their sick at la Couvertoirade in the twelfth century. But Philip le Bel suppressed the Templars in 1311, having charged them with sorcery, and the Hospitallers took over the causse, protecting the pilgrims in transit. The names of the villages recall them, la Cavalerie, l'Hospitalet, la Couvertoirade.

La Couvertoirade is one of the most exciting things to see in all the south-west, if you care for the fortification of the Middle Ages. Here is a settlement of the military orders, left almost as it was.[1] Viollet le Duc, thank God, did not lay his all too restoring hand upon this, nor any other well-intentioned patcher. Time has wasted it; and there is a small old village of houses inside the walls. But that is a natural thing; the knights must always have had serfs to till the shallow soil for them and wait upon their needs; and when the pilgrimage to Compostella ceased and the Hospitallers went away, their peasants fell heir to the place.

It was not a town, but a circle of towered walls. The knights had their church, of course, and a castle for their own habitation but otherwise the space was mostly left open, with ground for the pilgrims and their beasts, and no doubt cooking-fires and arrangements for shelter in bad weather. The plan was that of the modern *caravanserai* of the East, and likely enough the Templars brought it back from Syria.

As you approach la Couvertoirade, it stands on the causse like an immense castle; a ring of walls towered at intervals. When you enter, it is by one of the two gates. One is intact under its tower, the other shattered by lightning a generation since.

Inside the gates the buildings are set upon the stony ground, as they were in 1300 when they were built. The little church is plain Romanesque. It is possible to mount the stairs up the

towers and walk round the battlements for some way, till they are barred because the path has become dangerous. The streets have sixteenth-century houses, with outside stairs, miniature remises, and upper sun-rooms. One large house is lived in by 'grands propriétaires', big farmers. La Couvertoirade is emptying fast, Madame at the café will tell you; although, as she says: 'Here at least one eats. During the war we had enough, while the folk of Béziers would walk all the way up from the plains to find something to eat.'

There is nothing, not even the churches, for they reflect the continuing life of all their generations of existence, which gives so sharp an impression of the Middle Ages as this fortress. La Couvertoirade has but two phases: the time when a group of pilgrims groomed their beasts in one corner of the walled enclosure while their pots boiled over the fires, after the escorting knights had showed them their quarters for the night; and the succeeding unchanged life of the farming people, making a meagre living out of this desert land, and coming home to their houses at night within the walls.

Three miles south of la Couvertoirade is le Caylar, a village built under a tall needle of rock. This is almost the southern edge of the causse, for just beyond the road drops sharply down a huge circle of red cliffs to the Bas Languedoc country. But as far south as la Couvertoirade the streams are still running north to the Tarn; the source of the Sorgues is near to it; it joins the Dourdou just below St-Affrique.

Roquefort on the causse is the capital of the famous cheese. It is ripened in a cavern in the ridge of rock above the village; and for some reason the same results cannot be got elsewhere. The cheese is made of ewes' milk, from the herds which pasture the causses in great numbers. The lambs are taken from their dams almost at birth, in order to leave the milk for the Roquefort. It is their skins which go to the glove-makers of Millau, as the wool of the sheep goes to the cloth-mills of Lodève. The whole elaborate interlocked business from the shepherds to the cheese-merchants is organized upon a profit-sharing basis, in order to interest the whole of the workers engaged in it in keeping the standards of the cheese above imitation, and the demand for it effective.[2]

The road over the causse joins the main road west from Millau at la Cavalerie. Presently, red sandstone ridges begin to crop out, and the soil becomes more fertile. Round St-Affrique the valley slopes are dotted with two-storey huts. They are the summer-houses of the people, who have the excellent habit of owning a parcel of land in the country, where they cultivate a vine and some vegetables. On Sundays they take their families and a cold luncheon, and spend the day on their tiny estates. The tools are kept in the bottom room, but the upper one is for repose and refreshment. This civilized recreation, for people who live far too close together with their neighbours in these cramped ancient towns, is characteristic of the sensible gaiety of French ideas.

The road switches down and up river gorges, and along the lessening causse. St-Sernin-sur-Rance has a good church with finely carved altar-rails, and a Renaissance high street. And so to Albi.

Conversation at Peyrelau

Peyrelau stands on a ridge above the Jonte, opposite to le Rozier. Its old streets are stairs, climbing to the remaining tower of the castle. On the way down, I met an old lady, resting a faggot of wood in the shade of a barn. We exchanged greetings.

Her face was covered in wrinkles, but she had the indestructible beauty of fine bone and perfect proportion; the gracious charm reserved for women who have been lovely and beloved all their lives, and young, brown eyes.

'You find Peyrelau interesting?' she said.

'Yes, Madame, and very pretty. The view is splendid.'

'Ah! It is a beautiful panorama, indeed. But it is a poor corner, all the same. Nothing grows here. Now down there in the valley'—she waved her hand towards the lower gorge of the Tarn, a mile away—'there they grow plums, and all grows well, the soil is rich. Here we fall in ruins and the people vanish.'

Opposite: The fortified pilgrim church at la Couvertoirade.

1 It remains almost untouched. The ramparts are open daily from March to the end of November.

2 The caves at Roquefort can be visited every day except Christmas Day and New Year's Day.

'Yet they are rebuilding some of the houses, are they not?'

'Yes, but they are houses of which the owners have died, and there are no heirs. Then rich persons from Bordeaux, from Toulouse—how does one know where from?—buy them and reconstruct them for summer vacations.

'At least, that must bring some money and work into the village?'

'Well, yes. But it is not the same as the real people. It is not our friends, and there is nobody in the houses in the winter. And then since the war—'

'You suffered greatly here during the war, Madame?'

'Ah! What we have suffered. We were rummaged by the Germans. Of course, we all had French people in our houses' (*des Français!* thought I. My torture! That goes back to the Middle Ages!) 'and the Germans came and asked if we were sheltering them, but of course nobody told, and they could not distinguish who were the strangers. And we had a real battle here. Yes, Mademoiselle. The Maquis was up there,' she gestured at the Causse Méjean. 'They thought themselves safe, the poor boys, because they thought the German lorries could not ascend the causse. But somebody betrayed them. And the Germans came. All night and all the day after, the lorries came and went on the roads. It was a Sunday, the day of our fête; and we were all at Mass praying for them, and the Germans came and surrounded the church and the village. They threatened to kill us all. But the curé went out to them. He offered himself as guarantee for the village, saying that he would be responsible for his people. And they took him away in a lorry. Think, Mademoiselle, what we suffered; the Germans were killing people everywhere, and we thought he would never return. But after some days they released him and he came back. But on that day we heard cannon firing on the causse from before dawn. They surrounded the Maquis and killed most of them and the rest afterwards, at Mende.'

The beautiful brown eyes were full of tears.

'Ah! Mademoiselle, we must pray every day that war does not return. It is too cruel, too hard for us to bear.'

She told the truth. The Maquis Bir Hakim, camped on the causse, so secure, as they thought, that they had not even posted sentries, were surprised in June 1944 by the German garrison from Mende and surrounded. Only one or two escaped under cover of the dark. Most of them were shot down, and the rest taken to Mende and shot in the public square the next day. A column on the causse tells the tragedy.

Najac, Cordes, Penne

The main roads connecting Villefranche-de-Rouergue, Albi, and Montauban contain a triangle of wild little-populated country. The Aveyron is its river, running south from Villefranche to Laguépie, and thence roughly west through many windings to join the Tarn below Montauban. It is causse country, and the roads keep the heights as much as they can, for the streams either flow in narrow gorges, or are apt to flood the land where it opens to a riverain valley.

The Villefranche–Montauban road is as straight as a Roman causeway. A few miles west of Villefranche it passes Loc-Dieu, one of the Cistercian abbeys of Rouergue. This looks from outside like a castle, but the severe abbey church is Romanesque. It is in private ownership.[1] There is another Cistercian abbey church which can be best reached from Caylus; a beautiful building, recently rescued from use as a hangar, it is called Beaulieu[2]. Caylus itself, where the road drops to the Bonnette, is a little town built in an amphitheatre, with a street of fourteenth-century houses and a fortified church with battlemented buttresses.

It is the other side of the triangle, where the road switches up and down the ridges running west from Rouergue, that it leads to a group of places singularly little affected by modernity. The river here wriggles like a snake through gorges, which can be seen in places from the train, when it emerges from a series of tunnels. But the road lies away to the east, on the heights, and you must leave it to follow a by-road to Najac. This village is built on a promontory of rock jutting out to divert the river from the curve of a volcanic crater. It connects with the plateau

Opposite: A final flicker of evening sunlight tinges the château of Najac, perched above the village.

1 Loc-Dieu is open morning and afternoon daily, except Tuesdays, from 1 July to 10 September.

2 Beaulieu is now a contemporary art centre and hosts an annual festival of contemporary music. It is open morning and afternoon daily except Tuesdays from Easter to the end of September.

The main street of Cordes, leading up from one of its fortified gateways.

1 The entrance fee is now collected at the postern gate. The castle is open morning and afternoon daily from May to the end of September, and on Sundays only in April and October. The church is shut from mid-November to mid-March.

by a narrow ridge, and then rises to a cone. There was a much older castle there, but it had been destroyed, when Alphonse de Poitiers, it is almost needless to say, spotted the defensive strength of the place, and built the present castle in 1269. After all, he was a foreigner, and the local lords, whose fathers had either been defeated by Simon de Montfort or been among his tough crusaders, were almost as likely to fight the French crown as the English. So he made the fortress, which was peculiar in that it never was lived in by a feudal family, but was merely inhabited by a commander and his garrison. He built the church at the same time. It is a fine simple building, interesting because it was the first Gothic church of Rouergue, for that conservative province clung to the Romanesque style

for a long time. All this, however, is history and not description of one of the most dramatic castles in France. If you come from the road, you arrive at a long market-place on the plateau. Some of the houses are propped on stone pillars. As you descend it the castle dominates the view with its high donjon-tower. Then the street runs along the connecting *arête*, between little ancient houses, from one of which you collect the key of the castle from the Garde champêtre.[1] At the narrowest point a fine Renaissance house precedes the postern gate, and from there the path runs up to the castle on its peak. It is badly damaged, for after the Revolution it was sold for twelve francs, and a contractor carried away much of it to sell as building material. But the towered outer walls remain, and the great tower, its top repaired because it was struck by lightning. From wherever you look at Najac, even more from the river, or from the rise on the opposite side, it remains the child's vision of a feudal castle.

At Laguépie the road divides and the main road to Albi runs south to Cordes. Cordes shows what could be done in the Middle Ages by a town commanding crossroads, even in this poor country. It is built on a hill starting out of the valley of the River Cérou. It is a fortified town, and its main street leads uphill, sometimes by flights of steps, and through a couple of gates before it gains the square on top. The old town had three rings of wall, of which several gates remain. The houses are of any date from the fourteenth to the sixteenth centuries; it is fun to notice round and pointed arches in their doors. At the top are the finest houses. A handsome mansion called the house of the Great Huntsman is carved with hounds, obviously the ancestors of one which you have passed slumbering on a hot door-sill with a kitten asleep between its paws. The house of the Great Falconer is the town hall. It is clear that Cordes had enough trade to make fortunes for the merchants who built these handsome houses; it is a *bourgeois* city in miniature. The whole town is *classé monument*. 'But we don't make a fuss about that,' says the girl who brings you a *citron pressé*. 'We are used to living in houses of the Middle Ages. Only floors and ceilings of the Middle Ages are not so good as they once were; and the Beaux-Arts don't give us any help in restoring them.'

The next group of interesting places is reached either by the road west from Cordes, a pretty forest road, or by the parallel road, farther north from Laguépie by the Aveyron. The latter traverses Varen, where the tower and gate-house of a castle stand beside an early Romanesque church. Its east end has three little round chapels raised above crypts, and massive square pillars; the west end has no door because it was part of the town wall. Huguenots and Catholics fought bitterly over the possession of this strong-place.

Presently the Aveyron begins to run under cliffs on its south side, and St-Antonin appears. This is a charming little spa, with a mineral spring called the Source of the Black Prince. The rocks above the Aveyron are called the Rochers d'Anglars; there is a pleasant walk up them to some odd walls on the causse. They suggest sheepfolds or possibly some ancient village rather than anything the English may have done. The river view with its old bridge is good. The tiny town is pure medieval, a tangle of narrow secret streets, with thirteenth-century and even Romanesque houses. The former town hall is Romanesque, and treasured because twelfth-century civic buildings are very rare.[1] Unfortunately Viollet le Duc got his hands on it, and restored it with his customary, over-elaborate care, taking away the appearance of its real age.

There is a beautiful new road in the gorge, made in 1958. The old road crosses the bridge, and climbs the causse to join the route from Cordes, out of sight of the left bank. Here begins the forest of the Grésigne, a pleasant mixture of oaks and wych-elms. At Vaour the road runs down to Penne.

Penne is the strangest of all the castles.[2] Its two big towers and ruined keep are built on a limestone horn, a great rock whose peak bends over space. The castle is so improbable that you do not believe in it even as you look at it. You reach it by the ancient village. When you walk round the castle, you are constantly looking down into the abyss of empty air. Of course this is partly true of many castles. The feudal *seigneurs* built them on peaks precisely because the more inaccessible the situation, the easier was defence, before the days of artillery. But the whole of Penne overhangs, except the gateway. How did they get water, if they were besieged? However did women bring up babies on this platform suspended in mid-air? They must have tethered the toddlers like goats; and the children must have grown up with heads like steeplejacks.

But it cannot be real. Nobody in their senses could have built such a place. So you say to yourself as the fantastic castle is lost to sight, and becomes merely a name on the map and a startled memory.

The road runs along the edge of the causse above Bruniquel. On the other, the north side, a long cliff rises straight for 300 feet above the river, and the castle crowns it. After you have crossed the Aveyron, the road climbs to the old town. The castle was called after Brunehaut, a Carolingian princess, but this building is a mere seven hundred years old. There is a ruined Knights' Hall, a broken tower, and a Renaissance gallery through whose pillared windows you overlook the river and the valley.

A few miles down-stream is Montricoux, whose Romanesque church and donjon form one mass of building. The church has a fine octagonal fourteenth-century tower. From here you may seek sophisticated Montauban. But you may prefer to return to the forest of the Grésigne, to eat your lunch under its green shade, and to meditate upon the life of the Middle Ages in those old places, where the abbeys have towered gates, and the villages defensive walls, and everyone is glowered at by a castle. War and danger were the daily life of the people. The abbots have vanished, or have lost their rights of pit and gallows. The *seigneurs* are gone, and where a noble still owns a château he cannot levy the men for war. War is still the constant overhanging danger of life; but its compulsions come from farther away. The enduring resentment against power which takes the young away to perish, and makes a livelihood so difficult to earn, is transferred from 'him', *le seigneur*, to 'them', the authorities, described in the small word *on*.

Overleaf left: The gorges of the River Aveyron, seen from the D 155 between Penne and St-Antonin-Noble-Val.

Overleaf right: The tiny walled village of Penne, with its ruined château looming above the rooftops.

2 There are *son et lumière* presentations at Penne during the summer months.

Albi and Moissac

The hill-roads to the north and east of Albi look down at the city, where it lies at the edge of the plain of Toulouse. From them, the town seems a carpet of red roofs, a child's village of toy houses round the immense bulk, the soaring tower of the cathedral. This distant sight is astonishing. Then it is lost, as the road runs into a modern industrial town, its new quarters encircling the boulevards which, as usual, replace the former walls. Within them there are old narrow streets with surprisingly good shops, and here and there a close giving a glimpse of a Renaissance court. Then they emerge in a great open space, and there is the cathedral again, more astonishing than ever.

It is a red-brick cathedral. Toulouse had no good stone near by, and built itself of brick, and Albi imitated it. Red brick has been so much abused in England that we unconsciously identify it with architectural shame. But in Albi it is a good material. The bricks of the cathedral are large and long. They have been baked and tinted by the southern sun for seven hundred years, till they have taken tones of purple and rose. They are set, like Roman brickwork, in thick layers of mortar. The mortar throws a delicate rectangular net of white over them all. None the less, every time you look at the church, you are surprised at its redness.

Then there is its shape. The main body of the church is a huge mass rising to a battlemented wall that hides the roof. The sides and east end are formed of twenty-nine towers, each showing a quarter of its circle in the outer wall. Between each pair of towers is a recessed panel of plain wall, with lancet windows, slightly pointed, set high up. This curved and flat alternation in the walls is decorative in the extreme. The west end has no door, but is made of the base of the tower, which rises 250 feet, flanked with turrets carrying its spiral stairs, and with an outside gallery round each storey. The turrets look small from below, but when you get up beside them they are big, solid towers in their own right. From the tower roof you see the whole country, with the Tarn linking away to the south-west below the foothills of the causse.[1]

The building is, in fact, a huge fortress, with the attributes of a church, but mainly and in function a fort. The impression is strengthened by the two towers of the bishop's palace beside it. Dwarfed by the cathedral, they are nevertheless a formidable double donjon; and the slope down to the river is set with wall after wall of defensive *enceinte*.

Only on the south side is there a startling departure from the grim militarism of the cathedral. There the door is approached by a wide flight of stone steps, leading first through a fifteenth-century gate flanked by towers, and then under a Flamboyant porch. It is made of white stone, curvilinear, complicated as lace. It was added in the Renaissance and is called the Baldaquin. Its white traceries make a strange ornament to the red wall, as no doubt was the intention of the designers.

Now the military design of the original cathedral of St. Cecilia was just as intentional. Albi was not in fact the centre of the Albigensian heresy of the eleventh and twelfth centuries—though its citizens booed and laughed the great St. Bernard himself out of their town when he came to persuade them of the error of their beliefs. The Albigensian Crusade was long over, and the smoke of the mass burnings had cleared away before the cathedral was begun in 1282. But the tortures of the Inquisition had aroused the South to revolt in 1234. In that year the infuriated people of Albi hunted their bishop into the former cathedral, from which fastness he excommunicated the citizens *en masse*. So when Bernard de Castanet became bishop he decided to build a new cathedral in which he could be secure. He was the Holy Inquisitor for the diocese, and under the treaty ending the Crusade, the bishop was also the secular lord of Albi. The rules of the Inquisition worked straight in favour of his evil nature. For the Inquisitor was both the prosecutor and the judge of a person accused of heresy. The victim was always tortured; if he 'recanted' under the torment and submitted to the Church, he was imprisoned indefinitely. If anyone accused him of 'relapsing' into heresy, even a common criminal, he was handed over to the secular arm for burning, and his property shared between the Church and the

Opposite: Houses near the cathedral in the medieval quarter of Albi.

1 At the time of going to press the tower was shut for restoration work. On July and August evenings the Syndicat d'Initiative organizes guided tours of the illuminated cathedral, which is also the setting for concerts during Albi's annual music festival.

Opposite: The walled formal garden of the Palais de la Berbie at Albi, overlooking the Tarn and the medieval Pont-Vieux.

state. So Bernard the Inquisitor condemned the heretics, or anybody who had money, to prison in the bishop's castle, arranged for them to be denounced as relapsed, handed them over to de Castanet, the secular lord of Albi, killed them and received their forfeited wealth. Those who were too well known as orthodox he merely kept for years immured in tiny cells without light or ventilation till he had wrung their last *sou* out of their kin. At last the people appealed in desperation to the distant king in Paris. A batch of bishops was sent to conduct an ecclesiastical inquiry, and reported the facts. Bernard de Castanet, in the proper hierarchical manner, was promoted to the see of le Puy, and died a cardinal. It was the money obtained in this way, added to the yield of taxation, that began the cathedral in the form it kept till the tower was raised in the Renaissance. Albi was not like the bastide churches built by Capet and Angevin kings against each other; it was a church built against the people.

The centuries passed, and Albi grew rich again. Its canons belonged to well-born families of the city. They shared the rage for building of the fifteenth century and the Renaissance. They called in three successive groups of artists to adorn their bald red church. These men left the interior ablaze with colour and decoration.

It offered a wonderful background. The nave is the type of southern Gothic at its purest, a simple hull, 60 feet wide and 100 high. The chapels are the recesses between the towered buttresses of the walls. Unfortunately they have been roofed in below the level of the upper windows, which breaks their soaring line. The roof-arch is just pointed enough to take the strain of the wide span. Painters and carvers, seeing these immense stretches of surface before them, must fairly have licked their lips.

First an unknown artist painted the west wall, in the fifteenth century, with a gigantic 'Last Judgment'. The fresco is spoiled now, because some ecclesiastical vandal cut out its middle to make an entry into the chapel beneath the tower, and later the organ was put into the hole where the figure of Christ

ought to be. What remains is a frightful vision of the damned, shrieking and writhing in terror as they are sucked into the mouth of Leviathan. It has considerable interest in the history of painting, especially of the nude. But its effect is that of a religion of horror.

The later artists worked in a totally different spirit. One group were Italians, of the school of Bologna. They covered all the walls except that occupied with the 'Last Judgment', and the roof, too, with gay colour. An exquisite sky-blue predominates, the azure of heaven as a background to scenes of biblical history from the Old and New Testaments. It would be inaccurate to call them devotional pictures, for the whole is completely secular in effect; as is common with painting of that date, the floriated designs holding the composition together are classically pagan. The chapels are painted with large murals, much and unluckily restored, for the restorers had not either the pigments or the skill of the original painters. These at least were competent workmen producing school-work that is pleasant though devoid of genius. There is some modern stained glass, on a regrettably low level of colour and design.

The dazzle of colour makes the interior very gay. But what the canons, and still more a bishop of the great house of Amboise, wanted for their own choir stalls was more than just a cheerful scheme of decoration. They hired what must have been a whole workshop of the Burgundian carvers whose work is common enough in central and eastern France, but rare in the south. These craftsmen made what the French call a 'jubé', and we a choir.[1]

It is in painted stone. The choir-screen is wrought with the most complex and delicate tracery in the Christian world. The statues are gone from it save for the topmost figures of Christ and the Blessed Virgin. The whole structure is set in the east end with a passage round it allowing its exterior carving to be seen. The outside has statues of Old Testament characters. They are not mysterious figures, like those of the early carved saints. They are purely human people, and many of them, you feel quite certain, are portraits of the Albi worthies of the time.

1 The choir is shut at lunch time.

The most lovable is Isaiah, a little priest with a kind and humorous old face. Judith is among them. She is human too, and the sculptor used her for all his women; she is repeated in the Virgin Mary and the St. Cecilia, the patron saint of the church. She is not only unsaintly, she is not even good, as any woman will observe at first glance. Men however, will spend the same instant in falling in love with her. Lovely, lazy, easy, sensual; a possible Judith, an impossible St. Cecilia. She must have been the sculptor's wife, or his *bonne amie*, thinks the woman looking at her. Lazy enough to pose for days and days. Sensual enough never to lose that scent of allurement, even when she was translated into stone. Only the very end of Gothic carving, and only priests who cared more for art than for religion, would have set that slant-eyed slut above their services. She is a permanent type of French beauty; she reappears in Watteau's 'Embarquement pour Cythère', unchanged.

Inside the choir her face recurs many times; for the choir stalls are crowned by a frieze of child angels, on one side carrying scrolls of texts, on the other musical instruments. This angel choir is almost entirely composed of a childish version of the Judith—a little daughter, one wonders? The lovely little girl is not, of course, a wanton like the woman. She is often pretty sulky, and pouts above her viol; no doubt posing bored her, and it must have been tiring to carry that weight of draped robe, and to hold out her instrument while the sculptor got her hands right. Here and there is another face, of a much shyer child, stiff with nervousness, a friend, perhaps, pressed into duty to give the first angel a rest? But the angel choir is delicious, though not at all heavenly, and it must have given great pleasure to generations of canons in their magnificent seats.

There are apostles and saints in the choir, which with the prophets outside repeats the theme of the Old and New Testaments. Charlemagne is there too, and Constantine.

The whole interior ornament of Ste-Cécile is of a detailed complexity so extreme that it is bewildering. But the colour is gorgeous; and much of the detail, if you have the time and courage to study it, is of an accomplished art; that of the *jubé* of a technique trembling on the edge of decay.

It is a relief to go from this stupefying masterpiece to the old church of St-Salvy with its Romanesque door, its stone pillars, and its broken cloister.

Albi holds other treasures. West of the cathedral is an old quarter with houses of the Quercynois type, on the way to the Pont Vieux, which is eleventh century, and claims to be the oldest bridge in France, how correctly I do not know. The public garden in the cathedral enclosure is one of the most beautiful walled gardens in France. It has rose arbours, seats under nice silly eighteenth-century statues on the battlement wall, a court with great plane trees and a running fountain. Look up at the tower, and down at the Tarn. Here is peace.

The Palais de la Berbie, the bishop's castle, contains a remarkable picture gallery. It is best known for its collection of the works of Toulouse-Lautrec, who left them to his native town. The more publishable are hung, showing the brilliance of his draughtsmanship. There used to be a wonderful collection of the Post-Impressionist and Fauve artists, now there is only Toulouse-Lautrec.[1] This is a pity, for the work of a mannerist like Lautrec gained, not lost, by the neighbourhood of his contemporaries. An artist should not be shown *en masse*.

The road west from Albi runs through country whose simple lines are soothing after the richness of that city. It leads through Montauban, a pleasantly set town, with an interesting market-square and a fine old brick bridge. It was the strong-place holding the approach to the Tarn, and was constantly fought round in the Albigensian and Religious wars, so that it has not much remaining of its ancient buildings. From Montauban the short road down the Tarn cuts south of the river by Castelsarrasin, whose romantic name should not deceive the tourist. There are no Saracen remains, but a much-altered Romanesque church, and a nice market. Then comes Moissac.

Moissac is a quiet town with a southern air, built between the river and the edge of the causse. It is a retired situation

which possibly accounts for the survival of its famous abbey church. Not that it escaped the attention of the local warriors. Richard Cœur de Lion sacked it, and so did Simon de Montfort, for its people were Albigensians. On the other hand, Henry III sent money to help restore its damage—for Moissac belonged for long to the Angevin dynasty's lands, so that they may take some credit for its glory.

The church itself has been much rebuilt, and is rather uninteresting under its heavy tower. The west end is fortified, and there is an upstairs guard-house. But it has two unsurpassed treasures, the south door and the cloister. The south door is counted the type of the carved Romanesque doors of the School of Toulouse. Its round top is carved with a wonderful Christ in Glory. The central figure is a seated figure of God; majestic, awful, the God of Judgment, with the Sea of Paradise beneath His starry throne. About Him are the Gospel-Makers, Man, Lion, Bull, and Eagle. Their necks are turned, their eyes bent upon their Lord, and so are the eyes of the tall angels behind them and of the Elders seated on either side and below. The adoration of their gaze welds the great design together, within its borders of delicate foliage and rosettes. The lintel is upheld by a column of intertwined lions, on the front side, and of apostles on the other three. The carving of the door is extraordinary in the quality of its tool-work, apart from the splendour of its composition. On either side of the door are more carvings. Those of the Virgin, especially of the Annunciation and the Visitation, are delightful, but not the master-work of the door itself. Inside the porch the pillars have storied capitals, of which the strange animals, sharing two bodies between one head, are the most interesting.

An inconspicuous door opens into the abbey cloister.[2] It is large and low, enclosing a garth with an old tree shading it. The pillars are set upon a plain wall. They are alternately double and single, giving them the grace which la Merveille owes to the same order. At the corners and midway in the sides are plain square columns bearing the bas-reliefs of abbots and saints. One is dated 1100. The capitals of the marble pillars are

1 The museum now also houses a collection of nineteenth- and twentieth-century art, including works by Corot, Dufy, Matisse, Rodin and Bonnard.

2 The cloister is open morning and afternoon daily except Christmas Day and New Year's Day.

later. They are delicately carved in low relief, with very small designs of foliage, people and animals, wrought like the finest Arabic work. Indeed, except for the human figures, forbidden to artists of the Sunni sect, those pillars might well have been carved by a Saracen from Spain. Their carvers were certainly influenced by Arab art, so the learned say. Their source, however, matters little to the ordinary spectator, what matters is their fineness, the sensation of meditation created by their delicacy, and the peaceful proportion of the cloister.

For a few miles west of Moissac, the road runs high above the flood-mark of the Tarn. Then to the south a spit of land covered with grey-green bushes narrows to a point, dies into a white sandbank, and the Tarn flows into the Garonne, wide and quiet at its end.

The cloister at Moissac, with its finely carved capitals.

109

CHAPTER TEN

BEFORE HISTORY

The Painted Caves

Les Eyzies in Périgord is called the 'university of prehistory'. It is a village lying below the prow-shaped cliff where the River Beune flows into the Vézère. It has a street with a few shops, a few hotels, a fortified church, even a railway station. Summer visitors come to fish; and all the year round, students come to learn about early man.

Les Eyzies and its district, like the hill-slopes of northern Spain, have offered rich finds to prehistorians. Also this part of France has been the scene of the work of the great French savants in this science. The Abbé Breuil, and M. Perony, are but the most famous of living names known to the learned world. But to the unlearned it may be helpful to sketch the nature of their school.

Prehistory is one of the newer studies. It began only about a century ago. Before then, the nations of Christendom had largely accepted the dating of the Bible, and thought that the world began with the Seven Days of Genesis, and the divine creation of man, fallen from the perfection of Eden only because of the wilful sin Adam and Eve committed through the temptation of Satan. This Middle Eastern mythology was imprinted upon the popular mind, long familiar with the Bible story, which was regarded as a unity and all equally historical. It was fused with scholastic theology by the doctrine of the Fall and the Redemption. In spite of a century of enthusiastic historical research, the mind of Western man was little

prepared for the revolutionary discoveries which were to prove that the earth is far older than 4157 B.C., the date ascribed to Genesis, and man far older than Adam. So old that he had himself long forgotten his past, a past stretching back for thousands of lost years.

The famous skull of primitive man, the first to be recognized as such, was found at Neanderthal in Germany in 1857. But this was only a third part of the triple origin of prehistory. Firstly the geologists showed that the age of the substance of earth must be reckoned not in thousands, but in millions of years. Then the biologists, under the inspiration of Darwin, revealed a world of primitive living creatures developing into more complex forms; and of these, most thrilling of all to his descendants, man, an animal slowly learning skills and adaptations through many generations. Lastly the historians, some of them, began to discover traces of man before written history.

The shock to orthodox beliefs was terrific, at least as great as that when Copernicus proved that the earth was not the centre of the universe. It was not only that the learned had to readjust their conceptions of time, for the learned, if they are worth their salt, are trained to mental readjustment. But the simply devout had to accept that the Bible, taken over wholesale from the Jewish scriptures and believed completely for so long, must be sifted into the parts which are myth, symbol, and

Caves and houses built into the cliffs at la Roque-Gageac.

propaganda written long after the event, and the parts which remain historically true and essential to the Christian faith. There are still sects which refuse to abandon the word-for-word authority of the Bible, and many honourable thinkers who find the doctrinal implications of prehistory profoundly disturbing.

Meanwhile, as is its way, knowledge increased. For the desire to learn the truth is so strong that men will always follow it like a light. And while the majority of our fathers were led by other torches, a few caught sight of a candle burning in the black entrance to a cave. It was the cave where prehistoric man made his home.

South-western France offered particularly convenient caves to early man. The limestone hills were hollowed by the swirl of water collecting deep in volcanic faults. The rivers, which had worn the cliffs of their beds into curving overhangs, had shrunk away from the rocks, leaving admirable natural shelters from wind and weather. Some of them, as the traveller sees when he walks down these green river-valleys, are only shallow concavities in the cliffs; others run right into the rock, connecting with underground passages and caverns. Some open at valley-level, while the black mouths of others gape halfway up the precipices.

Man, as he appears in the cave times, was already very different from the other beasts. Like many of them, he was a hunter; but he used weapons, even if for long they were merely round stones chipped to fit his fist, and employed to bash his prey or his enemy. He lit fires. He covered his poor hairless skin with the furs of beasts, though it was long before he learned to sew. He sought food and comfort for his naked frogs of children, so that he took to building his fires, and installing his mate to mind his young, in the mouths of the caves. He was not the only creature who liked the caves; there were bears, too. But while a bear was stronger than a man, the man was more cunning than a bear; they were well-matched in the competition for lodging. And if he contrived to kill the bear who lived in a desirable cave, the man would eat him, and use his pelt for a cloak, and throw his bones, with those of the rest of his prey, into a heap on the floor.

It is these rubbish-heaps of early man, a crude eater and an untidy housekeeper, which have yielded much knowledge to the prehistorians. For their method is to cut a section through the 'middens' they find in the cave-mouths, which witness that men have used them for shelter. They cut the section carefully, straight down, like cutting a loaf of bread. And the layers of soil show age before age of human habitation, from the lowest, which is of course the oldest, to the most recent. The layers contain not only meat-bones, but tools and weapons, carved bones and stone jewellery. They show the advance of human skill, the increasing number and improving quality of flint tools, the beginnings of personal adornment. Sometimes there is a 'sterile' layer, an age when no man lived in the cave, and for thousands of years the dust collected and settled in unbroken solitude. The passing of whole races of living things can be proved. The earlier layers may contain the bones of mammoth and types of elephant long extinct, or lions, hyenas, and other beasts which died out in Europe—or perhaps left for the south—in the 'Great Freeze' of the last Ice Age. Or of reindeer and other grazing beasts driven away when the forests overwhelmed the pastures. This is the lore of the cave-shelters.

Then there are skeletons of men. These occasionally turn up, either because they are unearthed by chance, where a human being lay down and died so long ago, or where they have been ceremonially buried. For it is believed that the cult of the dead, later so marked when chiefs and priests were buried in carefully-built barrows, began in the days of prehistoric man. These bones vary in type, especially in skull-type, and on them are based theories of the various prehistoric races, some of which have left no descendants. The savants have chosen to name these early types of man after the places where their skulls are found. So that they are given picturesque names, extremely difficult for us who are ignorant to remember. Perhaps the easiest to recall are Cro-Magnon Man and Magdalenian Man. These are called, the one after a shelter at les

Eyzies, where a whole group of skulls was found, and the other after a shelter at the village of Tursac on the Vézère. Les Eyzies itself has an excellent museum,[1] in the remains of its medieval castle, which shows skulls, or models of those taken to other museums, for purposes of comparison. It shows, too, the different ages of flint tools, as well as the tools of American Indians, and Australian Aborigines, who recently lived, or are still living, in local survivals of the Stone Age. But unfortunately on the terrace-wall of the museum stands a statue of prehistoric man looming over the village. He is represented as half beast, half human, standing with his face towards the dawn. It is easy to see the intention of the image, the wakening of intelligence, the birth of the soul, whatever one may think of it as a work of art. But this was certainly not the man who made the cave-drawings, and who was completely human, and indeed modern, in type.

But it is the decorations of the caves which are far the most interesting to most of us. For early man was an artist, and a good one. He had sharp flints as tools, and he could engrave pictures on the smoothish limestone walls of his cave. He lived by chancy and dangerous hunting; could he not invoke a lucky kill by making a magic picture of the beast he was going to chase? Game was growing short; could he not carve cattle and horses, deer and bison, heavy with young, and so cast a spell of fertility? The artist in man is as old as the first child who stamped his foot in mud and showed the print proudly to his playmates; the magician in man is as old as his brother who thought out how to make fire.

Of course, the earliest carvings on the cave walls are simple. They are scratched on smooth spaces; they take advantage of curves and bumps in the rock which roughly resemble the curves of an animal's back or belly. They are, besides, mostly deep in the dark interior caverns and passages, where it is damp and chill, where man did not live; but where magic fear filled the stone-cold air. The artist-priests must have worked by the light of fires or torches, perhaps of splinters of pinewood. With their flint gravers, so soon worn blunt, the work must

have taken long to do. Plainly it was believed to be of the greatest moment, or otherwise it would never have been undertaken. For the artists could, and no doubt did, make transitory drawings on sand, on tree-trunks, on out-of-door stone surfaces. These have worn away, washed away, thousands of years ago; they have perished and left no trace. But the magic of the clan demanded the making of power, of a power greater than that of humanity, over these creatures whose images were drawn for ever, whose spirits were prisoned on the walls in the dark.

The extraordinary thing is that the drawings are so good. Go into a cave like that of la Laugerie-Basse, les Combarelles, or Font-de-Gaume.[2] The walls are covered with outlines, bas-reliefs, in the last with paintings still faintly visible. There are mammoths, elephants, lions, reindeer, horses. Most of all bison, which must have afforded some pretty pickings. The figures are not only recognizable, they are lively. Often enough they are imposed one upon another, for suitable walls were not so common, and men of successive ages used them again and again. In fact the quality of the art improved till the Magdalenian Age, from about 30,000 to about 17,000 B.C.

Till 1940, the most advanced cave-art of the region was to be seen in the Abri-du-Cap-Blanc on the Beune.[3] Here there is a great frieze of bison, deer, and horses, done in bas-relief on a large scale. The excursion to Cap-Blanc is rendered pleasanter still by a couple of castles; one the medieval keep of Commarque, the other, the inhabited Renaissance château of Laussel; so that the visitor can see, set close together, three different ages of human dwellings. It was at Laussel that two carvings of human figures, the 'Venus' and the 'Hunter' were found; but they are now in the museum at Bordeaux.

To diverge for an instant from Les Eyzies, it should be said that the next most important group of carved caves in the south-west which make a series from very early drawings to the naturalistic Magdalenian art are in the valley of the River Célé, especially at Cabrerets and Ste-Eulalie; they can be best reached from Cahors or Figeac.

1 The Musée Nationale de la Préhistoire, open morning and afternoon daily except Tuesdays.

2 La Laugerie-Basse is open daily from 1 June to 30 September. Les Combarelles and Font-de-Gaume are open morning and afternoon daily except Tuesdays throughout the year. Both limit the number of visitors per day for conservation reasons. Details of the many other caves that can be visited are obtainable from any of the local Syndicats d'Initiative.

3 Cap-Blanc, near Marquay, is open morning and afternoon daily from 12 April to 11 November, and all day in July and August.

Right: The 'Grand taureau' in the caves of Lascaux.

To most people, the cave-art is interesting, queer, rather frightening. Nobody can look at it without an overwhelming sense of the immense age of the world, in which for so many thousand years man has thought, in reality, much the same thoughts about himself and his surroundings. But the impressions of all the other caves are dimmed by the sight of Lascaux.

This astonishing cave was only found in 1940, by a strange chance. Four boys of Montignac, the little town on the Vézère, went walking in the wooded hill to the south of the town. One of them, Ravidat, took his dog Robot, and presently Robot disappeared down a hole. It was overgrown with brambles and half-hidden by a bush. The boys called, but the dog did not return. Then they dropped a stone down the hole, and thought it fell a long way. Ravidat widened the opening with his knife and crawled in head foremost. The passage led down and presently he tumbled down on to a heap of rubble. When the others followed him, they saw, by the light of a very tired electric torch, that not only had they got into a cave, but that it was painted with animals. Of course, every boy in this part of the world knows about painted caves, and they presently confided their find to their former schoolmaster, who was incredulous, till he went down and saw the paintings himself. Then he told the Abbé Breuil, who was staying near at the time, and who came to confirm the greatest find of French prehistory. After the war, the Ministry des Beaux-Arts opened an entrance to the cave—for its real entrance has never been found; that used originally by the boys was merely a crack in the roof—and lit the caverns with electricity. It was a pleasant thing that two of the original discoverers used to be the guardians of the caves and explained them to visitors. Very well they did it, too, with a pride in their trove which was charming to see, and with expert knowledge. It is sad that the pre-historians, who owe so much to them, as indeed all France does, did not at the outset arrange a university training for them, to enable them to enter the career of archaeology.

When it became obvious that the paintings had suffered greater damage from two decades of respiration by visitors than during the previous 300 centuries, the caves were closed to the public. Only six people per day are now allowed inside, and only with the authorization of the department of Monuments Historiques at Périgueux. (The proprietor of our recommended hotel at Montignac has been known to obtain this for his clients out of season.) In the meantime there is an exhibition with illustrated commentary at the entrance to the caves during the summer, and the hope that in a few years a complete artificial reproduction of them will be built alongside.[1]

Lascaux consists of two winding corridors, joined in the middle by a wider passage; the whole forming a sort of irregular H. Almost the entire surface of the walls, and in places the roof, is covered with paintings of animals. They differ greatly. Some of them, and these are the earliest, are outlines in black, especially of deer's heads. Some are great red cattle, larger than life-size. There are numbers of horses remarkably drawn, of which the most lovable are a frieze of little horses, with a fat roundabout pony, like a Shetland, in the centre of the line. One horse has fallen on its back—there is an idea that this depicts a method of killing horses by driving them over the cliffs.

The techniques of drawing vary, and are peculiarly interesting because they employ many of the devices of stylization used by artists of the Post-Impressionist and later schools. Some of the beasts are outlined in a heavy black pigment, while

1 The replica, Lascaux II, opened in 1983. It can be visited morning and afternoon daily except Mondays from 1 February to 30 June and from 1 September to 31 December. In July and August it is open daily from 9.30 to 7. Tickets are available from the Office de Tourisme in Montignac, and numbers are limited to 2000 per day. Out of season tickets are sold at the site. An exhibition about the making of Lascaux II can be seen at the le Thot Centre of Prehistory, open morning and afternoon daily except Mondays; closed in January.

the rest of their bodies is coloured in red or ochre yellow. The hoofs of the bison are picked out in black with the pale stone left for the highlights. In some cases the softness of animal fur is rendered by what seems like blowing or spitting the paint on to the rock, with a pointillist effect.

The pictures have been preserved by geological chance. At some period the walls sweated a film of crystalline damp, which afterwards dried and formed, as it were, a transparent glaze over the colours, which has kept them as fresh as the day they were painted. Only in one part of the cave roof, the sweat from the roof was greater, and the oozing deposit obliterated the paintings.

The animals are instinct with life. Look, for instance, at the cow which is trying to leap over a fence or trap. She is picking up her heels exactly as her sister does today when she is jumping the wall of her field. There has been no such living representation of beasts in movement in any surviving human art, save perhaps that of the T'ang horses and camels of China, till the high Renaissance.

The frescoes give a vivid religious impression. A high proportion of the animals are pregnant. One of the mares has a tiny foal standing upright in her belly, a bold bad guess at animal obstetrics. Those who believe that the animals were drawn to induce fertility must surely be right. But there are other signs of what Mr. Raymond Mortimer has dubbed 'wishful painting'. There are the mysterious magical signs which one grows to expect in the caves; scratchings somewhat like masons' marks. There is one great creature who is not naturalistic at all; it is a hideous composite monster, the ancestor of the hippogriffs which haunted the imagination of Babylon. And strangest of all, there is the 'prehistoric tragedy'. This is down a pit, where the ordinary visitor is not allowed, as yet, to penetrate. It shows a bison, pierced with a javelin, its entrails hanging out, stiffening for the fall of death. But before it is a man, falling backwards, whom the bison has just gored. The man is drawn, unlike the animals, in a formula such as a child draws on his slate, with lines for body and limbs, and a bird-mask over his head. He is the only man of the cave. Is he not the first picture of the tragedy which forms the core of so many religions? The human sacrifice, the vicarious suffering of the chosen victim for the many? This conception reappears so often in the Egyptian hierarchy, in the Middle Eastern myths, in Indian tales of the gods, in later Mithraism, in Christianity. Such are the thoughts which this terrible painting awakes in our minds. But we are ordinary people, free to indulge our fancies. The prehistorians are far too cautious to voice these speculations. They occupy their writings with the dating—within a period going back to about 30,000 B.C.—for the paintings. They disagree among themselves gleefully as to such matters, but there is no need to be alarmed by their battles, which are those of Tweedledum and Tweedledee. Controversy is the way in which the learned keep the claws of their minds sharpened; to spectators it should be taken in the spirit of a tennis-match. For us, it is surely enough to see the Lascaux paintings; to submit to their overwhelming impression; to realize that here is one of the great works of art of the world. It would be worth crossing France to see them if there was nothing else to bring us to Périgord.

Troglodytes and Caverns

There are modern cave-dwellers in south-western France. They use the same grottoes as Stone Age man, but they have added a number of amenities. For they generally build a neat front, with windows, on to the cave mouth, and lead a chimney up through the roof. The prehistoric shelter of la Laugerie-Basse, near les Eyzies, belongs to M. and Madame Maury, who with their son have done much of the excavations, and who live in a house built into the rock and wreathed in wistaria.[2] At Brantôme there is a whole street of such houses beside the River Dronne, with apple trees planted in front of them, and hazels growing out of their rocky roofs.

All over the country there are caves which the people used as refuges when invading bands, bent on pillage, swept through the valleys. They gape halfway up the cliffs, roughly fortified

2 La Laugerie-Basse is now owned by the Société Chimique de France and leased to a descendant of the Maurys. Their troglodyte house is empty and the wistaria has taken over.

with walls, approachable by a narrow path, or sometimes only with ropes or ladders. Les Eyzies and la Roque-Gageac have such shelters. The Roque-St-Cristophe on the Vézère is carved into a series of chambers connected by steps; it was used as a fort when the Vikings rowed up the river.[1] Sometimes these defensible caves were built into small castles. From the road at Brengues on the Célé and from the ravine of Autoire near St-Céré they can be seen high up, their crenellated walls rising to meet the bulge of the precipices. They are queer, sinister places; and the country people, who have a muddled and mythological idea of local history, call them 'Châteaux des Anglais'. This is because it is customary to attribute anything old and odd to the period of the Hundred Years' War; 'the time of the English', as they say. But the English certainly did not build these eyries. They, or the barons who followed them, raised castles and forts by the dozen, but not in places such as these.

There are even churches hollowed out of the rock. The most famous is the monolithic abbey of St-Emilion, the wine town near the Dordogne estuary. It must have been a lofty cave, originally. But for centuries the monks mined it and enlarged it till it became a church supported on ten pillars of the living rock. They made chapels and a passage-crypt for their dead. It is a dark, gloomy, and, it must be owned, a hideous church. The monks must have continued to use it, out of a perverse conservatism, long after the days of hermit-evangelists; for they made an elaborate belfry-tower, rising from the terrace above the cave roof, as if to show that they could follow architectural fashions if they chose. The town has a fine parish church as well, and several chapels. There is another monolithic church on the Dordogne below Domme.

The caves which in ancient and modern times have served as dwellings are those which are dry, relatively comfortable, and more or less open to light and air. But they form only the more accessible part of the vast underground network of caverns. Some of these are among the sights of the region.

The French are essentially stylish. Everybody knows this in connection with women's clothes, for which they have imposed fashion, and its very language, on all the Western world. But their liking for formality, for a mode clearly defined and generally accepted, extends even to their likes and dislikes in beauty and amusement. Nothing, you might suppose, could be more irregular and primevally natural than those rocky accidents which we call caves. But they became popular in the nineteenth century, in the wake of the romantic movement which accepted savage and curious nature as something to be admired. Indeed, in a minor way, even the eighteenth had a taste for fancified 'grottoes'. But the generations which accustomed themselves to looking at mountains and finding them beautiful, and not, as formerly, frightful and abhorrent, were willing to turn their eyes downwards, too, and to regard caves as exciting. Besides, there is no denying that they appeal to the child who never grows up in the breast of most of us, and who adores feeling frightened, brave, and adventurous in the dark.

Once the idea that caves were interesting in themselves had taken root, the French took to exploring them in their whole-hearted way. They began to penetrate the openings in the cliffs, and to follow the branching passages as far as they led into the hills. They descended the 'avens'. This is the country name for round holes in the ground, not uncommon on the causses, where the roof over an abyss has literally caved in. They were well known, of course, since the shepherds had to fence them with brambles to prevent their beasts from falling to their destruction; but they were never thought of except as a nuisance to husbandry. But when 'speleology', as cave-hunting is pompously called, became the fashion in the eighteen-eighties, the *avens* came into their own. The great leaders were E. A. Martel, a lawyer who deserted the courts of Paris to devote himself to his passion for caverns, and Louis Armand, the locksmith of le Rozier, a little Tarn village which cannot have provided a strenuous whole-time employment for his craft. These two and others spent days underground, following the passages, crossing mysterious chambers where unexpected

1 La Roque-St-Christophe is open morning and afternoon daily from Easter to 11 November.

fissures might engulf them. They had no light but candle-lanterns. Nowadays the caves are lit by electricity, and their entrances are managed by inclines; the day of the explorer has given way to the day of the tourist. The cave-clubs explore remote and little-known sites, in the hope of finding either a Lascaux or a Dargilan.

Almost every valley has caves, and the traveller is invited to see them by roadside notices—'à la Grotte'. Here are three of the most famous.

Halfway up the Grand Roc at les Eyzies[2] is a corridor which winds into the cliff. On either side are formations of spar, delicate and small, shaped like coral and seaweeds underwater. Many of them have electric lights set behind them, which show the translucent amber colour of the crystal. Le Grand Roc is always crowded; you will find many more people there than in the prehistoric caverns like les Combarelles.

Far to the south, on the desolate Causse Méjean, is the Aven Armand. With the neighbouring Grotte de Dargilan, it has the finest stalagmite formations in France.[3] It is an immense globe-shaped cave, formed by the swirling of an underground torrent long since vanished; in truth a gigantic pot-hole. It is over 100 feet high, and the slow-dropping limy water from the roof has fallen and splashed through millions of years upon the rounded bottom. The stalagmites formed by the splashes are strangely varied and complex, like curly greens, like bracken fronds, like tall tree-ferns. The lighting of the cave changes colour every few minutes, and so unlikely, so dreamlike is the scene that the stagey effect of the light seems appropriate as in the transformation scene of a pantomime. The lights apart, the cave is left almost as it was discovered; and it makes an impression of the timeless, hidden work of stone and water which is deeply moving.

Padirac—that is a name familiar through all France, and indeed outside it.[4] For miles around signposts on the roads of the Causse de Gramat point the traveller to the Gouffre de Padirac. Even on weekdays there are many cars running to it. On Sundays there is a steady procession of charabancs, bicycles, even walkers; tours, clubs, schools, Scouts, a sprinkling of foreigners. Here is the car park, as full as that of a racecourse. Rival restaurants proclaim their satisfying and expensive menus. A queue waits at the turnstile for tickets; you squeeze into a lift; change into another lift which plunges deeper still; get out and descend a long staircase set upon the rocks, look up at the circular patch of blue sky blazing at the top of the gulf, and enter the cave of Padirac.

This is a river-cave, the bed of a stream running in a narrow fault, more than 500 feet below the ground. After a series of steps descending to the water, the visitor is taken aboard a punt, with rows of seats facing forwards. The boatman rows down the stream whose current washes perpendicular walls of rock; the lights set along the cliffs at intervals do not throw a strong enough illumination to reach the high, narrowing roofs. The stream, if you put your hand into it, is deadly cold. The Styx must have been like this ice-dark river; the boatman might easily be Charon; and the French girls crying in delicious terror, 'O mon Dieu! O là là!' in their high treble are like the bird-like twittering of the souls of the dead. The boat rows for about half a mile, and beyond that there is a series of small lakes, one below another, divided by rocky waterslides and overhung with stalactites. You go round them on iron gangways, return to the boat, and begin the ascent of the river. Beyond the farthest lighted point, says the boatman, it has been explored for five miles; but the going is hard; they believe that its final exit into the valleys is at a resurgence twelve miles away.[4] You are cold when you leave the boat, but you will be warm before you have climbed the staircase leading up the debris at the foot of the open gulf to the lift. If you count the steps they come to two hundred and eighty-three.

In spite of the crowds and the lifts and the restaurants, there is still the real cave-feeling about Padirac; about its chill, dark river and its scenery like a madman's dream. Caves, after all, are not for the sophisticated, who will find them boring or absurd; they are for children and for those of us who have not lost a child's sense of mystery.

2 Open morning and afternoon daily from 1 April to 1 November, and all day in July and August.

3 Dargilan is open daily from Easter to 1 November and on Wednesday afternoons the rest of the year. Aven Armand is open morning and afternoon daily from the end of March to 1 November, and all day in June, July and August.

4 Padirac is open morning and afternoon daily from 1 April to the second Sunday in October, and from 8 to 7 daily in August.

CHAPTER ELEVEN

THE PEOPLE

Western Europe is peopled by the descendants of tribes of nomads, hunters, and fighters who have come into it from age to age and settled down. Nowhere is this truer than in south-western France, where the shifting nations found their advance barred by the Atlantic. Here the tides of their wandering met the tides of a sea which nobody in these latitudes thought to cross for many thousand years. Here they must stay, or turn back to the steppes and the forests, to the poor soil and bitter winters of the East. So they forced their way among the people already settled, they intermarried, sometimes no doubt they cleared ground still uninhabited.

It was all long ago, and a country so continuously lived in and worked over shows few traces of the racial movements. Yet it still gives some clues to that shifting of the nations, which continued till the settlement of the Normans in the tenth century A.D.

The men who succeeded the cave-men, and who used first stone tools, and later bronze and iron, seem to have preferred the hill-ridges as habitations. The valleys were still filled with marsh and jungle. So the new Stone Age men built their villages, traced their paths, set up their standing-stones, where a slope gave drainage, and a ridge shelter from the wind. It is characteristic of the oldest tracks, many of which still exist, or form the base of modern roads, that they run just below the highest level of the hills. Here and there as you cross the slopes,

you will meet a standing-stone; sometimes surrounded by a patch of wild, uncultivated grass, as if the country-folk still have a feeling that it is not canny to meddle with those ancient things. Megaliths, as they are called, are not uncommon, though there is nothing to compare with the great avenues of Carnac in Brittany, or with the British circles. After all, this is a matter in which the learning of the wise is not much greater than that of the ignorant. All we can do is to look at the standing-stones and to wonder what were the thoughts which caused men to set them up from Cyprus to the Shetlands.

The Romans summoned France into the record of written history; and when they came they called the people 'Gauls', and described them as tall and fair. This is the origin of the famous lesson, mocked by so many writers, in which a class of tiny dark-eyed children recite 'Our ancestors, the Gauls, were tall in stature, fair of hair'. The Gauls were a Celtic race, divided into tribes, each with its own name. They were cultivators, traders, and miners. They had villages and even towns, for instance at Périgueux, Cahors, Rodez, and many other places where later cities overlaid them. Here and there they can still be traced, by lines on the hillsides which the chances of history have left undisturbed; although it is far less easy to be sure of them in this land of terraced cultivation, than it is on the English downs. Near Luzech, on the Lot, a Gaulish town was succeeded by a Roman camp; they have both been excavated. But those

A farmer in the spring pastures surrounding the village of Besse-en-Chandesse.

Right: The trees in a village square cast welcome shade in the hot summer sunshine of the Tarn gorges.

who are interested in this ought to go to the Ville-des-Murs—Murcens—on the River Vers, which runs into the Lot east of Cahors. There, in the loneliest region of the Causse de Gramat, the fortifications of a Gaulish city have survived almost completely.

The impact of Rome upon France changed all its history. Here in the south-west the most vivid memory is that of the actual conquest. After Julius Caesar had defeated Vercingetorix at Alesia, a battle in which a large contingent of Gauls from the western side of the Massif took part, the south-west still held out. The legions marched across by the Languedocian plain to finish it off, and the native army prepared to stand siege in the stronghold of Uxellodonum. The Romans failed to take it by assault, when Julius Caesar himself came to the attack in 51 B.C. He diverted the stream which fed the spring of the fort. The Gauls thought that their gods had abandoned them, fell into despair, and surrendered. Caesar, furious at their insolence in delaying his schedule of conquest, had the right hand of every fighting man cut off. This brutality, while it may have accounted for the completeness of the submission of the people to Rome, was never forgotten. It throws a darkness on the heart of that brilliant portrait of the noble and civilized Caesar, painted by historian and poet. Yet strangely enough, nobody is sure where this final defeat took place. Archaeologists have disputed bitterly for the claims of various sites. Nowadays there is a strong majority for the Causse de Martel, on the sharply escarped height east of St-Denis called the Puy d'Issolud.

The river-country has a few notable Roman remains. Périgueux has a broken round tower, the Tour de Vésone, which is said to have been the temple of a Celtic variant of Artemis. It has, too, an amphitheatre in a public garden, and a wall built later for defence, into which pieces of temple carvings and Roman masonry are incorporated pell-mell. No doubt the people adopted the Roman hierarchy of gods, finding it easy to identify their reverence for trees and springs with dryads and nymphs, So it was that the spring of Cahors became the goddess Divona. But the Druidic religion had

allowed no graven images; and the Gauls of the south-west did not succeed in reproducing the art of Rome. Gallo-Roman statues and carvings hereabouts are coarsely wrought, and generally displeasing; there is a good collection in the museum of Périgueux. Ussel, in the Limousin, has a great granite eagle, the symbol of the legions, in its garden.

None the less, the Roman peace, and Roman trade, greatly enriched the land. There were two provinces of Aquitania, the first centred on Bourges, the second on Bordeaux. The cities, linked with the great system of paved roads, acted as trade outlets for the country. Périgueux became a city. So did Cahors, which sent wine and linen to Rome. Millau on the Tarn had a famous pottery. Rodez, the capital of the Celtic 'Ruthenes', became a Roman administrative centre. These places are still the local capitals.

A notable reminder of the Gallo-Roman times is the names of places. Everybody is struck with the number of names which end in 'ac': Souillac, Salvignac, Moissac, Jumilhac; the list is endless. This ending was the way of saying 'belonging to'; the people called the estate of Jumil, 'Jumilhac', just as later they called the farm of Robert, 'the Robertie'.

But the real legacies of the Roman period were two. Firstly, language. The people lost the Celtic tongue, which in this part of France only survived in place-names like Dordogne, the 'avon' or water of Dor, 'Puy', a height or a hill. They took to that form of Latin which developed over centuries into the Langue d'Oc. This endured through all the flooding invasions of the Dark Ages, to flower into poetry with the troubadours. It has survived even the centralizing linguistic policy followed by the French state, ever since Francis I, in the sixteenth century, decreed that northern French should be used throughout the land. The line between the Langue d'Oil, the northern form, and the Langue d'Oc runs through the northern edge of the river-basins. Everywhere, the people are taught the French of the north in the schools; they must use it for examinations, in the courts, for all official purposes. As a written language, the Langue d'Oc is almost extinct in this region. It is called 'the patois', as though it were just a dialect, a peasant accent. But it is far from extinct as a spoken tongue. Nearly all the older country-people are bilingual. They use French for their communications with the outer world.[1] In the villages and the smaller towns the patois is their ordinary speech. It is somewhere halfway between French and Spanish; a musical language, without the twang of the Provençal 'accaing'. Except in Cantal, where it must be owned that the folk mew the patois through their noses like New England cats.

The second and greater gift of Rome was Christianity. This revolutionary faith, with an emotional appeal far transcending the official deference paid to the materialistic Roman Olympus, came to this part of France in the third century after Christ. That is to say, as far as verifiable history shows; for the local traditions attribute the evangelization of Périgord to St. Front, one of the seventy-two disciples of the Book of Acts; and the hermitage of Rocamadour is said to have been founded by Zacchaeus. Naturally Christianity met with persecution. Caprais, the bishop of Agen, and a little girl called Foy were martyred under Diocletian, and became saints held in reverence; the abbey of Conques is dedicated to Sainte Foy, and the town of Ste-Foy on the Dordogne is under her patronage. But on the whole Rome was tolerant of any faith which did not conflict with her governmental system. And the Christian Church organized itself on the model of that system, with bishops in the cities exercising authority over the neighbouring priests. This constitution was rooted firmly enough to stand the fall of Roman rule. And none too soon, for the first invasion of France by the barbarian hordes who breached the wall of the Empire was the ruinous incursion of the Alemans in A.D. 276. The shock of their pillage and burning of the peaceful, rich cities and farms shows in the fact that France has kept the name 'Allemand' ever since for the enemy from over the Rhine.

Roman law, and Roman education for the nobles, had been shaping the minds of the Gauls for three centuries. The tribal chiefs had become landholders, their followers farmhands or slaves on the manses, the great estates. For those who know the history of the Scottish Highlands, there is a striking likeness to what happened there in the nineteenth century, with the same effect of outer betterment and inner decay. The saving element in the situation was the Church. In the fourth century and after, one barbarian wave succeeded another. Cities and temples tumbled. Officials and legions left; and even the

1 The Langue d'Oc, or Occitan, has enjoyed a revival in recent years, and is now taught at the universities of Toulouse and Montpellier. Occitan street signs and graffiti can be seen as far north as Figeac, and many bookshops stock a range of books in Occitan.

merchants who had brought them in the beginning. The Church remained, for its priests were recruited not from Rome but from the people. Its language was Latin, far nearer to the speech of that day than it is to modern French. The manner of thought, the logic of the Romans were continued by the Church long after the Empire had become no more than an uneasy ghost haunting Europe. France takes for granted that its civilization is Latin, as its language is. Yet to the British observer of the river region, it may seem that this Latin form is inhabited by a spirit which is not that of Rome.

Nobody can tell how much of their blood the Romans left after their long occupation. Nor what the admixture was when Goths and Vandals, Swabians and Visigoths flooded across the Languedocian plain and took everything they did not ruin. The Visigoths were the least savage of the invaders, for they had collected Latin law and Arian Christianity on their way from the East. After the preliminary atrocities, they ruled well for a century. But the Catholics hated their heresy, and called in the Franks from the north to expel them; thus setting one invader against another, and beginning the long process of northern domination of all France.

The times were Dark Ages indeed. The very scarcity of Roman remains witnesses to the devastation of a country which had been thoroughly Romanized. Still, the people continued to exist and to make their livelihood out of the soil. In times of racial war, the men are lucky, for they are killed in battle. It is the women who must live on, and bear the children of the conquerors. A. E. Housman, the English poet, put that misery into four lines, recalling the same time in Britain:

> When Severn down to Buildwas ran
> Coloured with the death of man
> Couched upon her brother's grave
> The Saxon got me on the slave.

Yet in their forced submission, the women have their power still. The language the children speak will be their mother-tongue; the prayers they will learn will be of their mother's faith. Small doubt it was that capture by captivity that joined with the tradition of the Church to keep remnants of Latin civilization alive beneath the aliens.

It was when the endless rivalries between the intruding nations had produced some sort of unstable provincial division that the Arabs came sweeping up from Spain. They were capable of making themselves masters of France as they had of North Africa, but the founder of the Carolingian line, Charles Martel, stopped them at Poitiers in 732. Between then and Roncesvalles, when Charlemagne's paladins retreated from Spain and left Islam its master, the Arabs occupied part of the south, leaving behind them a memory of learning and building superior to that of the country, in places such as Castelsarrasin near the Tarn.

The last of the great invasions was that of the Vikings, who began to raid the rivers in the ninth century. They pillaged towns and monasteries; took Bordeaux and turned it into a pirates' den. Their speciality was robbery; but they habitually burned villages and monasteries, which was easy enough as they were built of wood. Their incursions went on for eighty years, and penetrated as far inland as Rodez, for wherever a river ran, the Norsemen could follow it up-stream. Local lords fought them off, and bought them off with land in 911. They were finally defeated in 982 by a Gascon duke, and turned their unwelcome attention elsewhere. They cannot have settled to any great extent, or they would have given the south-west that infusion of energy and genius with which this extra-ordinary nation transformed Normandy, England and Sicily.

This was the last of the racial invasions, for the later 'Anglais' were, in fact, mostly Frenchmen. The long tale of immigrant peoples ended; from that time the rivers sent their sons away.

Clearly it would be absurd to call this people a distinct race. Apart from the Gauls—not to mention earlier strains—the invaders included Romans and Teutons, some with Mongol blood, some Arabs. They have been living together and intermarrying for a thousand years, and must by now be inextricably mixed. In any case, no serious attempt has been made to disentangle their ancestry. All the same there are things about it which the people believe.

The conquerors, as a rule, while they helped themselves to the women of the country, kept the highest positions and the status of lords and landowners for their own stock, as each nation came in. Some of the old aristocracy may have survived as such, because of the habit of tribal enmity which caused them to side with the newcomers, often enough against their own nation. The Romans especially exploited this Gallic tendency to the full. But on the whole the later conquerors, the Teutons in particular, remained as a succession of master classes. As the records emerge into the Middle Ages, the names of lords and bishops, like Waifre, Guilhem, Theodebert, have a Nordic ring. It was more significant, perhaps, that the ideal beauty of the French romances was a slender, yellow-haired maid. It was her figure which was woven into tapestry, painted into the glass of church windows, carved as the Virgin Mary. But the girls of the Périgord villages remained obstinately brunette. This identification of a ruling nation and a general idea of beauty occurs often enough. The Greeks of Athens spoke of grey-eyed Athene, though most of them belonged to the little dark type of the Parthenon frieze. To this day, the Serbs, many of whom are golden as Vikings, will condole with a slim blonde girl, because for centuries their masters' wives were the dark and ample Turks.

Personal observation is scientifically worthless. But there is no law against it. In this connection a tourist like myself will notice strong local types of physique. In Périgueux and the valleys of the Isle and the Auvézère, all the way up to Hautefort, half the people might be related, so nearly do they resemble each other. The tourist is nagged by a likeness to a face long familiar. Why does one recognize that countenance? The bright brown eyes with short thick lashes, not large, but well set under a prominent round brow? The nose aquiline and a shade too long for beauty, the thin-lipped mouth and oval cheek? One stares at a child in a bus, and suddenly realizes that this boy has one of the most famous faces in the world, the face of

Mona Lisa. True, she was a Neopolitan, one dimly remembers; well, it says something for the Latin theory, perhaps. For what it is worth I may record that I spent several weeks in Périgueux and never saw one person with light eyes save a Czech refugee. But as soon as one begins to traverse the upper reaches of the Dordogne, still more of the Lot, one sees many people with blue eyes, and with faces which may be either eagle-beaked or tip-tilted, as we expect to see them in Ireland or the Hebrides. Farther south, there are some who are so entirely Arab in type that they might have sprung straight out of an Islamic troop of 740. And in the Cévennes you will notice—indeed you would have to be blind not to notice—women whose beauty is pure Greek.

Pride of ancestry is queer. In Spain, it is held a sign of aristocracy to be fair, a fair Visigoth. There is quite a sprinkling of fair people in our river-valleys, but nobody ever mentions the word 'Visigoth'. But a blackavized man, palpably vain of his hooked nose and chin, of his fine wrists and ankles, will tell you that his family throws up the Arab type. It is *chic* to be descended from the Semites, but no one wants to admit to Teutonic blood, though it must be common. The word 'Frank' has been so naturalized as 'Français', that few remember its origin.

Then there is the matter of local character. Here, too, the trained anthropologist would be puzzled to analyse the facts. For national character, viewed at any given moment in time, is a real thing, which only sophism refuses to recognize, however shy we may have got of facing it since the Nazis talked themselves into aggression with racialism as a pretext. It is real; the problem is what causes it? It is stylized by tradition and propaganda till it is impossible to tell how much it is an accepted habit, and how much, if any, inborn. Of course science has proved that acquired characteristics do not transmit from one generation to another. Yet all plant and animal breeders mate for character as well as for appearance. The civilization of a valley is taught to babies at their mother's knee. But what, in the first case, caused that valley to adopt some habit, imported from outside, in a different way from that followed by the next valley? It might be a hundred things, a strong-minded teacher, or a general shape of mind inherited like a general shape of body. This seems a question which, in a people of mixed racial origins, is impossible to answer. Perhaps the only sure thing about it is that the people do believe in local character and live it. For instance it is important to know that the people of the Dordogne and Lot do not consider themselves southerners. A Périgourdin, and still more a citizen of Bordeaux, will be affronted if you call the region the Midi, or the people Méridionaux. Yet the Périgourdins, as they are delighted to tell you, are Gascons, a nation which originally came in from south of the Pyrenees. They have the name of being brave, gay, expressive, hospitable, warm-hearted and hot-tempered. Their types in literature are Cyrano de Bergerac, a figure whose original, regrettably, never lived in Bergerac, but whom Rostand drew as a Gascon *par excellence*; and d'Artagnan, who really did come from Périgord and who was historically captain of the King's Musketeers under Louis XIV. Now all this assumption about character may be merely legend, though a good deal must be allowed for communities which have lived and intermarried for a long time sharing common traits. As a proprietor's wife said to me, apropos of a First Communion party: 'There were a hundred guests; but if all the kindred had been asked, the whole Dordogne valley would have been there.' Yet it is one of the pleasures of travel in Périgord that the people are gay, friendly, polite and conversible, and extremely hospitable, as I have reason to know.

The Rouergats are very different, as are the Auvergnats and the people of the Limousin Montagne. They are shy and reserved. Say 'Good-day' to one of them in passing, and you will receive not a cheerful smile, but a stately acknowledgment. If, however, you can gain their confidence and convince them that your desire for knowledge is not impertinent curiosity, they reveal themselves as cultivated people and outstanding talkers. The Rouergats are Gauls, as they believe. The argument is that their valleys were so difficult of access and their plateaux

so barren that the invading hordes, who naturally came mostly by the coastal plains, passed them by. Stray rievers possessed themselves of the lordship of the more eligible places; but they vanished with the suppression of the old bad barons by Richelieu and the Revolution. The Celts remain, they say, people wedded to old custom, proud, with a sharp wit which covers an immense secrecy about the things they truly care for.

Then you go down the Tarn, and diverge through the southern gorges, where the Tarnon runs up to Mont Aigoual, and the Jonte divides the Causse Méjean from the Causse Noir. And you will notice that the village inn, as often as not, bears the sign 'Hôtel du Midi'. Here at last are the southerners, the Méridionaux; merry, imaginative, graceful. Here you will stop and talk to everyone you pass; partly because their talk is entrancing, partly because they would think you uncivil if you did not. Soon you will begin to feel that these lyrical people are more democratic, more sure of themselves, than those farther north; that under their gaiety they are tough. They are the same people who endured centuries of persecution for their faith when their leaders had gone over to the winning side, when human justice was dead, and rescue unimaginable.

The differences in local character account for the custom of the people in adhering to the old provincial names. The departments, as they are now, were decreed in 1790. When you are addressing a letter, or bringing a law-suit, or sending a child to high school, you think in terms of your department. But nobody would dream of describing himself as a 'Dordogn-ais'—I do not think the word exists. He is a Périgourdin, or a Quercynois, or a Rouergat, or a Cévenol, because these words mean local tradition, character, and civilization. For this reason I have used the old provincial names throughout this book.

When you return home, you will not say so lightly as before: 'I love the French.' For the words will die on your lips as you remember how the French vary within so small a space. And after that there are the French considered as individuals. It is enough to make you give up generalization, if you had not picked up the habit—in France.

CHAPTER TWELVE

THE LAND AND THE PEOPLE

Trees

South-west France is farming country. The large majority of the people are cultivators, or are engaged in trades directly dependent upon agriculture. This lends the region much of its charm, for the life of the people fits the soil as closely as the soil fits the rock it covers.

The land, in return, has been fitted through thousands of years to the life of man. The trees show it better than anything. In the Middle Ages it was said that a squirrel could swing from branch to branch from the Monts Dore to Bordeaux, without ever touching the ground. That is far from the case now, and yet the landscape has a strong feeling of forest; only the trees that cover its slopes and colour its horizons are grown for the use of man.

The native beech and birch trees have been driven to the high wastes. In the wildest of the gorges, where cliffs and stony chaos make even a footpath impracticable, there is a sort of primeval jungle. Cattle breeders are still clearing the woods in the Limousin 'Bocage', the Bush, to extend their pastures. Some of the Cévennes slopes are bare of trees, though they were forest till the Revolution. Since that date the land has belonged to the peasants, and the trees have been devoured by that pestilential though handy beast, the goat. The Great Causses grow nothing bigger than juniper bushes. Down in the seaward plains the vine-growers have left few trees standing; there the landmarks are the avenues shading the highroads, and the tall poplars along the watercourses. But the farmers are great tree-growers through most of the country. One of the main products of Périgord and Quercy is walnuts, and the graceful trees are planted at intervals through the fields, and often along the roads. There are innumerable fruit trees, especially plums and apricots, in Quercy. Chestnuts cover many hillsides; they grow in a zone up to two thousand feet in the north, but much higher in the Cévennes. The chestnut was only introduced about a thousand years ago, it seems, and it made a vast difference to the standard of life of the peasants, who used it for food if the rye failed—and still do, at a pinch—and were able greatly to increase their stock of pigs. With their dark trunks, which wrinkle and warp with age, their wide shade, their leaves transparent in spring, vivid in summer, and glorious in the fall, the polished wealth of the nuts, the chestnut groves are by far the most beautiful of the woodlands of the south-west.

Nobody can travel this region without noticing that where they are allowed to grow to their full stature, in the deep-soiled river-valleys, the trees are immense. The Dordogne water-meadows have rows of giant poplars, both the lean dark kind and the whispering Lombardy poplars. But the characteristic trees of the uplands, where the soil is too thin to allow cultivation, are scrubby little oaks; obviously planted by man, and yet poor specimens of the royal tree. This is entirely intentional, for the oaks cover—or so their owners hope—

Dairy cows graze on the pastures near Besse-en-Chandesse to provide the milk for the creamy Auvergne cheeses.

buried treasure. They are truffle-oaks. When the terrible phylloxera epidemic of the 'eighties destroyed the vineyards of Périgord, the farmers were in despair. But they were saved by the truffle. This fungus, as was discovered quite recently, is a disease of the roots of certain young oaks. The countrymen grow copses of the right sort, and with luck, and the scent of a truffle-hound or sow, they find them and dig them up at the beginning of the winter. Périgord swears that her truffles are the finest in the world; Quercy that just as good lie under her trees. There is an insatiable and a paying market for the queer black lumps, the most delicate of all the fungus tribe, of which a slice will give a *pâté* a delicious flavour, and a few specks translate an omelette into ambrosia. But when the oaks grow beyond a certain age, their roots cease to throw off truffles, and they are ruthlessly cut down.

The French state has an active and intelligent forestry policy. Wherever the land is too poor for the plough, it gets the consent of the proprietors, often a village *commune*, and plants trees. And it is far too statesmanlike to follow the idiotic habit of the British forestry department, and to confine itself to a monoculture of pines. There are considerable stretches of forest west and south of Périgueux, and another south of the Dordogne, where the main plantations are of chestnut and acacia, both used for stakes, although there is a good deal of live oak, and of maritime pine that has come colonizing inland from the Landes. In the Grésigne forest of the Aveyron gorges the main tree is the oak. Much the most extensive forestry of the region is on the high slopes of the Lozère and the Cévennes mountains. These were due originally to the work of one man, Georges Fabre, an official of the Waters and Forests service. He found the Cévennes naked after a century of pasture, and the hillsides washing away in the floods caused by thunderstorms. He set to work to replant first the ground beside the springs and along the watercourses, and then the main ridges. The early plantations were of fir trees, but later, as humus accumulated under the groves, he planted beech trees. This great work was begun in 1875, so that the Cévennes forest is

still young. But it has given rise to a forestry industry, and also to a summer tourist season, adding immensely to the wealth of a desperately poor population. That is not to say that it was easy to do. The shepherds, naturally, opposed it furiously. The *communes*, where they are strong, still refuse their agreement to afforestation. Often enough the pastoral defenders have taken to the attack. It is wonderful what a couple of goats let loose in a young plantation will do in the way of sabotage. As a last resort, there is always the twig, set alight on a dry summer night, and no evidence left as to the incendiary. Even without intentional arson, the danger of forest fires is acute on these dry heights. The drought of 1949, which saw miles of the Landes pinewoods in flames, did not entirely spare even the rivers. When the firs of the Tarn gorge caught fire, the cliffs acted like the flue of an oven and the trees, painfully grown on the screes below them, were reduced to charcoal.

Forestry produces its own dependent industries. Every here and there throughout the region there are saw-mills. Furniture, railway sleepers, palings, walnut rifle-stocks at Montignac, tannin for leather, which unfortunately means the destruction of walnut groves; all these are made from the trees. But they are first and foremost a part of farming. Even the pines are planted mainly to conserve the soil. As to the rest, some of the most paying exports from the region are chestnuts and *marrons glacés*, fruit both fresh and preserved, jam, walnuts, and above all, the black and perfumed truffle. These are humanized forests. When a farmer speaks enthusiastically of trees he does not say: 'Fine old trees!' He says: 'Yes, we have walnuts, and beautiful ones—young ones.'

Animals

In a country which ranges from 5,000-foot mountains to sea-level, farming naturally varies immensely. It is, of course, true in the main that the higher land is pasture and the lower cultivated. But there are many local specializations.

The Monts Dore, the Cantal slopes, the Monts d'Aubrac, the high Cévenol valleys feed cattle. The Limousin is largely given over to cattle breeding, especially of baby beef for the city markets, but also of draught oxen. When the snows melt from the high pastures, the cattle come up from the plains, and come out of the byres, for the summer pasture. Cantal produces an excellent cheese from the milk of the red cows that pasture its slopes. The most curious, and the most ceremonially stylized of the cattle migrations is that of the Monts d'Aubrac. These bleak, rounded hills, snow-covered in winter, lie silent and shivering under the winds for months of the year. Their farmhouses, surprisingly large, stand almost without surrounding fields in the vast grass uplands. In April the snows melt; in May the grass becomes an incredible garden of flowers. On the 25th of May[1] the cattle cross the Lot bridges and come up to the pastures. Each herd comes separately. All the cows wear garlands on their horns, and the leader a big bell, too. The cattle are the lovely beasts of the Rouergue, fawn-coloured with dark points. These herds will not rent the pastures as you might suppose. It is the Aubrac farmers who hire the cows for the summer. Through the summer months the herds graze the grassy hills with a posse of men looking after each of them, from the overseer, who directs operations, to the herdboy who keeps the bunch within the limits of their grazing-ground. For dogs are not allowed in the Aubrac; there are no fences, and they would fight. The cowherds milk the cattle, and make cheeses which are sold at the end of the season. The money they sell for must pay the wages of the herds, and the hire of the cattle, as well as giving the farmers their profit for the whole year. This strange economy dates back to the days when the Aubrac was owned by the Domerie, an order of military monks who protected pilgrims on their way to the shrine of Compostella over these lonely and bandit-ridden heights.

A feature of the high pastures, as of the causses, is sheep-pasture.[2] Many of the upland villages have a communal herd of sheep. Throughout the summer it is tended by a shepherd, who folds it in a different farm each night, for the sake of a just distribution of manure, and gets a few extra nights for himself as a reward. But the great shepherding is on the causses, when the 'transhumants' come up from the

pastures of the Mediterranean marches. All through May, the stranger meets small flocks of sheep on their way uphill. They are attended by a herd, often by a family, a man and his wife, and a son or daughter, and always by two dogs. They are moving slowly, eating the wayside grass as they go. If they include goats, they are more experimental. An entire herd may be seen standing on its hind legs devouring the tender foliage of a beech copse. The clever goats give the example, and the sheep, who might not have thought of it for their silly selves, are quite bright enough to be inspired by propaganda. The flock is probably on its way to a grazing on the causses which the family rents year after year. When they get there, they can be seen bunched in a close ring, cropping the fine scant grass, with the herd leaning on his staff, and the dogs watching every movement. They will only be allowed to eat for a period in the morning and evening; they will be taken to drink at a dew-pond—ponds are the only surface water on the causses—and they will be folded for the night. The sheep, to British eyes, are very queer. They have no wool on their bellies, and only a short moth-eaten-looking mat on their backs. Even that is shaved off by July. This poor wool is the basis of a weaving industry at Lodève, which makes the scratchy cloth of French army uniforms. Many of the sheep are bred for the market, and if mutton in France is scarcely eatable for us, since Anglo-Saxon jaws cannot negotiate meat so tough, we should remember the muscles the sheep develop on that long trek to the causses. On the other hand, lamb in this part of France is delicious; for the sheep of the great Causse du Larzac are dedicated to providing milk for Roquefort cheese. The cheeses are ripened in caves on the southern edge of the causse, and the lambs are taken from their dams soon after birth. On the Causse de Gramat the goat replaces the sheep, and the little round cheeses sold in the markets, each lying on a leaf, are very good.

The cattle and sheep herded carefully through their morning and evening outing, the sheep feeding so closely gathered that they look like a rugby scrum, are strangely unfamiliar to us,

1 Or the Sunday nearest the 25th of May.

2 Except the Monts d'Aubrac, which are now given over entirely to cattle.

Fields of maize beside the Dordogne. The crop is grown extensively for animal and poultry feed.

pairs. They ploughed and harrowed in spring, and the fields resounded to high-pitched yells of 'Aah! Aah!' 'Go on! Go on!' and 'Arré! Arré!' 'Stop! Stop!' Later in the year they drew the hay and corn harvests home, walking along the roads, their neat feet, shod with iron shoes, planted elegantly in their slow, invariable gait, their eyes veiled from sun and flies by a hempen sweat-rag. They are beautiful creatures, and usually look well treated. In the southern valleys there were more horses used in farmwork, but almost everywhere the tractor has now taken over from both beasts of burden.

Every farm has poultry. Hens as a matter of course, often confined in far too small a space, and in miserable condition to northern thinking. The ducks and geese which are hatched out in May and June are a very different matter. They are petted like children, fed on grain and greenstuff, taken for walks to water twice a day, given the most agreeable life. Till the time comes when they are considered fit for the market. Then they are fattened by forcible feeding till their livers degenerate, when they are sold for the production of *foie gras*. Their meat is conserved too. You may buy it, or the *pâté*, in extremely expensive tins in Sarlat or Périgueux. But every farmer's wife keeps some of her geese for the use of her own household. For poultry is the woman's perquisite—and work—and the money earned by it is the wife's affair. So much so, that in metayer farms, where the farmer pays a proportion of the harvest price to the owner instead of a fixed money rent, poultry does not count in the divided produce. The countrywoman does her own preserving. She tins *foie*, but she usually preserves joints of goose and duck in great jars of lard, from which she will take out what she wants for Sunday lunch on festal occasions.

The rabbit forms another resource of animal husbandry. It is astonishing how few wild rabbits are in this region of pasture and woodland. Even before its near-extermination by myxomatosis, the race was kept low by the hunter, for French countrymen are as devoted to 'la chasse', the hunt, as they are to 'la pêche', fishing. They shoot many birds that do not count as game in Britain, and certainly as many rabbits as they can.

used to seeing sheep on the hills widely scattered, and cattle in the fields all day, and in summer all night too. In fact, the foreigner may be puzzled to know where the animals are, in a country where he will be given two meat meals a day, milk in his morning coffee, and all sorts of *pâté* on a basis of pork. The truth is that the beasts have finished their morning bite before he is out of his bed. In the evening he will meet an old woman in charge of a cow, which is eating the wayside grass, or a little herd of mixed sheep and goats stuffing themselves as full as they can in their brief pasture-interval, or a horse being led to drink at the fountain. As to pigs he may never see one at all, for they seem to live entirely in their sties; unless he encounters a farmer going to seek truffles, with a preternaturally intelligent-looking sow following the guidance of his long wand. Oxen were the only farm animals which were ever much in evidence. They used to be everywhere in the valleys, always yoked in

Seedtime and Harvest

Dogs and cats abound. The dogs divide into sheep dogs, which are work-animals and respected as such, and dogs kept for hunting, as house-watchers, and as pets. The hunting dogs are usually mongrel hounds, such as are carved on houses at Cordes. They have the sad faces and sentimental nature of hounds. The mixture of breeds is shocking; many dogs are deformities hardly able to walk, so badly bred are they. And a terribly large proportion of the dogs are starved; it is quite common to meet one that cannot hold itself upright for more than a moment, it is so weak with hunger. This seems to be partly due to the myth that only a hungry dog will be a good watch-dog; but it is a barbarous thing. The same is true of cats; they must be the smallest on earth, and they are always miserably thin; on the farms it does not seem to be the custom to feed them at all. Add this to the dirty state of many of the cattle, and the foreigner often thinks that the population of the south-west is in dire need of education in animal hygiene, and of a new St. Francis to teach it Christian mercy to the beasts.

Field crops in the south-west include several kinds of grain and vegetables. The principal crop is wheat, followed by oats. A good deal of maize is grown at the lower levels, as poultry food. Rye used to be the crop of the poorer land, but it is rather rare now, for the liming of the soil has rendered the cultivation of wheat possible. An important crop is tobacco, again in the lower ground of Périgord and Quercy. The farmers gather it, tie the leaves in twenties, and take it to the state tobacco stores to be weighed, for it is bought according to quality and weight.[1] The towns with stores, like Sarlat, would be glad if there were cigarette-factories attached to the stores, to provide employment for some of the townspeople. But so far this has not been done. Fruit and nut cultivation is carried on in all the agricultural districts, combined with the ordinary crops of mixed farming; the trees are grown widely spaced through the field.

Harvest is a season of intense activity. For such a dry and hot region it is set very late, perhaps just because the people can count on fine weather, except for the dreaded hailstorms. They leave the hay standing in the fields till long after it has seeded and withered; to the British mind, almost all the good must have gone out of it. The farmers have a saying: 'The hay should be carried by the 14th of July, the *fête nationale*.' Considering that it has been ripe since early June, this does not seem to be unduly prompt. The same is true of the corn, it stands till it must have dropped much of the grain. Until recently it used to be cut and stacked, with a straw cross to top each stack, till the itinerant beating-machine came round and threshed it.

The climate is favourable to vegetables like tomatoes and artichokes, which grow to great size. It is really too dry in summer for roots. Potatoes are treated as a luxury vegetable, washed meticulously before being sold in the market, and cooked with care. If they are served at a meal, there will not be another vegetable, probably. The most delicious of all the vegetables are the peas, eaten as they should be, very young and small.

To speak of the cultivation of the vine is impertinent of any foreigner. But it is worth observing that the Biblical phrase about sitting under his own vine and his own fig tree carries a delusive implication of effortless luxury. People do sit under their own vines, for they are often trained to shade the terraces. But they do not sit long at ease. From the moment when the transparent shoots begin to waver out of the black stocks, the vine-grower is at work. He trains, he prunes, he sprays with a succession of chemicals, till the exquisite green of the leaves is dyed a metallic peacock shade. The vine is a delicate fine lady among plants. It is threatened with phylloxera, with many insect plagues. If there is a day's rain after it is growing, it will get mildew. If it hails, the soft fruit-bearing shoots are broken off, and good-bye to the vintage. When at last the fruit has passed these manifold perils and is ready to gather, the work of vintage is terrific. Town boys and girls stream out to the country to help cut, for the period when the grapes are just right for the press is brief.

1 Tobacco is still an important industry, but the traditional crop is giving way to *tabac blond*, which requires considerably less labour. Bergerac has Europe's only museum of tobacco, open morning and afternoon daily except Sundays, Mondays and holidays.

Proprietors

Most of the land is farmed by freeholders in these parts. There are four kinds of farmer, known as big proprietors, small proprietors, metayers, and farmers.[1] The really great landowner, as we know him, is rare. A few of the old nobility still hold part of their ancient estates, and some new families have regarded land, especially vineyards, as a good investment for money made in trade or manufacture. Landlords on a large scale sometimes rent land to 'fermiers', farmers in the strict sense to which the French confine the word; a farmer is a cultivator who pays a fixed rent for his land. But even the big proprietors usually prefer to use the metayer system. There is no English word for 'metayer', since we do not have the system; and the American 'share-cropper' has a bad sound because of the starvation share-cropping of the southern states. The metayer of France is probably a prosperous man. He pays the value of a proportion of his harvest to his landlord. This the French consider just and logical, for in a bad year the owner's share is less, in a good year more, so that the metayer does not run into debt for back rent. At the same time, it is easy to see that there are temptations to juggle with the figures, and perhaps it may be the metayers who, together with the landlords, sustain such a large number of notaries in the little towns.

Figures on this subject would be dull. But a big landlord is one who has a property of over 90 hectares, or 220 acres; only 23 per cent of the owners of the Limousin, for instance, exceed this acreage in property, although that is a country of extensive cattle-farming.

The great majority of the proprietors are smallholders. They are by far the most important element of the people, because they are the essential element. A family may own five hectares of arable and five of grazing (25 acres), in which it grows a little of everything. It subsists quite comfortably on this acreage, with enough surplus to sell to endow the daughter with a dowry, and to give the younger son his 'share'. Such a family used to bake its own wheat into its own bread; it still eats all its vegetables from its own garden; makes its wine and has some

to sell, grows its own fruit and nuts. The pigs and the poultry furnish meat; very rarely does such a family enter the butcher's shop. Coffee, sugar, and salt are the necessaries to buy. Clothes, tobacco for the men, and the church collection, are the less needful expenditures. Taxes? Well, the French proprietor is opposed in principle to paying taxes. He has never got out of his blood the old days when it was he, and not the great landowner, who paid them all.

With extreme caution, the proprietor sidles in the direction of co-operation. The wine-growers of Bergerac run a co-operative.[2] Threshing is a service supplied by a travelling team. The form in which co-operation would appeal to the small owners would be in the purchase of machinery. Already they have a habit of working in village groups at harvest time, finishing one field and then going on to another, the families combining to help each other. This is an incidental result of the small-family social system. But if anybody dared to suggest the collectivization of the farms, he would meet with a resistance which, if needed, would take the form of civil war. So when you hear that co-operatives have sprung up in these provinces, it means for the purchase of machinery and for selling some kinds of produce, but not collectivized ownership of land.

It is easy to realize why the countrymen feel so deeply about land-ownership. For centuries their ancestors were serfs, tied to the soil, and to the service of the 'gentle' class that owned the land. They were not quite chattel-slaves, for the customs of the country left them some rights. But they could not go away without their *seigneur's* leave. They were taxed and tithed, subject to forced labour, allowed to till their fields, in which they had no ownership, only after the *seigneur's* land was prepared; bound to follow him to war if required; they were about as free as the Russian collective-farm labourer of today. As in the rest of western Europe the process of their emancipation was slow, and not much is known about it. The manpower shortage caused by the wars, and also by the Black Death of the fourteenth century, gave them some bargaining power, and it seems that by mid-fifteenth century serfdom, in

1 Metayer farming is on the decline. Most farmers in the south-west own their own land, however small the plot may be. Recent years have also seen a considerable drift away from the land, as young people head for the towns and cities.

2 This of course is now the norm rather than the exception.

the formal sense, had ceased. But feudal land-tenure, and with it the economic and personal insecurity of the peasants, continued till the Revolution; and human relationships between landlord and tenant grew worse in the reigns of the later Bourbons, because the highly artificial civilization of the gentlefolk, always absent at court if they could manage it, widened the gap between rich and poor. The Revolution, which gave freehold ownership to the peasants, meant not only better living standards than the drain of rent and tithe had ever allowed, but liberty, status, self-respect. The majestic manners of the proprietors have not only the charm of courtesy, but the pride of free men secure in the possession of their land.

The Code Napoléon introduced a rule of succession theoretically just, but economically ruinous, when it decreed that the property of a family must be left in equal shares to all the children. When there was nothing to share but the land, this meant that division and sub-division threatened to reduce the holdings to parcels so small they would not even feed a family. The same process may be seen today in the land reforms of eastern Europe, where the land is divided into uneconomically small holdings, in order to furnish a pretext for later collectivization. The French proprietor faced this problem and solved it long ago. This is the position, described by a Périgourdin proprietor:

'What happens in a family like the Fauchers, where there are two sons and a daughter? When the "Maître" dies, will the land be divided?'

'Mademoiselle, decent people, *les gens bien*, do not divide the land. Before the Maître dies, in fact, when he wishes to repose himself a little, there will of course be a family council. They will settle the heritage *à l'amiable*—that is to say without calling in the advice of a lawyer, which only multiplies costs. The eldest son will be designated as heir of the land. But as long as he lives, M. Faucher will still be the master. The daughter is married and has no doubt received her share as dowry. The younger son will receive a sum of money which the council will recognize as just, so that he may buy a farm for himself, or if he

marries a girl who is heiress to a property, he may enter her property without feeling himself empty-handed.'

In practice a family of three is rare. One way of solving the difficulty of the law of equal inheritance, has been to restrict families, and birth-control has been the custom of French working people for over a century. The ideal family is two children, a boy to heir the property, and a girl to marry the son of a neighbour and with him to inherit the neighbour's farm.[3]

The traveller should remember that it is rude, hereabouts, to say to a man 'You are a farmer—'fermier'?' The proper address is 'Monsieur, vous êtes propriétaire?' 'You are a landowner, sir?' For it is the status of *propriétaire* that gives the countryman his power of work, his constancy, and his immense dignity.

Hens scratch around every cottage doorway and farmyard in this region of France.

3 With the many inducements which the French government offers couples to encourage them to produce more children, this may now be changing.

CHAPTER THIRTEEN

WEATHER AND WIND

The south-west is a long slope to the Atlantic. And it lies in the latitude of north Italy; Périgueux at about the level of Turin, Albi of Florence. These two factors make its climate, for its draws its rainfall from the west, and its temperature from its southern position.

The winter is long and sometimes severe on the heights. But as few travellers will visit the country in winter, this does not concern us. There is still a good deal of snow lying on the mountains in April, when spring has begun in the valleys. The spring of Aquitaine comes flying from the west in a swirl of flowers. It has to hurry, because summer is hard on its heels and will pursue it by the rivers and catch up with it on the ridges in June. No wonder that the troubadours always began their lays with a passage in praise of spring. Even wicked old Bertran de Born obeyed the rule, though he hastens to say that he loves spring because then the tents of the knights are spread out in the field and the horses neigh for battle. But the other poets sing of the flowers.

They include nearly all the wild flowers of Britain, and many that we do not know. They are bemusing in their extravagance. Gorse and broom actually colour the hillsides yellow, and cowslips do the same to the way-wastes. You think you have gone colour-blind and are seeing the green fields blue, till you look closer and see that they are blue with scillas. Flowers that we are used to weeks apart blossom in a mad simultaneity. Here is a record of a day in May, begun high on the Monts d'Aubrac. The field where I lunched was white with narcissi, with an under-layer of cowslips. The way down by a stream, through beech woods whose leaves were at their luminous silken unfolding, passed through banks and swathes of gorse, broom, yellow dwarf genista, gentians, rock-roses, bugloss, marguerites, columbines, alpine pinks, wild roses, many meadow florets which in my ignorance I could not name; and

Above right: Wild thyme grows in profusion on the rocks in the valley of the Tarn near le Pont-de-Montvert.

Left: Summer storm clouds clear momentarily over the Maronne valley near Salers.

Right: Tall horse chestnut trees in flower on the Rouergue uplands near Villefranche-de-Rouergue.

Opposite left: Summer flowers outside a cottage near Villefranche-de-Périgord.

Opposite right: Trees beginning to change colour in late October on Mont Lozère between le Bleymard and le Pont-de-Montvert.

down by the Lot a long wall covered with crimson valerian startlingly interspersed with scarlet poppies.

In the river gorges there are quantities of rock-flowers, from lavender and sea-thrift, pinks and campanulas and saxifrages to the exquisite flowering grasses. Two of these in particular give the russet rocks a delicate veil. They are both of a pure blue, one the size of a small convolvulus, the other a smaller star. They cannot be gathered. If you try to pick one the flower comes off the stem and floats away like the blue butterfly whose tint it shares. Nor will the inquiring foreigner find it easy to discover the names of these flowers. French education, deplorably urban, neglects to teach the children the natural lore of their surroundings. I asked the landlady of my hotel. She giggled: 'Ah! I do not know its dictionary name. It has a name in the patois'—but she would not say what—'we say that if the goats eat it they give more milk.' The smaller is in fact wild flax, but I failed to trace the other.

Last of the spring flowers, the hedges bloom with honeysuckle, drained of its scent till after sunset. Then the summer turns the flowers to seed; only the late small after-blooms of poppy and ragwort and pimpernel make points of colour among the withering grass.

Autumn is set alight by the turning of the woods, bright against the wreathing mists when the rains begin. Some find the long stretches of russet and umber sad. But if the tourist cannot see the marvel of the spring he had best come in the autumn, after the middle of August. From mid-June till then the sun is a tyrant, forcing the whole land down into silent burning endurance for the noon hours. The only way of passing them is to sit immersed in a river, or to lie flat and naked on a bed with the shutters closed. But the nights are balm.

Sometimes, in the summer months, a strong wind blows out of the west. The foolish tourist says to himself: 'West wind, from the Atlantic; thank the Lord there will be rain.' But the wind blows and blows, tearing the tender shoots and the dead branches from the trees till the roads are scattered with sticks and leaves; and no rain falls. He then asks the local Authority, the hotel proprietor perhaps, what sort of a wind is this? At that, a glazed expression comes over the face of the Authority, who merely says: 'Ah! There is a wind, in effect!' For this wind is the Autun, the scorching summer wind from the hot Atlantic, which does no good and sears the crops. It is as indecent to mention the Autun, in the presence of an hotel-keeper, as it is to mention the Mistral at Avignon. At last, after days of the Autun, there may be a storm. The electric storms of high summer are not to be taken lightly. The huge cumulus clouds climb widdershins against the low air currents, boiling up the sky's bowl. One may cross the zenith, spitting lightning without either thunder or rain. Then the sky rends apart, and the lightning forks as the hail beats down. The countryfolk, who have taken all their beasts under cover, watch it in despair. If it is rain their feeling may be mixed. Its weight may do damage and lay the corn, and it will harm the vine, but it will save the maize and potatoes. But if it is hail it is fatal. In 1950 a hailstorm lasting twenty minutes devastated twenty

Opposite: A summer storm brewing in the hills above the village of Orcival in the Auvergne.

miles of the Dordogne valley. Three feet deep of hailstones as big as half-crowns beat the crops to a brown mat, tore off the vines and shattered the stocks, split the young apple trees through their trunks. The country looked as though it had been swept with fire. The sole remaining trace of the fruits of the earth were carpets of unripe walnuts lying under the trees. A storm like that is very rare; it was the worst in seventy-five years. But most seasons see some quite limited area severely stricken by hail.

Here it is perhaps sensible to say that if you get caught in an electric storm you should ask for shelter; any farm will take you in. If you are driving a lonely road, stop, away from trees. The rubber of the tyres is said, I hope truly, to act as insulation. The road will be running like a torrent in a couple of minutes and will be dangerous to drive; blind, too, for no windscreen wiper can contend with that weight of rain or hail.

After this account of wild weather, fortunately rare, it is right to sketch wild life. The guide-books hint that there may still be some wolves in the high forests, but I failed to get any local confirmation of it. In the eighteenth century they terrorized the country, and the woods were cleared partly to get rid of them. There seem to be few of the smaller fry, except for hedgehogs, which one meets fairly often. There are quantities of snakes. Most of them are harmless grass-snakes, but there are adders in stony places, and some snakes whose sting is fatal. Even the guide-books say of some places 'Attention aux vipères!' 'Look out for adders'. So it is wise to inspect the place where you mean to sit for lunch. Fortunately snakes, unlike the silent flickering lizards, are noisy movers, and their rustle gives ample warning as a rule. You will sometimes meet a snake in the morning lying right across a road, so that you can neither pass beside it nor miss it with your wheels. It lies so flat and still that you may think it dead. Do not be misled, it is just having a nice hot sun-bath on the tarmac. I am not frightened by snakes, but I respect them; and my technique is to stop and shy little pebbles at the creature, till it rouses and undulates reluctantly off the road.

Birds are more common than in many parts of France where the hunters have almost exterminated them. The commonest include the magpies, at least on the roads, where they peck voraciously at the tar for insects. The largest I happened to see were buzzards, two couples in the high country. There are ravens in the gorges. But the greatest and simplest pleasure is given by the nightingales, which sing in springtime both by day and night. If you choose to spoil yourself, you need never stop for a meal where there is not a nightingale to make music for you. I have rested on the bank of the Lot, watching the fish rise in the clear water, with a nightingale in the chestnut above my head. He set his claws on a forked twig, braced them and sang till the twig vibrated and shook.

For those who like me are lazy, there is no more pleasurable way of wasting time than watching fish. This is easy, because the water is so limpid that you can sit above a pool and see them waving in the stream.

Insects are seldom amiable. Some are harmless, like the cicadas, but a frightful nuisance and the enemies of sleep. The cicadas on the causses, where they have few natural enemies and multiply exceedingly, can make a racket like a machine-gun barrage. They are less noisy in the river valleys because, I suppose, the birds who live there for water, eat the grasshoppers. There are mosquitoes in damp places, so that some insect-preventive is essential. There are also horse-flies, and a sort of small hornet called by the people 'les grosses tonnes'; we do not have these alarming rocket-flyers. There are real hornets, too, to be avoided like the plague, for their sting is painful and can be dangerous. This all sounds frightful, but in fact the terror of the insects has been defeated by modern science, and they are nothing to be afraid of.

This is enough zoology. The pleasure of flowers in bloom, the song of the nightingales, the small brown trout slipping past the boulders, far outweigh the annoyance of the cicadas. What is common to them all is the vehemence of life in a climate where the rushing movement of spring gives place to the languor of the heat of summer.

CHAPTER FOURTEEN

THE BUILDERS

Churches

Church and castle, town and farmhouse, this part of France is full of good buildings. They belong to a series of styles and to many dates. Some of them are very old, and only skilled local archaeologists can date them correctly. Stone, once it has weathered, keeps the same tone for centuries and gives no guide. And conservatism makes country builders continue to use a style long after it has been discarded in the cities. The Roman arch, for instance, lingered in remote valleys for centuries, and it is agreeable to note that even when the diehard masons had ceded to Gothic for churches they went on building it into houses, even to this day. Now nobody needs to know when a town was built, or why, in order to find it pleasant to see. But it adds immensely to the pleasure to be aware of the background of the building.

These places as we see them today do not go back farther than the eleventh or twelfth centuries. Many of them existed before that, of course. Some had been considerable towns under Rome. But for hundreds of years they had been wasted by one invasion after another, ending with the burnings of the Vikings. Moreover, it was not only the barbarians who destroyed the Roman buildings. The early Christian Church was determined to wipe out the earlier faiths, and took care to break the heathen images into pieces. It was not for nothing that Roman temples were built into the town wall of Périgueux. The country was shattered. We hear of a bishop of Rodez who

went to Spain to collect some of the learning of the Arab schools, and, so it is claimed, introduced Arabic numerals into France on his return, as part of an effort to restore some civilization among the ruins. In the tenth century there was a slow recovery from miserable poverty. But it was generally believed that the world would end in the year 1000, the millennium of the Apocalypse, and what point was there in building on an earth about to shrivel like a fiery scroll?

But the year of judgment passed; and what mattered more in a practical way, France had an interval of comparative peace. Two hundred years of intensive building set in. Ralph Glaber, who died about 1044, gives a contemporary report which appears in every history book:

'So on the threshold of the aforesaid thousandth year, some two or three years after it, it befell throughout the world, but especially in Italy and Gaul, that the fabrics of churches were rebuilt, although many of them were still seemly and needed no such care; but every nation rivalled with the other which should worship God in the seemliest buildings. So it was as though the world had shaken herself and cast off her old age, and were clothing herself everywhere in a white garment of churches. Then indeed the faithful rebuilt and bettered almost all the cathedral churches and other monasteries dedicated to divers saints, and smaller parish churches.'

He goes on to say that many relics were discovered, 'revealed

The château which dominates the village of Najac on an outcrop above the Aveyron.

Opposite: Ste-Enimie on a late October afternoon, from the road which climbs up on to the Causse de Sauveterre.

by divers proofs and testimonies'. They were indeed, and they made the fortunes of the new churches.

The river region is full of Romanesque churches built in the eleventh and twelfth centuries. They can be recognized at a glance by the rounded east end, the plain round-topped windows, by a simplicity of mass later ages do not reproduce. Their great number was due to two causes. The south in general was a rich and advanced country, and till the Albigensian Crusade wiped out its civilization Languedoc was the most artistic part of France. The outlets for energy were few. If the lord, or the people, had any small wealth to spare, they would tend to build a church for the honour of their village. The immense influx of men into the church encouraged building, too, for it became possible to serve even remote hamlets with a resident priest.

The attraction of the Church must have been extraordinary. The monastic orders, constantly increasing in numbers, and augmented in the twelfth century by the mendicant friars, enlisted many thousands of members. It was not only the true religious vocation that drew men and women to the cloister. It was also the longing for peace, for a life free from the brutal materialism of the age. Learning was almost confined to the Church. Theology engaged the minds of all thinkers, for there was no other subject for intelligent thought, except for kings trying to create civil law. Art was the creation of the Church, apart from the songs of the troubadours. Even business opportunity was greater in the administration of the convents and their possessions than elsewhere. In a society dominated by the increasingly rigid caste system of feudalism, there was some modification in a career open to a certain degree to talent. Consider the story of Sainte Enimie, who hunted the devil down the gorge of the Tarn.

She was a Merovingian princess, very lovely, so the tale goes. Her father, the king, offered her one after the other of his followers as a husband, but she refused them all. At last, losing patience, he forced her to betroth herself to a young noble. But she fell sick with leprosy, and was covered with the dread disease. She thought she might be helped by the waters of Bagnols-les-Bains, and set out to make the long journey to the healing wells. On her way from the main road south she had to go through the Tarn gorges, and climb the Causse de Sauveterre to the Lot valley. As her train reached the point in that savage ravine where the path took off for the ascent, they saw a spring gushing out of the hillside, and stopped to drink. The water was cold, and pure as the air of the solitary place. Enimie drank and felt strangely better. She told her followers that she would stay here for a little, and say her prayers in thankfulness for this mercy of cold water. And she was better; almost at once the pain and corruption of her illness began to heal. Presently she was as clean as a child. So she turned back to face her father and her bridegroom. But as soon as she reached the mouth of the gorge, her disease smote her again. This she experienced not once but several times; till it was plain to her that God wished her to stay in the gorge and live a life of prayer. So she founded a small abbey, and lived there all her life as its abbess; and the place is called Ste-Enimie still.

I recounted this story to a doctor, as we sat above Ste-Enimie. 'Yes,' said the doctor, 'she was a sensitive—look at those visions of the devil. And also that uncommon thing, a naturally virginal woman. The prospect of marriage fretted her with so much horror that, as we should say now, she developed nervous eczema. The leprosy of the Middle Ages must often have been that. And the account of her cure is clinically perfect; a cure produced by the feeling of security, of protection from the drunken toughs of her father's court in this wild ravine; the return of the disease when she turned back and picked up her worry again, and its gradual disappearance when she found her shelter from the world once more.'

The later centuries of the medieval Renaissance saw not only many religious in need of convents and churches, but the presence among them of men who took a pride and delight in building beautifully. Distances were great, though it was surprising how soldiers and pilgrims got about the world. Under the widespread impulse of construction there grew up

local schools of architecture, still apparent in the churches. Hereabouts the schools of Périgord and Limousin, and towards the north-east that of Auvergne, are most marked.

All the builders used the round arch, the legacy of Rome, in civil as well as in ecclesiastical building. But the local divergencies of church architecture are the subject of terrific controversy among scholars. This account is based upon the most generally accepted assumptions.

It is certain that monks built some of the churches. The pillar-capital at Conques showing the brothers building a tower is evidence of this, and so is the life of St-Etienne of Aubazine, for it describes him directing his monks in the building of the abbey, and helping them with a little miracle at a crisis. Many churches which serve as parish churches today began as small abbeys, like St-Léon-sur-Vézère and Carsac. But there must have been lay masons and builders, too, for monks did not build castles. These doubtless could build a village church, or a cathedral if need be.

Périgourdin Romanesque, with its domed roofs over nave and transepts, looks Oriental. Some of the great churches, like the cathedral of Cahors, St-Etienne of Périgueux, the abbeys of Souillac and Solignac, have those domed roofs, as well as many of the village churches. Nobody knows for certain why this region was alone in building churches so closely modelled on those of Byzantium and Syria. The most probable explanation is that of the influence of the Crusades. During the First Crusade of 1096, for instance, the French Crusaders descended like locusts on Constantinople, and spent a long time besieging Antioch, which had had Christian churches for centuries. Surely Crusaders whose motives were sincerely religious must have been struck by churches more splendid than any at home. Among them were some capable of drawing plans and bringing them back to France. An analogy is the Templar round churches, copied from the Moslem Dome of the Rock at Jerusalem. Perhaps the domed Périgourdin churches may all have sprung from the ideas of a group of men who wanted to build as closely as possible upon the model of the churches of the Holy Land. Some, but not all Périgourdin churches, have towers. With the exception of the beautiful tower of the abbey of Brantôme, they are mostly simple square structures. Many churches in little villages throughout all this region do not have towers, but the simpler and no doubt cheaper device of a west wall raised above the level of the roof, with round-arched holes for the bells. These belfry-walls are not beautiful, but odd.

Limousin churches have barrel-roofs, and give an impression of being narrower and taller inside than those of Périgord. Sometimes, as at Beaulieu or Uzerche, they continue the pillars supporting the aisles round the back of the altar, so that there is a path for processions between the altar and the chapels built out from the semicircular apse. This processional passage is also part of pilgrimage churches like Conques, for it allowed pilgrims to pass round the altar where relics were kept. Limousin churches have more important towers than those of Périgord; often a square becomes an octagon, to finish in a spire.

The churches of Auvergne are somehow less graceful than those of the lower valleys. Their chapels are detached more abruptly from the line of the apse, so that the east ends, always the most beautiful exterior part of the Romanesque, are less fluently composed. It is true, too, that the dark stone of the Massif Central is less lovable than the coloured limestones of the country farther west. The best Auvergnat church of the river country is Mauriac. Conques is allied in style, but it seems to have been the work of its own monks, originally a colony from Cluny, and it is alone of its kind.

It is the simplicity in mass, and the strong straight lines containing the circular east ends, doors and windows, that render Romanesque delightful to the eye. But simple as these churches are, they have their own kind of decoration. It is concentrated upon carved doors and corbels outside, and on pillar-capitals within. It has the effectiveness of a fine jewel worn on a plain dress.

The doors may be adorned in many ways. Sometimes they are made of a series of semicircular rings set one inside the other, as in the parish church of St-Emilion. Sometimes they are surrounded by a band of carving on the wall, as at Besse-de-Périgord. The medieval carver was far too good a craftsman to bore himself or his customers by repeating his patterns. But here in the south-west there was a great early school of door-carvers, called nowadays the School of Toulouse. Their work at Toulouse was destroyed by nineteenth-century vandals, save for some pillars, preserved in a museum, and the Abbey of St-Sernin. They must have been a workshop of skilled men, directed by at least one or two designers of genius. They carved the great 'Christ in Majesty' of Moissac, the heart-rending 'Ascension' of Cahors, the 'Last Judgment' of Beaulieu. Lesser but still fine doors of this type are at Carennac, Collonges, and Martel, which may have come from the same source. They have marked similarities. The most striking is that the central figure is always that of God. He is the Syrian bearded Christ, a man robed in a garment that folds in tiny flutings close to the body—the folds taken by hand-woven linen. The figure is full of life and of stillness, as though an instant in eternity were crystallized. Round the still centre is a whirl of violent movement. Angels bend backwards in their adoring flight, saints and devils and mythical beasts gesture in wildly emotional activity. The artist will notice the fine sharp technique of the bas-relief. The historian will observe that the Virgin Mary is not an especially outstanding figure among the lesser characters; it was too early for that; her rise to a position scarcely less than that of Christ belonged to the era of Gothic art. The merely ignorant, like me and some of you, will find it entertaining to look for likenesses, such as the resemblance between the devils of Souillac and those of Beaulieu, between the flighty angels of Beaulieu and those of Martel, or of the reliquary tomb of St-Junien. But of course the learned would be shocked at us for this pastime, for what can we know?

Violet Markham, in her enthralling book, *Romanesque France*, discusses the problem of the origins of these carvings. She thinks it likely that the workmen of the School of Toulouse were summoned to Paris by the Abbot Suger of St-Denis,

whose patronage of the arts favoured the flowering of Romanesque into Gothic. He learned what they had to give, she thinks, and sent them or their pupils to make the most beautiful door in the world, the Royal Portal of Chartres.

The other carvings outside the churches are corbel-ends. The French call them 'clous', nails. They are, structurally, supports for the roofs, carrying them outside of the line of the walls so that the rain may not drip down and rot the beams. They offered the carvers the same chances to have fun as the later Gothic gargoyles. They form a decorative pattern even when

Above: The doorway of the abbey church of Carennac, on the banks of the Dordogne.

Above left: A detail of the carving of the Last Judgment on the tympanum of the twelfth-century abbey church of Beaulieu-sur-Dordogne.

they are plain. But often they are carved into human, animal and diabolical heads; sometimes even into scenes with several characters. Those on the soft limestone churches are much worn by rain; the best are on the granite churches of the Limousin like Vigeois, where they have kept their sharpness. Perhaps the most striking series is at St-Yrieix, where they are carved inside as well as outside the abbey.

Pillar-capitals, inside the churches, are naturally better preserved. The Romanesque capitals are of three main kinds, floriated, animal, and human. The floriated capitals are classic and formal, based upon the acanthus of Rome, and palm and lotus motifs more reminiscent of Egypt or Syria. The human capitals are called by the French 'historiés', storied; and that is just what they are. They depict Bible stories, or events in human life like knights fighting, or workers gathering the harvest. Their purpose is usually didactic, but if the carvers ran out of subjects they would put in some that they were used to regardless of context. Thus a common subject is a man between two lions. This is naturally called 'Daniel in the Lions' Den', but it seems that it is really an ancient Mesopotamian demi-god greatly senior to Daniel. An age devoted to symbolism could turn almost any design to a moral purpose. After all, it had endowed the four Evangelists, on the strength of a text in the first chapter of Ezekiel, with the attributes, Man, Lion, Eagle and Bull, of four Babylonian gods.

The animal capitals are extraordinary. Some of them are naturalistic, like the famous bat of Moissac cloister, though the French carvers had great difficulty with beasts they had never seen. Lions are sometimes like sheep, and sometimes like pug-dogs. But there is an endless variety of monsters. Often they are intertwined, and are busy eating each other, or crunching the naked bodies of men and women. All round them are patterns of interlacing lines, leaves and knots, of such complexity that the eye cannot follow them from beginning to end. These are so common that some archaeologists have a pet name for them, 'Aquitanian interlacings'. Illuminated capital letters in manuscripts of the time have them too. One of the

puzzling things about them is that they closely resemble the art of the Celtic church, some centuries older. The 'entrelacs' are very like the Celtic fret we know on the old crosses of Scotland and the Kingdom of Strathclyde. The twining beasts are there in the Book of Kells, supposed to have been illuminated in Iona in the eighth century. The resemblance is too close to be fortuitous; and scholars think now that both came from the East.

Byzantium was the centre of Christendom for long before the rise of the bishopric of Rome to the primacy of the West. It had churches which moved the admiration of pilgrims from Ireland and Gaul alike. In the eighth century the Iconoclastic Movement banned human images from the churches of the East for about a century. But carvers have to earn their bread, and they took to carving animals familiar from their presence on old temples of old gods. These, and twining designs also woven into textiles and graven on caskets exported to the West, were copied by monks illuminating their copies of the gospels and prayer-books. Either from these books, some of which survive, or from direct observation of the Syrian churches, the carvers copied their fabulous monsters. They made a fine curly pattern. They could be better stylized than human figures. If they might seem rather too cruel, the answer was that they were demons, or the Deadly Sins, showing the pains of hell and entirely moral in their effect.

However, the Romanesque carvers had to reckon with that ruthless ascetic, St. Bernard of Clairvaux. He held that the Orders, especially that of the Cluniac Benedictines, of which his own Cistercian Order was a reformed offshoot, were far too rich and luxurious. Reformers divide roughly into dreamers and scolds; St. Bernard certainly belonged to the latter category. It was in about 1125 that he wrote his famous and acid letter to the Abbot of St. Thierry, saying:

'In the cloister, under the eyes of the brethren who read there, what profit is there in these ridiculous monsters, in that marvellous and deformed comeliness, that comely deformity? To what purpose are these unclean apes, these fierce lions, those monstrous centaurs, those half-men, those hunters winding their horns? Many bodies are there under one head, or again many heads to a single body. Here is a four-footed beast with a serpent's tail, there, a fish with a beast's head. Here again the forepart of a horse trails half a goat behind it, or a horned beast bears the hinder quarters of a horse . . . For God's sake, if men are not ashamed of these follies, why at least do they not shrink from the expense?'

St. Bernard described the capitals better than anybody. And so great was his influence that they were not only forbidden in the monasteries of his own order of the Cistercians, but they died out of fashion in others, too. When, some time later, the habit of adorning pillars rose again in Gothic art, it took the form of naturalistic leaf-patterns, and equally natural human portraiture. These were often beautiful, but 'never glad confident morning again'. The riotous imagination of the Romanesque, its barbaric vigour, were killed in their youth.

The next stage of church-building, the Gothic, is nothing like so common in our region as Romanesque. It is not here that lovers of Gothic will come on pilgrimage. There are several reasons for this. Firstly, the country was well supplied with churches in the twelfth century and they were far too good to pull down just for the sake of fashion. Then, Gothic with its dreaming fancies was more attuned to the misty north than to the lucid south. There are some who say that the architecture of the pointed arch and the flying buttress never took root in the south at all. This is an exaggeration. It would not be fair to cite St-Flour, or Rodez, both deliberately built on the northern model, and both with an alien air. But a simplified form of Gothic is found in the south. It is without aisles as a rule, for who would bother with supporting pillars if the broken arch could take the strain of the roof? The cathedral of Albi, internally, is a stupendous example of this construction. And besides, there are Gothic churches in plenty, built by the French and English overlords in their domination of Aquitaine. Under Henry III of England, under Alphonse of Poitiers, regent of the Toulousaine, the bastides were built, and every one has an Angevin church, often a fine one, with a noble hull, and those enchanting lancet windows that frame stained glass as well as the rounded Romanesque. Look at the fortress-churches of Beaumont or Monpazier, of Villeréal or Monflanquin, of Rudelle or Villefranche-de-Rouergue or Martel, and you can see this early Gothic, in most cases built under northern influence.

Why is it that the Gothic churches are fortresses? And why are there so few of the later Gothic, so that there is a gap between the thirteenth and the late fifteenth centuries? The third reason is war. From Eleanor of Aquitaine's marriage to Henry of Anjou in 1152, the power of the descendants of the Dukes of Aquitaine met that of the ceaselessly ambitious Capets. English history books write of the Hundred Years' War; but in fact the war lasted off and on for three hundred years. And nobody did much church-building in wartime, except in bastides. Their people naturally could not be left without a church, and it could be made to serve as the inner fortress of the strong-place. The traces of the wars can even be seen in many of the older Romanesque churches, which have had their doors blocked and their walls built round with battlements in the later Middle Ages. The early abbeys were built in open and indefensible places like Beaulieu and Sarlat. Later they furnished themselves with defensive walls and gates, such as the tall Gothic arch defending the Romanesque abbey of St-Amand-de-Coly.

After the final defeat of the English, there was something like a revival of church-building in the south-west, though it was mainly confined to ornament. Flamboyant, the style of extremely curvilinear Gothic roughly contemporaneous with the fastidious English Perpendicular, is found here in a window, as at Martel, there in a porch, as at Albi. The greatest example of the style in the region is probably the tower of Rodez. But there is a good deal of interior statuary, especially the choir of Albi, and the naturalistic and elegant, though somewhat morbid Pietas like those of Carennac, Rodez, and churches here and there throughout Rouergue.

The slightly later style sometimes called French Renaissance, with its flattened arches, is commoner in castles than in churches. It exists occasionally as at Issigeac and at Assier. But in truth this was a period of decay in the Catholic Church. The creative spirit in art was pouring into the Reformation. Clément Marot from Cahors, Bernard Palissy the ceramist and saint from Lacapelle-Biron, who died of neglect in the Bastille because he was a Huguenot, were the regional artists. The Church was on the defensive; it did not build, it was intent on extirpating heresy.

The Wars of Religion did enormous damage to the churches of the south-west. The whole of the region was deeply involved in the struggle. The Calvinists destroyed images which they considered superstitious—it is lamentable how little medieval stained glass remains, for windows were all too easy to break. But it was by no means only the Protestants who besieged and broke the churches, for they served as shelters for the fighters of both sides, according to the local party in the majority. It is also probably due to these wars that there are so few old statues in the churches. English eyes miss the tombs we are used to, but their absence may be due to a difference of burial custom.

Or they may have gone in the Revolution, since they represented the aristocracy.

After the Religious Wars, the country was far poorer in churches and especially in their decoration. It was the task of the Counter-Reformation to reconvert the rivers, the 'Flues of Heresy' as Monluc called them. As to the gentry it was simple enough. Few posts under the Crown, in the army, at court were open to anyone but a Catholic; a generation or two sufficed. The working people and the middling *bourgeoisie* were more difficult. The day would come when the party of force would be strong enough to get the Edict of Nantes revoked and apply persecution wholesale. Meantime the church depended partly on the method of persuasion. It was necessary to refurnish the despoiled churches. This was done at a time when France was dominated by Spain, both through its Spanish queens and its half-Spanish kings, and through the leadership of the Society of Jesus. Many churches were repaired with the curving roofs and characteristic little bulbous spires of 'Jesuit' architecture. That purely seventeenth-century bulb may be seen crowning a Romanesque tower like that of Sarlat or that of St-Geniez. Again there was a minor movement of building new churches. Guilds of Penitents were formed, with the idea of attracting the workmen of the towns, always the backbone of Huguenotism, and chapels were made for them. They are usually small and simple outside, topped with a bulbous dome, and richly decorated inside with 'Spanish' gilding. Perhaps the neighbourhood of Spain contributed as much to this as the work of the Jesuits and their Spanish tradition. In any case the churches abound in this work. A church like that of Turenne was given a Spanish altar to mark its conversion to the Catholic faith. Gilded altars are found in the only over-decorated chapel of Conques, and in most Penitents' chapels, especially in Villefranche-de-Rouergue, where the work reaches its height. It is especially marked in the valley of the Lot, where it is easy to imagine that it was done by a single group of craftsmen. It is Baroque in date, of course, but not at all like the cheerful Baroque of Italy or Austria. Here there is not that irresistible

impression of witnessing a ballet performed by troupes of rotund, double-jointed, haloed acrobats. On the contrary, the saints of the Lot are in deadly earnest. They gesticulate, but stiffly. Their faces and attitudes are astrain with the resolution to prove that they are just as serious-minded as the Huguenot pastors. At Ste-Eulalie on the Célé a vast 'Assumption of the Virgin' is framed in multicoloured scenes of the life of Christ. The little angels watching Him, decently clad in shifts to the knee, are portraits of a plain little girl with a thin face dominated by far too long a nose. At St-Geniez, farther up the Lot, she is there again as the Angel of the Annunciation, older and less plain, for she has grown up to that Bourbon feature. The Spanish altars are freely gilded, no doubt to give them an air of richness. When this is done with discretion, in small villages like St-Julien-d'Empare near Capdenac, where the panelled chapels have gilded swags of fruit, it is charming. But as a rule the gilding is far too heavily laid on.

There are no Protestant churches, of course, earlier than the Revolution, for they were all razed after the revocation of the Edict of Nantes. A sign of Protestantism common enough in the countryside is a tall cypress tree, with a tomb below it; for heretics were not allowed to bury their dead in the church-yards. In the Cévennes, such tombs are frequent; and some places even have a Protestant cemetery. But their occurrence is no guide to the faith of the present people.

The eighteenth century was mainly notable for frightful additions and reconstructions, by a generation of clergy who thought the medieval churches uncivilized. The Revolution caused a good deal of sabotage. A city like Rodez, never Huguenot and thus untouched by the Wars of Religion, had its Flamboyant cathedral porch smashed by the Revolutionaries. The choir of Albi was only saved by a courageous canon who appealed to the crowd not to destroy the treasure of their city. The nineteenth century threw down many an old church and relegated more to uses as shops and stores, when the clergy diminished, and the monasteries emptied.

But the mid-nineteenth century saw a revival of religion in

France, and a strong movement to preserve the churches. It seems to have set in later than the similar movement in the English Church, but it shows much the same features. Broken churches were mended, new ones built, and much decoration was added.

Broken churches—this raises the vexed question of restoration. To restore or not to restore? Well, the Middle Ages had no doubts. If they happened to want to restore or to alter a church the medievals did it regardless of the incongruity of the newer style they were adding. It is a pity, in churches like the cathedral of Cahors, but all the same, good building added to good building is not so bad as letting a church fall down. I have no sympathy in my heart for the weak classicism of the eighteenth century in this region, which would cover up Romanesque carving in favour of feeble Roman as at Souillac. But it is equally hard to bear the efforts of the nineteenth century impertinently to recreate old building and sculpture. The would-be-Gothic of Viollet le Duc was less disastrous here than elsewhere, though he lifted the face of St-Antonin's hôtel-de-ville. But looking at St-Front of Périgueux, one imagines that M. Abadie is employed carrying the stones of his good intentions to build the walls of hell. This is a supreme example of how not to restore.

The region happily includes excellent examples of how to restore. The modern method of the Beaux-Arts, like that of the British Office of Works (and how characteristic are those names, in either case!) is to save the structure without attempting to imitate decorative work. In this spirit St-Martin at Brive has been extensively patched, but not deformed, and there is no effort to hide the repairs. Conques was dilapidated, and has been lovingly restored by an architect whose historic imagination was so sensitive that he mended it as the monks would have done themselves. From outside one can see that the roofs are new and that there are new stones; but not one that spoils the great abbey, or that seems strange to its old walls. My third example is the work not of the Ministry, but of

a devoted and artistic priest. At Carsac a Romanesque east end had been added to in the late French Renaissance-Gothic style. When the present curé, M. Roger Deltreil, came there the two parts had come away from each other, and the whole church was in a dangerous state. Besides, as so often, its walls were covered inside with stone-hard plaster, under which twelfth-century carving and Renaissance bosses could be faintly discerned. M. le Curé practically rebuilt the romantic ruin. He and his relations scraped off the plaster with their own hands; he raised money somehow for the necessary mason-work to seam the old church together again. He cast out the plaster saints which nobody looked at because they had long lost their meaning for the people and were hideous to see, as well as the customary pastry-cook's altar of pseudo-marble. Instead he set a plain block of stone in the beautiful little apse, under the carved pillars. He has installed a modernistic 'Stations of the Cross'. The church has come to life under his hands, and breathes a spirit of pure peace; and the proof of it is that it is difficult to get inside its doors for High Mass on summer Sundays, for its parishioners regard it as their own, and strangers come to it from far away.[1]

As to the modern churches, there is nothing to say which could not be said of similar buildings in Britain or America. They are conscientious, machine-made imitations of old churches. Here in the south-west, there are two models, one Romanesque, the other Angevin Gothic. Both are characterized by better workmanship in detail than their English equivalents, but both are totally uninteresting.

Lastly there is the decoration of the last century. It is deplorable. The windows are especially bad. When it can be said that they are worse than Victorian glass in England, it may be imagined how bad. The glass is only too obviously mass-produced by some factory in the north, where a manager says: 'St. Caprais; which is he. Ah. Number 253, the type with the red gown and blue boots.' Some windows seem to have coloured paper stuck over plain glass, peeling away in places. A

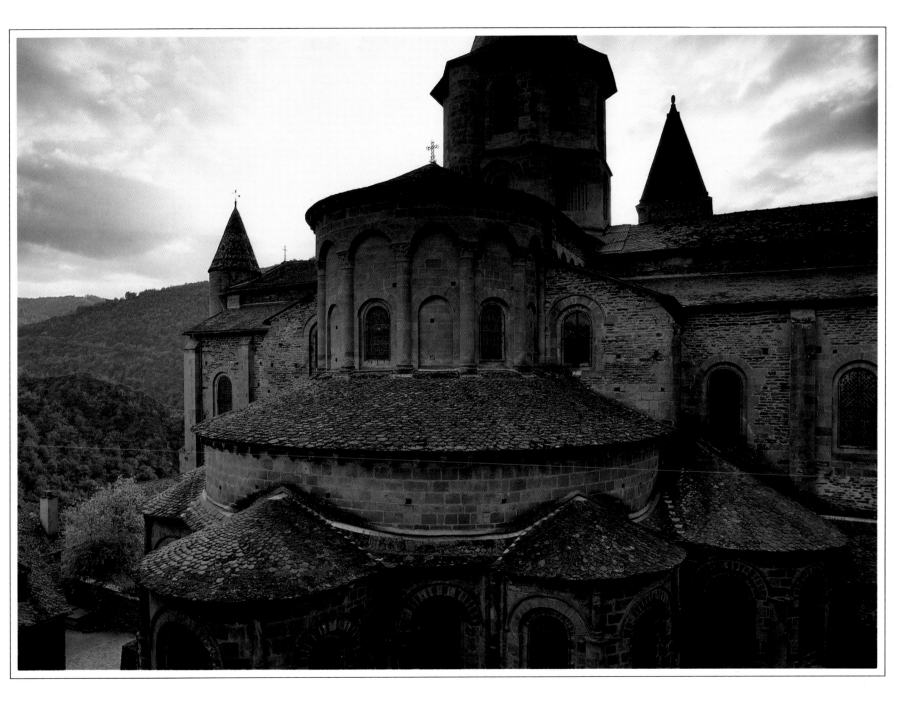

Limoges firm has been trying to do something better of late, and has captured most of the more progressive orders. Unfortunately it does not have a good designer; his figures are attempts to reproduce Romanesque missals, with an unconvincing result of what Alice in Wonderland calls 'Anglo-Saxon Attitudes'. And the determination to avoid the crimsons and cobalts of the usual after-Raphael horrors has misled this glazier into what are called 'art shades' of a nasty false range. It is a pity that this firm was let loose on Conques. There is ample room in France for a real revival of the art of glass-making in which she was once supreme; but there is little sign of it so far.

The churches are all too often hung with poor pictures. Except for one small Spanish 'Crucifixion' at St-Geniez, I do not remember wanting to give one a second glance. I am not an art critic, but it seems to me that pictures of such mediocrity serve neither decoration nor edification. They are frequently labelled 'Gift of the State', which means that they are throw-outs from some museum unwilling to spare wall-space for those huge and worthless canvases. They disfigure the walls notably of those churches which are not well looked after; and which are also sometimes covered with a sort of holy wallpaper remarkable only for its utter insignificance.

Then there are the statues. There are a great many of them; far too many. One may laugh, and sometimes feel cloyed, by the 'Spanish' propaganda statues, but at any rate they are hand-made and have a faint gilded charm. But the nineteenth- and twentieth-century statues are beneath contempt. It is quite interesting to go round a church and see how the saints are regarded by the people. The Virgin Mary is by far the most revered. Her candles burn; her statue is surrounded by plaques of gratitude, especially if she is a Black Virgin or one of the many Miraculous Virgins. St. Joseph commands a steady degree of liking, as is natural in a kind, elderly man, sympathetic to the parents of a problem child. The two 'official' saints of fifty years ago, Ste. Germaine and Ste. Jeanne d'Arc, command no interest in this country. This may partly be because the statues of St. Joan, standing with her hands clasped

in prayer round an awkward armful of banner and sword, make many women feel uncomfortable. But one might suppose that with the degree of celebration granted to her by the church authorities, with the processions of convent-school children on her Fête, and her established position as the party saint of the Right, she would have a few vases of flowers—but no, not one. Certainly at that date the most popular saint was St. Anthony of Padua, who has many a purple-lettered tribute beside him. He has fallen out of favour; often he is skied on some bracket in a dark side aisle. But he cuddles his Babe and seems as content as ever, and as kind. The saint who reigns supreme now, however, is Ste. Thérèse of Lisieux. If there is a church that does not contain her statue, I failed to find it; and it is always decorated with flowers, always surrounded with tablets of gratitude. It is a bad statue. Or rather two bad statues; for there are two models. In the worse the saint wears what can only be called a holy smirk; in the better she merely looks insipidly self-righteous. A crude model of the vision of Ste. Bernadette of Lourdes is now spreading to rival Ste. Thérèse. It is an insult to any saint to market these heartless commercial images under her name. If just one church had the courage to see that a better Ste. Thérèse would be carved by the village carpenter, working with his heart and a knife! The church used to be the patron of great art; now some big business industrial grows rich on these travesties of sanctity. The present position is pretty near to a sort of spiritual blackmail, for it would take great courage to free any parish from the grip of the image-factory. And yet such vision might start an artistic renaissance that would revivify the Church itself.

The decadence of modern ecclesiastical ornament, however, is not the right note on which to end a sketch of the river churches. The bad statues are like the dirt on a lovely child's face. One would like to wash it off; but what matters is the delight of the living beauty beneath it. The tawdry decorations cannot hide the strength and fineness of churches built when workmen held glory in their heads as easily as they held the tools in their hands.

The fortified manor of La Grande Filolie near Montignac.

Castles and Towers

Castles were built at the same time as churches, and show similar changes in fashion. When the French say 'château' in ordinary conversation they may mean a medieval fortress or the modern 'big house' of the village. But historians divide the old castles into three classes: 'châteaux-forts' or castles properly speaking, 'manoirs', or manors, and 'gentilhommières', or gentlemen's houses.

The early castles were military forts, built for defence, not to live in. Yet the lords who inhabited them used them to house their families and those of their men-at-arms and their domestic serfs. Najac is the only castle in this region constructed simply to keep a French garrison in an alien and unfriendly country. A great castle like Bourdeilles, constantly taken, retaken, and repaired in the wars, was still lived in by the barons of Bourdeilles in the mid-sixteenth century. Even a solitary peel-tower such as crowns some of the hills was inhabited by the local *seigneur*; there is one above Daglan in Périgord, whose fifteenth-century rooms have eighteenth-century fireplaces. And most of the *seigneurs* felt it necessary to fortify their manors, so that the difference between them and castles seems to be mainly one of size, after all.

Castles are not numerous, if you reckon only medieval forts

that are fairly complete. But there are hundreds which have left a shell of wall or a single tower. They are the enduring evidence of the insecurity of the Middle Ages. Christianity had become the official religion of France. But its peoples, in common with the rest of Western Christendom, were still in the main a pack of savages, the layered aggregate of tribal migrations. Writers of the humane nineteenth century, impressed by the quality of church-building and scholastic learning, tended to represent the twelfth century as one of high general civilization. They banished from their minds the records of brutality in war, of the oppression of the serfs. Or they treated them as mythical. How could people who listened to Anselm and Abelard, who witnessed the work of Bernard and Dominic, have tolerated such cruelty? We who live in the new Dark Ages are better able to realize what life was really like in the twelfth century—or for that matter in the sixteenth. People of ordinary intelligence were no more able to grasp the theology of the schoolmen than the same people today can follow nuclear mathematics. And the schoolmen themselves were just like the scientists now, impelled by contemporary morality and their emotions to commit deeds contrary to their reason. Clergy and laymen were to prove their barbarism, over a period of centuries, in the ferocities of the Crusades.

The castles were the nails that pinned the pattern of society in place. There is a strong resemblance between scholastic logic, involved in endless verbal argument, the interlaced carvings of the pillar-capitals with neither beginning nor end, and the network of the feudal system. It, too, was an unending circle of pattern. It rested on two logical principles: hierarchy and heritage. Each man was subject to his lord, each lord to his overlord, till the tenants-in-chief paid homage to the king. Heritage meant that land, and all the powers over people living on the land, passed from one member of a family to his heir by blood. But logic does not allow for chance, nor for the vagaries of human nature. Hierarchy broke down when a lord rebelled against his overlord. Was his tenant to stick to him or to the more distant overlord? And heritage broke down constantly.

For the gentry were trained to the profession of arms, and to nothing else, except for the tiny minority who went into religion. And having taken the sword, they commonly perished with the sword, to the last man of the kindred, leaving their lands to be inherited by some luckless girl, who became the victim of bargaining, intrigue, and often of abduction for her fortune. No wonder that the lords built high towers and surrounded them with walls, in order to live in some security from their enemies and friends.

As far as this region was concerned, the supreme instance of this breakdown was the fate of the dukedom of Aquitaine. The same train of events that diminished church-building augmented castles. The Carolingian kings exacted homage from the lords of Aquitaine. But it was independent in practice till the last of the line of Williams died and left his daughter, Eleanor, to marry the heir to the French throne and take her immense lands with her. She did, and was Queen of France till the virtuous Louis VII could bear her on-goings no longer, and divorced her in 1152. Within two months she had married red-haired Henry of Anjou. He soon inherited the kingdom of England, and the French lands of Normandy, Maine and Touraine. The pair ruled from the Tweed to the Pyrenees, and from the Atlantic to the Massif Central, including Quercy and Rouergue. From that marriage dated the continuation of the old conflict for power between the local lords and the French kings. Historians call its final stages the Hundred Years' War, but in truth it was a war that lasted from Eleanor's marriage in 1152 till the battle of Castillon in 1453. It had pauses and even peaces, but it never really ceased.

It was those wars, and the Albigensian Crusade, that destroyed a civilization equal to, though most unlike, the pious and learned society imagined by those who idealize the Age of Faith. There is no doubt that the south of France, for a while, led the world of the West in prosperity and the arts. The Gascon ports grew rich on the wine-export to England. The towns of Languedoc imitated the luxury and education of the Arab cities of Spain. This region was the home of all the greatest troubadours, the founders of modern European poetry. They sang in the Langue d'Oc, and came from any class. William IX of Aquitaine, his granddaughter, Eleanor, her son Richard Cœur de Lion, were all troubadours, as was Bernard de Ventadour, the son of a serf. Dante might meet Bertran de Born in hell, but he encountered Arnaut Daniel of Riberac near to the top of Purgatory, and makes him speak in his own dialect:

> 'Ieu sui Arnaut que plor e vai cantan'–
> I am Arnaut who weeps and goes singing.

The Counts of Toulouse favoured the troubadours. Unfortunately for its people Languedoc also favoured the Albigensian heresy. The people welcomed it because its initiates lived lives of extreme austerity, according to its mysticism of vicarious redemption. Their self-denial contrasted with the luxury and corruption of the contemporary Catholic Church. Here in the valleys of the Tarn and the Garonne, St. Bernard and St. Dominic preached a reformed Catholicism in vain.

At last the Pope proclaimed a crusade against heretics 'worse than the Saracens'. Northern nobles took the Cross and followed the bloodthirsty Abbot Arnaut of Cîteaux to the south to extirpate heresy and collect lands and loot. Simon de Montfort emerged as their leader after the more decent lords had gone home in disgust at the cruelties and perfidies of the war. From 1208 to 1229 the conflict raged. The Crusaders slaughtered the population of whole cities, and burned the heretics *en masse* 'with extreme joy', as their admiring chronicler records. The Inquisition was gradually organized, with power to judge people accused of heresy and to hand them over to the secular arm for execution. Its rules, which seem to assume that God cannot afford to be just, are described in the account of the building of the cathedral of Albi. Since the property of a man killed for heresy was shared between the state and the church, the Inquisition continued to try so-called Albigensians till the end of the century, for the south was full of merchants who could be accused and stripped of life and wealth. At the end, the heretics were, indeed, extirpated, and with them the civilization of Languedoc. The troubadours, what was left of them, had long gone to the small part of the lands of the House of St. Gilles that remained to them in what is now called Provence. The atrocious Simon de Montfort died during the war, and his conquests passed to the crown of France, under a treaty made by that formidable regent, Blanche of Castille. It was her younger son, Alphonse de Poitiers, who married a daughter of the last Raymond of Toulouse and had the task of consolidating the gains of France in a devastated country smouldering with hate. Hence the energy in building castles and bastides which causes his name to crop up so often in the traveller's path.

Simon de Montfort ravaged the southern part of the river region rather than the north; it was places like the abbey of Moissac that the Crusaders wasted. He did make one foray into Quercy and the Dordogne. That was pure land-grabbing, for they were hardly affected by the heresy, but he took the castles of Beynac, Castelnaud, Montfort, and Biron. But even as far north as that Simon de Montfort remains to this day a name of terror, much as Cromwell does in Southern Ireland. It is perhaps right to mention that this was not the Simon de Montfort who organized the first tentative parliament of England; that was a younger son of the Crusader.

The cities of the south took centuries to recover from the Crusade; some never did recover.

What the Albigensian Crusade did to Languedoc in one orgy of destruction, the conflict between the Angevins and the Capets did to the inheritance of Eleanor of Aquitaine. Lands passed from one power to the other according to the fortunes of war. Towns were besieged and burnt, castles built and taken. French historians, impregnated with the centralist nationalism of the schools of Paris, often make the mistake of representing the wars as the struggle of Frenchmen for freedom against alien empire. Even the *Guide Bleu* cannot speak of the English except as 'the enemy'. This is reading history backwards and upside

Overleaf: The ruins of the Tours de Merle.

down. Patriotism in the sense of French patriotism, did not exist here till near the end of the Hundred Years' War. For instance Froissart describes the Gascons appealing to the King of England in 1344 to send them an army to help them against 'the French'. Edward III won the decisive victory of Poitiers with the aid of a Gascon army under the command of a Girondin *seigneur*, the Chaptal de Buch. There was intense local feeling, of course. But the ruling morality was that of personal loyalty; and the loyalty of the people of Aquitaine went to the blood of the Williams, not to a foreign French dynasty who could not even speak the language of the people. The early Angevins did, for of course they were pure French not English at all—Henry of Anjou had one English great-grandmother as his sole strain of Saxon blood. His son, Richard Cœur de Lion, sang his songs in his mother-tongue, the Langue d'Oc, and spent his working life governing Aquitaine as Eleanor's deputy. In ten years as King of England he visited it twice, for a few months in all, to get crowned and collect money for his crusade. Even two centuries later, Edward the Black Prince only spoke English as a patois. The conflict was, in truth, dynastic and lay between two crowns. The Angevins and Plantagenets produced the better soldiers, and commanded the support of the wine-towns. But their communications were far too long, including, as they generally did, the Scottish border as well as that of France. The French kings were their masters in persistence and cunning. They fought on inner lines. They had the feudal advantage of the kingship; most of the rulers of the south-west owed them homage. Thus the Court of Peers, under Philip Auguste, found that John Lackland had forfeited all the French lands because he had omitted this ceremony; although later Louis IX proved his chivalry, to the disgust of his council, by returning most of them to Henry III of England because he disapproved of his grandfather's sharp practice.

The nobles took war as the normal condition of life and death. But the feelings of the people subjected to these struggles were divided. Froissart, who was a remarkably shrewd observer, and neutral, for he was a Fleming, tells how the Black Prince summoned the tenants of the English lands to join him on one side of the war for the disputed crown of Castille:

'To this council came all counts, viscounts, barons and men of ability, not only of Aquitaine, but of Saintonge and Poitou, Quercy, Limousin, and Gascony.'

When the council of Edward III had agreed, the lords at Bordeaux cheerfully consented to attend the Black Prince on the expedition. The other side in Spain was defended by a French army under du Guesclin; in fact it was simply the Capet–Plantaganet conflict at one remove, but the 'English' army was composed of loyal adherents born in south-west France as well as of Englishmen. Of course, in these long-drawn and inconclusive wars, feelings changed; at a later date Froissart records:

'In travelling from Toulouse to Bordeaux, there are many rich and beautiful towns. Some of these being English and others French, they carried on continual war with each other; they would have it so, for the Gascons were never for thirty years running steadily attached to any one lord. True it is, that the whole country of Gascony submitted to King Edward of England, and his son, the Prince of Wales; but it afterwards revolted from its English masters. King Charles, son of King John of France, by his wisdom, prudence, and kind treatment, gained the affection of the principal Gascon barons, which the Prince of Wales lost through his pride. I was at Bordeaux when the Prince of Wales marched into Spain, and myself witnessed the great haughtiness of the English, who were affable to no other nation but their own; nor could any of the gentlemen of Gascony or Aquitaine, though they had ruined themselves by these wars, obtain office or appointment in their own country; for, the English said, they were neither on a level with them, nor worthy of their society, which made the Gascons very indignant. It was on account of the harshness of the Prince's manner that the Count d'Armagnac and Lord d'Albreth, with

159

many other knights and squires, turned to the French interest. King Philip of France, and the good King John his son, had lost Gascony by their overbearing pride, and in like manner did the Prince. But King Charles, of happy memory, regained them by good humour, liberality, and humility.'

The Old School Tie manner has often been detrimental to English policy, and here, when the English treat their French fellow-tenants with rudeness, they begin to create what might perhaps be called a nationalistic reaction. And not for the last time. As a Scot, whose nation was constantly allied with the French throughout these wars, and whose sentiments are therefore biased on their side, I have felt it unjust to let my feelings run off with me as do most French historians. The point is that unless the English kings had commanded much local support, entirely justified by the rules of feudal hierarchy, they could not have held Guienne for a generation; for victories followed by the disbandment of armies gave no lasting position in the country. Yet there were always local lords who for one reason or another—and the English would have bitter reason to regret alienating the Armagnacs—gave their allegiance to the French kings, the overlords; and this meant that the land was distracted and the energy of the gentry put into strengthening their castles.

Even between campaigns, there was no peace. The country was infested by bands of unemployed soldiers. By the fourteenth century the mercenary army was a recognized system, only too well established. Its leaders were old soldiers, seldom noble, but experienced in fighting. They sold their services to any leader who promised them good pay and looting. Nationalism was not even a thought in their minds. Thus after the battle of Poitiers, when many French knights were captives of the Black Prince and their castles empty, the leaders of the 'routiers' seized the forts and held the countryside in terror. Geoffroi Tête-Noire in Ventadour was a Breton. At the same time Bertrand du Guesclin, also a Breton, was employed in rooting the free-lances out of the castles. He died of pneumonia, contracted in the siege of one such

company at Châteauneuf-du-Randon, near Mende. The *routiers* were an aftermath of the feudal system, with its mania for war; but they were worse than the landlords because they did not even have any interest in the continued existence of the peasantry to till the soil. They have left a faint echo in a nursery-rhyme, which French children still sing:

> 'Qui est-ce qui vient ici si tard?
> Compagnons de la Marjolaine.
> Qui est-ce qui vient ici si tard?
> Gai, gai, toujours gai.
>
> 'C'est les Compagnons de Gai
> Compagnons de la Marjolaine.
> C'est les Compagnons de Gai
> Gai, gai, toujours gai.'

The earliest castles were simple. One like the Tour de César at Turenne consists of a round tower, with a spiral stair so narrow that it could be held by a single man step by step, and with one small room opening off it on each storey. There were no windows, only arrow-slots. The roof was battlemented so that the defenders could shoot their bows from shelter. An outer wall contained a court with a well, if possible, and room for beasts to be driven in for food.

The chroniclers of the Albigensian Crusade tell how the knights were baffled by one castle with Saracen fortifications, very strong and curious; and it was partly under the influence of these castles, seen especially in the Near Eastern crusades, that the castles grew more and more complicated in their defences. The tall double donjon of Beynac is surrounded with little watch-towers; the walls round Bourdeilles are almost as high as the main block within; Castelnau-Bretenoux has deep ditches besides its formidable towered outer wall. The main defensive device however remained the choice of a high rock on which the castle was perched, and into which it was impossible to shoot arrows. Castelnaud, Najac, Penne-de-Tarn are among the most startling of these cliff-placed castles. In such cases the problem was always water; and some of the tall castles have immensely deep wells. The real crisis came with the invention of artillery. The French claim that it was first used by the English in the siege of the castle of Puyguilhem in 1339. The long range of cannon-balls, as well as their weight, was going to be fatal to walls built to withstand arrows. The castle of Bonaguil near Fumel was specially designed to stand artillery, yet it is clearly within range of the surrounding heights. It marks the close, near enough, of the era of the medieval castles.

After 1453 south-west France enjoyed a century of peace only disturbed by a belated revolt in Guienne in favour of the return of the English. The later Valois found an outlet for the energies of their restless nobility in the invasions of Italy. The south-west contributed its quota to these aggressions. Monluc, the later butcher of the Wars of Religion, learned his trade in Italy. Galiot de Genouillac of Assier earned his fortune supplying Francis I with guns. But the gentry for the most part stayed in their own lands. It was not till the reign of Henry IV that they invaded Paris in force; and not till the ever-tightening centralization of the seventeenth century that it was necessary to hang about the Louvre in order to get a post, or as a younger son to engage in the royal army. In the early Renaissance the squires had plenty to do building fine new castles.

The rage for building was extreme. Not that they abandoned their old castles. For one thing, they were the natural centre of the estates; for another their towers were as good as new, almost, and you never knew—Beynac built a tall new wing on to its two towers fit for the ladies to live in; Bourdeilles, a whole new house beside the donjon. Some of the old keeps like Commarque were just left as they stood. But as a rule, the gentry reconstructed their manors. The variation in opinion about how much of the older structure to include makes dating both expert and tricky, it may be said. Sixteenth-century castles like Losse and Bannes built practicable battlements in their new blocks, at the same time that Montal and Puyguilhem gave them up in favour of pure decoration.

A gentleman of the French Renaissance felt that he might as well be dead as not have a tower on his house. So if he could not incorporate an ancestral donjon, at least he had a spiral staircase, contained in a tower with a pointed roof rising above the main building. The *seigneur* of a tiny village like Autoire had a modest tower to mark his *gentilhommière*; the lord of Jumilhac-le-Grand fantasticated his roof with towers and high-pitched gables. The spiral stair is universal in houses of the fifteenth century, both in town and country. In the sixteenth it became the mode to build a stair in short flights, contained in a square tower, as at Puyguilhem and Montal.

It would be wearisome and interminable to give a list of castles with towers. Périgord alone has over a thousand castles classed as historic monuments. Exceptionally decorative castles like Fayrac on the Dordogne, la Grande Filolie near Montignac, Losse and Belcayre on the Vézère, la Lambertie in the north all have this feature that they were built on the site of earlier fortresses, kept their towers and added others. But they were not seriously meant for defence. Many of them, like Campagne near le Bugue, are quite unsuited to warlike purposes, and the big towers of Puyguilhem with their false battlements are for show not for strength.

Better windows were a modern amenity. The characteristic Renaissance window is a tall oblong, divided rather higher than the middle by a cross of stone framework. The upper windows are often used for decoration. They are built out from the steep roofs and are surmounted by gables of elaborately carved stone, sometimes in formal patterns, sometimes with statues as at Montal. There are such windows in towns too, as on the house of la Boétie in Sarlat. Castles with these gables include Jumilhac, la Lambertie, Bannes, les Milandes, Lanquais, Montfort, and Montal.

Farther south the castles have a plainer effect, because they usually have flattish roofs on their towers and living-rooms. This gives them almost a Spanish air. The château de la Caze[1] on the Tarn is a good example, or Cabrières near Millau.

Many of the castles cannot be visited, because they are

1 Now a luxury hotel.

161

privately owned; but there are usually some to let or sell, into which one can enter. Their most interesting feature is sometimes the chapel, as at Biron, Fayrac, or les Milandes. The fireplaces of the great rooms used for dining are often good. They become grander and grander, developing from the plain hoods of the medieval castles to overmantels on which a white cerf sits with more majesty than comfort.

It is one of the delights of the castles that they are all different. The builders had to design them to join the remaining part of an older structure. They had to fit a hilltop, or at the least to stand on a slope; for it is rare to find one like Campagne on the flat. Some are long and low, like Fénélon or la Grande Filolie; some square like Mercuès, some tall like Bannes, or slender lady-castles like Clérans or Lafinnoux. The secret of their beauty is perhaps that they combine straight and curved lines. The sensation of bruising and meanness combined in the cubic form of the Victorian prison and the modern office-block is absent, as is the too cloying sweetness of the Flamboyant church patterning.

We are taught nowadays to despise consciously picturesque building. The happier gentlefolk of the Renaissance had no such inhibitions. They set out to be picturesque, placing their castles where hill and stream displayed their towers to the greatest advantage. The castles are shamelessly, flauntingly picturesque; a child can see how pretty they are. It is an extremely agreeable sensation to recover the unjaded vision of a child, and to take pleasure in these pleasure-castles, built by owners who did not expect that they would ever be fought in any more.

They were wrong. The Wars of Religion devastated the south-west from 1562 to 1598, and were more destructive and savage even than the Hundred Years'. The castles were used for attacks and sieges for which they were never intended.

It is difficult to get a clear idea of the wars in the river-region. It was deeply involved, for Protestantism swept the country and divided the people from end to end. There is no want of information, rather a superfluity. The generals and politicians of the sixteenth century were as given to writing memoirs to justify themselves as are those of the twentieth. Naturally those of the Catholic Monluc give a picture totally opposed to those of the Protestant Sully. And later historians write with undisguised, though enjoyable, bias, each seeking to prove some thesis. The truth is that this question of the Reformation still lights such a flame of feeling in the breasts of the French that they cannot think of it judicially. A further complication is the desire to spare the sensibilities of the descendants of people engaged in the wars. This applies especially to the castle owners, for it was they who changed most promptly, under the pressure of royal disfavour after the death of Henry IV. The guide-books mention that Bergerac was the 'Geneva of the West', and lost first its buildings and finally its population because it remained Calvinist. But they are silent on the Protestant lords. When you go round the castle of Beynac, you may notice a portrait of the Protestant Baron des Adrets. But the guardian will not mention that Godefroi de Beynac, his friend, was a noted Huguenot leader, one of the stiff old Calvinists who presented an unmoved face to the last.

The Reform ranged the whole country on one side or the other. Turenne, a Protestant leader, ruled Bas Limousin and the upper Dordogne; la Rochefoucauld, another Calvinist, held estates in Périgord. The two Biron Marshals, father and son, were Catholic and Royalist. But the wife of the one and the mother of the other was Huguenot; her son repudiated her almost at his scaffold's foot. Among the other lords, Bourdeilles was Catholic, Beynac Huguenot. Indeed it is interesting to give a list of the clustered castles of the Dordogne and the Vézère. Fages was Catholic, it backed Monluc; Beynac, les Milandes, Fayrac Huguenot; the last was Geoffroi de Vivant's castle. On the Vézère Jean de Losse was an able Catholic leader, and Belcayre and Clérans followed him. The two fine new castles to the east were governed by two resolute women; Montal by the devout Catholic, Jehanne de Balzac, and Assier by the heiress of Galiot, who felt honoured to entertain Calvin as her guest.

The towns and villages were split in the same way. Périgueux was occupied by the Protestants for some years, but seems to have had a strong Catholic majority; the same is true of Sarlat. Bergerac and Ste-Foy-la-Grande were solidly Huguenot, as were Beaulieu and Argentat up-river; Turenne had to besiege Tulle and Brive, which were Catholic. Cahors was Catholic, especially after it burnt its Calvinist citizens at prayer in a house in 1562—a massacre for which Henry IV took vengeance years later when he captured the town and let his army loot it, contrary to his usual humane custom. Fumel on the contrary murdered its Catholic *seigneur*. Figeac was taken by the Huguenots and retaken by the Catholics; its abbey was destroyed in part in the process. Rodez and St-Flour remained Catholic. Millau was Huguenot, and Montauban the centre of Protestant resistance to Monluc. Nor was faith divided according to class. The *bourgeois* of Sarlat faced the *bourgeois* of Bergerac. Perhaps the craftsmen were especially attracted to Protestantism because of its emphasis on the value of individuality and of education for all; but not everywhere. The peasants of the forest of Vergt, after the defeat of the Protestant army in 1567, killed the wounded and fugitives. Two years later, Coligny took a horrible revenge by shutting two hundred peasants into the castle of Lachapelle-Faucher and killing them. But it was the peasants of the Cévennes who held to their Huguenot faith long after the gentry had turned their coats, and who endured the persecutions, ever increasing in ferocity, which turned to attempted extirpation after the revocation of the Edict of Nantes.

The wars combined the horrors of civil war and of foreign occupation. For both sides imported mercenary armies. Of those the ravages of the Spaniards of Monluc set a record of cruelty. Not that he had much objection, even when they filled the well of Penne d'Agenais with slit corpses of Protestant women and unarmed citizens. It was he, sent to put down the Protestant rising after the Catholic massacres of 1562, who wrote:

'You could tell where I had passed, for on the trees by the wayside you could see my signs hung out. One hanged man was worth a hundred killed in battle.'

The château of Larroque-Toirac in the valley of the Lot.

Sully, who served his apprenticeship in arms under Henry IV in this region, which belonged to Henry's inheritance, but was far from entirely obedient to his rule, gives both the funny and the atrocious side of the war. Villefranche-de-Périgord was Catholic, Monpazier Protestant:

'The citizens of Villefranche had formed the plan of surprising Monpazier, another little town near by. They chose for this attack the same night as the men of Monpazier, without knowing anything about it, had decided upon trying to capture Villefranche. It so chanced that as both troops took different paths, they did not meet. All was carried out with the more ease, because on one side and the other the walls were left defenceless. They looted, they were laden with booty; everyone thought himself in luck; till the day broke and both towns realized their mistake. The terms of peace were that everybody went home and returned everything to its own place. There is the image of the war as it was then (in 1576). It consisted almost altogether in seizing by guile, or by assault, enemy towns and castles.'

But Sully gives a very different tale of the taking of the church of St-Nicolas-de-la-Grave near Moissac:

'We pursued the enemy till meeting a church they barricaded themselves inside it. It was a large church, solidly built and provided with provisions, because it was the ordinary retreat of the peasants, of whom there were a large number there at that moment. The King of Navarre determined to take it and sent to seek workers and soldiers at Montauban, Lectoure, and other neighbouring towns. For he suspected that Beaumont, les Milandes and the other Catholic towns would send for their part a powerful reinforcement to the besieged, as soon as possible, if they were given time to. Meantime we set ourselves to sap the church, aided by our servants. The choir fell to my share. In twelve hours I made a breach in it, although the wall was very thick and the stone extremely hard. Then by means of a scaffolding set up to the height of the hole, I caused a number of grenades to be thrown into the church. The besieged had no water, and dampened their flour with wine; and what harmed them much more, they had neither surgeons nor linen for bandages, nor remedies for the wounds made by the grenades which were being thrown at them from every side. So they surrendered, seeing that a powerful reinforcement was arriving from Montauban for the King of Navarre. That prince was content that six or seven of the most obstinate should be hung. But he was obliged to abandon them all to the fury of the men of Montauban, who came and tore them out of our arms, and stabbed them without pity. We learned the motive by which they were animated, by the reproaches they heaped on these criminals, of having made six women serve the most outrageous debauchery, and of having made them perish afterwards by stuffing them with gunpowder, to which they set fire. Horrible excess of brutality and of cruelty!'

Brutality—the word is ill-chosen. Nothing in the brute creation is capable of the cruelty of men who believe that they know the absolute truth and have the right to impose their beliefs on others by force. The France of the south-west had been taught this in the Albigensian Crusade, and again in the Wars of Religion. It was to re-learn the lesson in the persecution of the Huguenots after the Revocation, and in the Second World War. And the other lesson, that cruelty begets cruelty. The reprisals of the Huguenots, after half a century of persecution and the massacres of 1562 had driven them into rebellion, were as bad often as those of the Catholics. It was a common thing, on either side, after a town or castle had surrendered for the victors to kill every man of the vanquished. On civil war, and foreign occupation, had been imposed the horror of a war of totalitarian ideas.

Of course there were moderate men between the extremists, who wanted peace either because they were practical or because they were Christian. But they did not succeed till Henry IV came to the throne. Meantime the country was devastated. The peasants, driven to despair by starvation and ruin, rose in a sort of smouldering revolt. They did not attempt to fight, but took to the woods and lived by banditry. In Limousin and Périgord they called themselves the 'Croquants', and later in Quercy the 'Tardavisés'. They only asked for justice and peace; for an end to the burning of their houses, the stealing of their harvests, and the rape of their women. Henry IV, who understood their grievances very well, tried conciliation, and when that failed to work put them down by force. Their leader was broken on the wheel in the market-place of Monpazier.

The seventeenth century saw France bled white by foreign wars and royal extravagance. It was the townsfolk and peasants that bore the cost of it all. The nobles tended to be absentee, since the hope for profitable posts lay in attendance at court. This was the age when a Comte de Lauzun might marry the richest princess of France—or did they never marry? A more modest Gascon gentleman like d'Artagnan might become a captain of the King's Musketeers. There was some castle-building. Hautefort in its present form dates from then, and elegant Laffinoux; Marqueyssac from the end of the century, since its gardens were planned by Le Nôtre. But the Dordogne was badly damaged by the Fronde, in which its gentry took part on behalf of Condé against the Italian Mazarin. The beginning of the eighteenth century saw the two years of the Camisard Rising in the Cévennes. Down here, the 'Great Century' showed itself for what it really was, brocade draped over a skeleton.

The region which provided, in the Gironde, an important party of the Revolution might be guessed to have been torn in pieces in 1789. But it was not. The gentry, or many of them, fled, but few of them were killed. The people seized the castles, but they usually confined their victory to battering out the coats of arms over the doors and breaking off the weather-vanes. Biron was an exception and was burned. Churches like Rodez suffered worse than castles, on the whole. When it was all over, the gentlefolk returned. Some of the inhabited castles are still in the possession of the old families. They are difficult and expensive to maintan, and when they fall vacant, it will usually be a rich *bourgeois*, a trader or industrialist, who can afford to buy them; sometimes an artist like the tenor who salved Castelnau-Bretenoux, or like Josephine Baker, one-time chatelaine of les Milandes.

One class of buyer is favoured by French land-law. If the farmland of an estate has been cultivated by a tenant, and it is for sale, the farmer has the option of buying at a fair price. You will notice castles here and there, as at Châlus in Limousin, or at St-Jean-du-Bruel in the Cévennes, where the towers are used as stores for farm machinery, and barn-roofs are built on to the walls.

The real revolution, as far as the castles were concerned, was not the burning of buildings, but the loss of the land. Once the farmland had passed into the freehold possession of the peasants, the day of the ascendancy of the gentry was over, and their power broken. Never again would a knight ride into battle covered with armour paid for by his tenants, and followed by a troop of men from his lands. The day of the castle as the power-station of the feudal system was done. The castles remain, apart from their use as magnificent though somewhat comfortless houses, as decoration in the landscape, and memorials of a half-forgotten past. There is an epitaph at Melrose Abbey, in the Scottish Borders which fits them well:

> *The Earth goeth on the Earth*
> *Glistering like gold.*
> *The Earth goeth to the Earth*
> *Sooner than it wold.*
>
> *The Earth builds on the Earth*
> *Castles and towers*
> *The Earth says to the Earth*
> *'All shall be ours.'*

Town and Village

Great cities, with about six exceptions in the world, are not places that any sane person would visit on holiday. The reader will observe that I have cleverly circumscribed my frontiers so as to exclude even the middling cities of Toulouse and Bordeaux. But small towns and villages are among the most delightful things in France. The towns of the river-basins have one common characteristic, and that is that they are principally market-towns. The largest, Périgueux, Bergerac, Brive, Villeneuve-sur-Lot, Albi, Montauban, Millau, have some industry, but not of the sort which obtrudes on the old town-centres. On the whole they all live on trading with the countryside, and are inhabited by a middle-class of shop-keepers, merchants and teachers, and a working-class of skilled artisans.

The main towns are described in earlier chapters as they occur on the road of travel. But it adds to their interest to look at them with some idea of their origins. There are the old provincial capitals, dating from the pre-Roman days of Gaul, like Périgueux, Cahors and Rodez. There are towns that grew up round an abbey like Albi or Sarlat, and those that owe their being to a castle like Estaing. It is rash to advance this theory, but it seems, looking at this region, that the abbey-towns stood a better chance of growth and prosperity than the castle-towns. Brantôme is livelier than Bourdeilles. It might be that they gained from the better education of the monks or it might only be that the *seigneurs* chose inaccessible situations for their castles. Of course, the abbeys settled in the old cities like Périgueux, too. And some abbeys set in incultivable places like Aubazine and Conques did not develop towns, but had to depend on their relics, and an annual pilgrimage, for their subsistence. So perhaps the situation of a town, more than any other factor, decided its fortune.

All towns and considerable villages had to be walled for safety in the Middle Ages. The larger towns have long lost their walls, though their line is still obvious in their present plans. Within the bounds of the old walls is a maze of narrow streets. The more prosperous the town was, the tighter the central knot, for houses were built higher and the street-space was encroached upon to allow more people to live in the city. An important place like Rodez has several streets round its hill-top market where it is impossible to drive a donkey-cart, though nearly all the old houses have themselves been rebuilt. When the walls were destroyed, they offered a chance which was nearly always seized, to make 'boulevards', the wide, pleasant avenues where the cafés gather the townspeople at the hours dedicated to conversation. They also share the shopping-quarters with the market-place, for it is on the boulevards that the best dress-shops, the bookshops, and in general the goods likely to appeal to the better-off customers will be found. But while a ring of boulevards is usual, the market-place is invariable, except in the tiniest hamlets. The church and the market are still, as they have always been, the heart of town life. There may also be a castle; there will always be a school, there may be a factory or two in the spread of uninteresting nineteenth-century streets outside the boulevards.

The bastides are in a class by themselves. Sometimes their buildings are all old. Yet as towns they are relatively new, dating usually from the thirteenth century. They were built all of a piece. They are early examples of town-planning, on simple lines followed by that later instance of a primitively-planned city, New York. The plan is a grid, of straight streets crossing each other at right angles. The rim of the chequer is formed of walls, sometimes doubled as at Beaumont, and pierced at the ends and the sides by towered gates. The middle of the grid is left open as a market-place, and surrounded by merchants' houses of which the bottom storeys form arcading round the square. This admirable device affords shelter from the rain in winter, and shade from the sun in summer. As the bastides were strong places garrisoned by their people, not by a lord, they did not have a castle; instead, the church was also a fortress. Some of the bastides, like those of Périgord Noir, are no larger than they were when they were built. Their situation was chosen for strategic, not for economic reasons, and they might be set on a cliff like Domme, or on a barren causse like Villeneuve d'Aveyron. Others had better luck in placing; and when the long insecurity of the Middle Ages was over, they burst out of their walls, as did Villeneuve-sur-Lot. Villefranche-de-Rouergue is the chief example in our region which prospered in the Middle Ages itself, and it grew upwards inside the walls, tall and cramped.

The frequent names of Villeneuve, Villefranche, Sauveterre, are signs of these bastide towns. They show that they were brand new, planted where there was not even a village to lend them a name of their own. Then they advertised the advantages of settling in a bastide. If a serf went there, he could gain his freedom in a year and a day. For the towns fought for the freedom of their people, and got it written in their charters; and the bastides had charters, too. If he were a prisoner of war, going as a colonist to a bastide might win him life itself. The rules of chivalry were applied only to the privileged classes. A knight, or even a squire of good birth captured in battle would be spared, because his kin would ransom him; ordinary soldiers were killed out of hand, there was no money in them. Unless they served the purpose of supplying

manpower, always short in those times, for the new towns.

Next to the bastides, the towns that have kept most of their old character are naturally those least touched by the early French Industrial Revolution, which was staffed by the same vandal breed as destroyed the beauty of the English towns. Entirely modern industry does not do so much damage, partly because the towns have awakened to the commercial value of beauty, so attractive to tourists, and partly because it is run on electric power, and is clean. But places like Uzerche and Sarlat, Martel and Estaing, are more interesting to look at than larger towns.

It is interesting to stroll about a town and shop-gaze. The shops are much more sharply specialized than in Britain, far more so than in the United States. The larger towns, it is true, have chain-stores called 'grands magasins', but they are not attractive, for their goods look poor species of mass-production.[1] But the real shops are small and selective. You go to the butcher for meat; to the charcuterie for *pâté* and all products of the pig. The grocer sells biscuits, of a sort; the baker bread and rolls; the *pâtissier* cakes and fancy rolls, especially the exquisite buttery *croissants* that make such a good foundation for a picnic lunch. It is only in a small village that you will find the baker and the *pâtissier* combined, and the combination is not a success normally, for it desolates any baker to waste his time on pastries, and a fine *pâtissier* despises anything but his elaborate art. The shopkeepers are, of course, middle class, *bourgeois* people, but in their commercial practice they are also among the craftsmen of France. The craftsmen properly speaking are perhaps the happiest of the people, when trade is good. The French are passionately individualistic, as every traveller in the country observes, and a skilled craft gives a man the chance to be his own master in his own trade, with no tyrannical employer telling him how to do a job, and with the fun of training 'prentices. For a thing about the French that fewer travellers notice is that they are born teachers. The result is a very high level of accomplishment. The tourist is likely to meet it in the motor-mechanic, the cobbler, the hairdresser. Handling machines appeals to most men, and a repair-shop where he can take an antique car to pieces, put it together lovingly nut by nut, and make it go, is the joy of the workman. The *cordonnier* will look reproachfully at your shoes, tell you that you have worn them too long and brushed them too little, and explain at length what can be done for them, as though he were a doctor prescribing for an illness due to neglect. He will

Left: One of the fortified gateways of the medieval hilltop town of Cordes.

1 This is no longer fair. The stock of the *grands magasins* is easily as good as and possibly better than that of their British counterparts.

then mend them well and cheaply. As to the *coiffeuse*, one can judge her work by the hair of the women of the place.

It is fun to buy books in France; not because the shops are well stocked, for they are not.[1] French literature is quantitatively small. New books, if they are any good, run out of print immediately. The remainder is a shocking show of translations of 'Westerns' and detective-stories, together with all that is worst in the sentimental novel of Britain and America. But the bookshops are staffed by people in whom even the over-bookish education of France has not killed the taste for reading. It is only in France and Scotland that it has been my experience to be refused a book on the ground that it was not worth buying, though it stood on the bookshop shelf.

But of course the best fun is shopping in the market, You can wander round the stalls, gazing at the piles of tomatoes and lines of lettuce, before entering on a profound discussion about how many you want. You can try on dozens of light wide straw hats made at Caussade, before choosing one which will be the very thing for the hot days, with an old dame from the country beside you taking turns with the hand-mirror. The townspeople do not wear hats, out of snobbery, and the more fools they.

The best day in the week is fair-day, and the best in the year the annual *grande fête*, the saint's-day of the town. Take Sarlat on a Saturday morning. The main street, the Traverse, is barred to motors for it is needed for stalls. All the shops have a stand of goods outside their windows, and the shoppers use the middle of the road. The big *place* in front of the Mairie is full of stalls shaded by white covers. There you can buy materials, pottery, hats, dresses, bobbins and pins, braid and laces, boiled sweets of terrifying hues of cerise and nile-green, gloves and string-shoes, knickers of the slightest degree of coverage and nightgowns with substantial sleeves. For it remains a mystery why the French, whose shorts are so short by day, seem to demand such an amount of drapery by night. But it is the food market, down in the old town, that is really thrilling. There is a row of old men, each sitting beside a basket or two containing rabbits, or young geese. There are meat-stalls, and butter-and-

cheese-stalls, and flower-stalls with pots for the balconies hung with flowers without which no house in Sarlat is complete. The square is full of men wearing wide berets and greeting their friends in the patois; and of women chatting confidentially. For the fair is the natural exchange of the news of the countryside, and the social as well as the commercial opportunity to relieve the monotony and narrowness of the life of the farm. Nobody would go to Sarlat fair, at the price of a bus-ticket, unless he had business to do; but it is surprising how one can spread out one's sale of produce so as to go quite regularly.

The climax is the *grande fête*. Then the fair is something terrific. Church and state, town and country are gathered to rejoice and to do business. Go to Mauriac, for instance, on the 8th of June, the feast of St. Maur, their legendary apostle. His chapel stands on a small hill outside the town. The hill and the road into Mauriac are lined with rails to which are attached horses, mules, donkeys and cows. One whole boulevard is given up to agricultural machinery, painted red and veridian green. The pavements of the high street are decked with goods from the shops within. The church square is occupied by the Forains, the travelling merchants, their white shades whiter than ever against the dark stone of Ste-Marie-des-Miracles. Emile's Great Lottery is propped against the church porch, and children look wistfully at the plastic dolls arranged as prizes. The music of the merry-go-rounds blares without cessation. On the fringe of the fairgrounds are the gipsy carts, where you can have your fortune told according to the wishful thinking of the country: 'You will live to be very old, Madame. You will be very rich. Only beware of the many jealous people who envy you your wealth.' 'How horrible!' you murmur to your companion. 'Did she say the same to you?' 'Yes, exactly.' Late in the evening the Forains fold their shelves into their motor caravans and drive off. The inns are crammed with farmers eating an immense dinner, the cafés with men sealing a sale with drinks. A farm-float, loaded with a reaper-combine, a horse, a donkey, five men, three women and a mountain of parcels, sets off amid cheers from the crowd. A gipsy cart,

1 This too is no longer true.

Opposite: An ancient stone cottage in the remote upland village of Castelnau-Pégayrols.

drawn by a miserable little nag, is pushed up the hill by a man, his wife the fortune-teller, and a pack of children as lean and shaggy as the horse they are aiding. 'Ah, Madame!' says a bystander. 'These are not the Forains, who have beautiful installations. These are the Bohemians. They lead a wretched existence.' Wretched, indeed, though there are many of them hereabouts. Nearly every village square has a notice: 'Nomads are forbidden to station here'.[1] You meet them encamped for the night on waste patches by the roadside; a small fire burning beneath a pot, and an extraordinary number of ragged children watching it. I do not know if gipsies are good Catholics, but they seem to be the only class of French people who carry out the instructions of the Church on the production of children.

Town and village people do not depend entirely upon the fête for their fun. There are the general church festivals, adorned with ceremony and pomp so old that it wears a casual friendly air. The Fête-Dieu, when the Host is carried through the streets in procession, is the prettiest, for the people strew the roads with flowers, and kneel as the procession passes, with the children of that year's confirmation wearing their first Communion robes. No family is too poor in France to afford a little girl her white frock and veil as 'la petite mariée'. On the Eve of St. John bonfires blaze on every hill, and the boys leap through the flames. The Bishop may bless the bonfire; but there is something anciently pagan about this feast. It is the same as the Celtic Beltane, and dates at least from the days of the Gauls.

The secular amusements of the people are few, compared with those of more urban societies. Partly, no doubt, this is because farm workers do not need exercise outside their jobs. Yet the universal passion for fishing does not by any means exhaust the local sports. Bowls are played in every large place. The ideal situation is on a reserved pitch of the *place*, beside the river, where the trees shade the players on Sunday and a café called 'Le Rendezvous des Boulistes' dispenses wine and coffee. Bowls has the advantage that it can be played at almost any age. For the young, the favourite sport is bicycling. Each little town has an annual competition, in which the youths, reckless and

sweating, tear downhill and wobble uphill in an interminable race called 'le tour de ville'. From winning the town race they may gain a place in the Tour of the South-West; who knows, perhaps the glory of circulating France in the Tour de France itself.

The nicest town houses dates from the sixteenth and seventeenth centuries. They are not the oldest. St-Antonin is by no means the only town with Romanesque houses still in use, and Gothic ones are common in places like Cordes, Martel, Turenne, and the bastides. But it was in the Renaissance that the turreted town houses, with the gay carved windows, became fashionable. Sometimes they belonged to the local nobles, like the house of the Dukes of Ventadour in Ussel, but often enough these houses would be lived in by the richest *bourgeois* of the city, like the house of la Boétie in Sarlat.

There is one good mark to be given to the nineteenth century, though whether it belongs to town or country I do not know. It is the railway viaducts. The main lines run south from Paris, and cross the river ravines at right angles, spanning them on long rows of tall columns. The builders seem to have taken the Pont du Gard as their model, whether consciously in imitation of the finest thing in Gallo-Roman architecture or not. At all events the viaducts are splendid. There are those who prefer the iron suspension bridge of Garabit on the Truyère, a work of Eiffel, but for my part I find the stone viaducts far more majestic.

There is a lot of thoroughly bad work in the towns, both nineteenth century, and worse, belonging to our age. Cement is a temptation to all the worst architectural passions. But there are some decent plain modern factories, notably the state tobacco stores such as may be seen at Sarlat and Figeac.

Villages, if they are old, are compactly built. They do not straggle, for the villagers had just as good cause to cling close for safety as the townsfolk. Isolated farms out in the country are generally fairly modern; and may, as in Limousin or the Ségala of Rouergue, mark better and more prosperous agriculture. But the village houses are normally farmhouses; and they are built

1 Few still do, though Villefranche-de-Rouergue has one in the last stages of decay.

170

Shutters, like these near Cabrerets on the River Célé, are a characteristic feature of houses in this region of France.

on the same plan throughout the region. They are two-storey buildings as a rule. The ground floor is devoted to farm uses, to byres and barns. A big door, often with the true antique Roman arch, leads into the 'remise', a large passage running right through the house. It is infinitely useful, serving as cart-shed, garage, shelter for horses and pigs for any short period, such as market-day in the village. A flight of outside stone steps leads up to the first storey, on which the family lives. The stair usually ends in a terrace, roofed with creepers, often set with flowers, with a table and bench where the man can sit for his evening drink, and the wife sew and mind the baby in the intervals of housework. From the terrace a french window takes you straight into the kitchen. This is the heart of the house. It is a very large room, furnished with a solid table flanked by benches, six wood-seated chairs and two cane-bottomed ones ranged round the walls, a long clock, a big shelved dresser-cupboard, a wireless set. The fire burns on a flat hearthstone, and never uses more than a small handful of sticks. It is under a narrow shelf where coffee, sugar, salt, and spices are ranged in pottery jars. From the chimney hang two chains with oblong links. On one the soup-pot hangs

permanently. An S-shaped bar of iron hooks it on to the links of the chain, and the smaller pots for which the second chain is used can be lowered or heightened link by link to regulate cooking-heat. There are inglenook benches inside the chimney on either side of the fire; the ingle is called 'le cantou' in the patois. From the kitchen there open the bedrooms according to the size of the house. Each bedroom contains a big bed, a hanging cupboard, a chair or two; in some rich farms a chest-of-drawers, a holy picture of painful artlessness, a mirror a foot square.

Above the roof rises the dovecot, like a miniature tower. The proprietor of Périgord Noir or Quercy would consider himself lowered if he did not have a pigeon-cot, though relatively few keep pigeons now. There must have been millions in the past.

The farmhouse is of a good size, roomy and solid. It may be lived in, and generally is, by the equivalent of a British smallholder, but it bears no resemblance to a British cottage. Indeed the only houses which could be called cottages are in the Limousin Montagne, which used to be very poor. Of course the size is partly due to the fact that the farm animals are housed in the same building on the ground floor, except in new and rich farms where there is a tendency to separate off the stables and barns into a wing built at right angles to the dwelling, making the whole half a square. But the first-floor living-rooms are large, and the kitchen a fine room, though furnished with extreme simplicity. The house-plan has not changed for centuries. The Renaissance farmhouses of remote hamlets have just the same rooms. There is the account of the will of a Périgourdin miller's wife, written in 1788, in Jean Maubourguet's *Choses et Gens de Périgord*, which gives every article in her house even to the pots. Even to the pots, the furnishing is the same today, except that the four-post beds of the will have given place to iron painted to look like walnut, and there is electric light and the wireless.

The farmhouses are charming. They owe their beauty partly to their shape, the outside stair, the steep-pitched roof, the dovecot towerlet. Even more to the building materials. In the limestone country the mason has an easy task, indeed many a farmer builds his own barn. The stone is so brittle that it can be split with an adze, a short hammer with one pointed and one cutting edge. The stone parts along the grain, in slabs of varying length but about the thickness of a large brick. The mason trims the edges roughly square, with a few delicate taps of his hammer, and then lays the slabs to make his wall. If it is for a barn he will lay it dry-stone; if for a house with discreet cement which does not reach the edges of the slabs, so that they keep the interesting irregularity of their formation. When such buildings are new, they are coloured a brilliant amber; in years they tone to honey, or rose-grey. This texture of stone-building is extraordinarily satisfying to the eye. The roofs in these parts are always red; the older tiles are curved, the newer, alas, flat. They are often corbelled out from the walls, in a way that makes them tilt up a little at the eaves, and this is very gay. The curvy tiles cast an indented shadow on the walls, like Romanesque billet carving.

In the Massif Central, the stone is dark volcanic grit, and the villages are made of it and are sombre in tone. Sometimes, as at Salers, they have used black tufa, which is rather grim. But the shape of the houses is the same, and the roofs are made of round slates, set in fish-scales pattern, extremely decorative. Towards the south the roofs flatten out, for the Midi is here, and the neighbourhood of the Mediterranean austerity.

The first thing that the tourist notices in town and village is the shutters. They make a constant note on every house, rich or poor; their faded blue turned back against the wall, or shut and blinding the windows. They are indeed essential in a country where winter is cold, but there is no weak concession to house-warmth except in the kitchens; and where summer is hot, and the cooler air of the night must be shut into the rooms or they grow intolerably like furnaces by day. The mechanism of the 'volets' is dangerous to foreigners; they fold and like nothing more than trapping a thumb and taking off its nail. But just as you get used to coping with this fiendish device, you cease to notice the shutters, till if you saw an unshuttered

A gariotte on the Causse de Brengues.

window, you would wonder what could be wrong with it.

You will notice here and there a queer circular hut, made of stone with a domed stone roof. Sometimes it may be a couple of feet high, sometimes rather larger. In some places in Périgord and Quercy there are what seem like villages of these odd beehive huts; for example behind Beynac, and near Salignac. If you ask the country-people what they are they will tell you 'hen-houses'; but the actual construction is better than that of many farms, and it is difficult to believe that anyone would build so meticulously for hens; and besides many of them are deep in the woods, far from any farm. Some writers say they are Gallo-Roman buildings; but no dry-stone huts would last for a thousand years; and anyhow the Gauls were not dwarfs. They are a mystery; puzzling and pretty wee things, whether they house hens or stand solitary under the trees.[1]

1 Puzzling as they look, there is not really any great mystery about these huts. Known as *gariottes*, *bories* or *caselles*, they were (and are) used as shelters for people and animals.

CHAPTER FIFTEEN

RESISTANCE

The story of the Resistance of the French has still to be told. But the south-western river region bears such visible scars of it that something must be said here. The region was south of the zone occupied by the Germans after the Armistice of 1940, though of course it was subject to the Vichy Government, whose policy wavered between passive acceptance and active collaboration. Some of the small towns were crowded with refugees from the north, their spirits too much shocked to allow of much resistance. But the people of the country soon realized that it was ideally suited to secret guerrilla warfare. Free French fighters from Britain, British agents, and even considerable supplies could be dropped by aeroplane on the flat causses. More or less all over the area young men and women began to prepare for the opportunity of fighting to liberate the nation. The Resistance was all-party, its main strength lying with the Catholic Left, the reformist Catholics later called the M.R.P., the Protestants of the Cévennes, the socialists, and after the invasion of Russia, the communists. An immense number of people who were not actively engaged in the Resistance movement helped it nevertheless, if only by failing to report to the authorities the mysterious movements of strangers about the country. But there were also those who were, for various reasons, obedient to the Vichy policy.

Then at last came D-day, 6th June 1944, when the Allies landed in Normandy. The Resistance rose, took openly to arms, and concentrated on sabotaging German communications with the battlefront. The Germans took swift vengeance. The Allied warning that they regarded Resistance members as soldiers, entitled to treatment as prisoners of war if they were captured, met with no response from the Germans. They took the line, justified by the strict letter of the laws of war, that civilians rising against the occupying power were outlaws, entitled to summary execution. The division called das Reich was sent on a punitive expedition through the country. It burned many farms and some entire villages like Rouffignac in Périgord. When it captured Resistance bands, like the Bir Hacheim on the Causse Méjean, the Germans shot all the survivors publicly on the square at Mende. At Tulle there was a pitched battle with some casualties. The town officials were forced to summon all males, even boys, and to choose ten of them for each German killed in the fight to be shot. As the division marched across the country it summoned all the people to assemble in the small towns and villages, picked out a large proportion of the able-bodied and sent them to forced-labour camps in Germany. On the average a tenth of them died before the Allied victory freed them. The taste of blood grew sweet in the mouth of the Germans, and they took to seizing every man they met, whether a Resister or not, taking him to the nearest crossroads and shooting him. Scores of crossroads have little boards, where, in fading letters, are the names of four or six

The Causse Méjean near the Roc des Hourtous above the Tarn gorges.

175

men, followed by the words 'Morts glorieusement pour la patrie, Juin 1944'—'Died gloriously for the country, June 1944'. If no men were available, for soon all the men fled on their approach to the woods and caves, they took women and children and killed them. At Paluel, near Sarlat, they took twenty-eight women of a hamlet, poured petrol over them and burnt them.[1] Their orgy ended by the massacre of the people of Oradour in the Limousin, where they wiped out the whole population, burning them in the church.[2]

Now it may be imagined what is the feeling left in the country not only about the Germans, but about those who were not Resisters. It is fair to give their point of view, too. They think that it was because of the Resistance that so many were killed, because it was true that guerrilla warfare has no rights. They say, too, that many of the Resisters were criminals; that they stole the money dropped by the British for themselves; that instead of fighting the Germans they—or rather certain communist companies of them—marched about the country satisfying private vengeance on people belonging to other parties; for instance that one company marched down the Dordogne robbing innocent people and looting castles.

Both sides, when talking of the Resistance, say at some point 'One could not choose, in such times. There were good and bad in the Resistance.' There were indeed; it is certain that the Germans managed to plant plenty of spies in the Resistance bands, and that they were often betrayed by their own members. On the whole, however, the story is one of astonishing courage and loyalty through the whole population. Any traveller will hear many tales; here are three typical ones.

'My factory makes every kind of steel tool. I was summoned to speak to a man who could not talk French. I went down, and there was an Englishman. He was, believe me or not, Mademoiselle, the legendary Major Henderson. He could not speak French, hardly a word. I had to make him draw a picture, and at last I gathered that he wanted a tool for cutting wire. Of course, I gave it to him; but the extraordinary thing was that he came strolling through a town, asking his way from

no matter whom, and into a factory, talking that unmistakable English. His only disguise, if you could call it one, was that he wore the blue jeans of a countryman. He spent three years in this neighbourhood, and nobody ever told the authorities, though he must have been recognized by hundreds of people as a British agent. *Formidable!*'

Second, a conversation near Paluel. I had left my car in the shade of a barn while I went to look at the castle. But it was locked, and no more than a shell, its Flamboyant chapel open to the sky.[3] Down below there was one of those heart-rending boards, on which the only decipherable word was 'Allemands'. When I returned to the farm, there was the proprietor whose leave I had asked, inviting me to rest upon his terrace. His wife and a pretty daughter were there, too, and a little old lady, with her head wrapped in the black turban-folded kerchief that is almost the only remaining trace of peasant costume left in the country. I asked the proprietor what had happed to the castle of Paluel.

'The Germans of das Reich burned it,' he said. 'It was empty, and there was nobody there but a man working in the fields. He was not a Frenchman, as it happened, but an immigrant Italian labourer. They shot him, and threw fire-bombs into the castle just for fun. I had hidden in the woods, and they did not get us. Then they went to Paluel village. All the men had hidden, but the women and children were there. See, mademoiselle, this lady was among them, one of the three who survived.'

The old lady nodded, looking at me with tired old eyes.

'She and her daughter were hidden in their cellar. The Germans went down and dragged them up and told them to run, and as they ran they machine-gunned them. They were both wounded, Madame's girl through her arm, and Madame herself through the body, a bullet grazed her heart. They both lay and pretended to be dead, and the Germans thought that they were dead and did not examine them. Then they took the rest of the women and children, twenty-eight of them, and poured petrol all over them and locked them in a house and set

1 The village is now called St-Vincent-le-Paluel. It has proved impossible to verify this story.

2 At Oradour-sur-Glane the women and children were killed in the church, the men in barns. Altogether 642 people died. The ruins of the village have been preserved as a memorial to them.

3 The castle is now being restored.

A LA MEMOIRE
DES
MAQUISARDS DU GROUPE BIR HACHEIM
MORTS POUR LA FRANCE
MCMXLIV

SOUVIENS TOI

men will do if they are obsessed by a creed which they believe is totally right, which they think they have the power to enforce on others? Here in our time is a repetition of what men in power did in the name of religion three centuries ago.

Here is the third story:

'They tell me that you were a Resistance leader, madame?'

'Why! That's to say much. Of course I wasn't a leader; I just did what anybody would do. After all, I had the hotel. When British officers came down by parachute in winter, naturally I fed them. When our boys of the Resistance were wounded, naturally I took care of them, I was the one in the town who had the resources.'

'Weren't you ever afraid?'

'No. You will think me stupid, but I wasn't afraid. I did not think ahead at all. One just did what seemed possible.'

'But they tell me that you were captured by the Gestapo. Were you betrayed?'

'Yes, I was betrayed. I must say when they took me to Paris and locked me in that hotel they used as the Gestapo headquarters, I was sure that I should be sent to Ravensbrück; and I felt pretty sick.'

'How was it you did not get sent?'

'I was ransomed.'

'Ransomed?'

'Yes. The Gestapo officers were very corrupt. The Resistance here communicated with the boys in Paris, and they bought me with that good money your agents gave us for the struggle.'

That woman left me speechless with admiration. Her courage was not only flawless, but gay; yet she had lived in danger of her life, at the mercy of any traitor, for years.

The monuments numbering the shot, the deported, the killed in battle, erected by the French Resistance in the towns; the boards that weep away their lettering at the crossroads; the obliterated name of that Italian workman;[4] the eyes of the old woman; the inn-keeper's heroism; they are the last layer of history. It lies on the top of all the other layers visible to the sight in this beautiful tragic country.

fire to it. One little girl of eight jumped out of an upstairs window at the back, all burning as she was, on the other side from the Germans. She was terribly hurt. Then they got into their lorries and drove away. And the Resistance came down from the woods and took Madame and her daughter and the little girl to Sarlat hospital.'

'Did the child recover?'

'Yes, but all the rest were dead.'

'How could they do such things?'

'Ah, mademoiselle. They were young men whom Hitler had driven out of their minds. A Frenchman would not have done it.'

'I am sure that is true.'

Am I sure? I said to myself as I drove away. Who knows what

4 There is now a memorial to Mario Perusin outside the church.

CHAPTER SIXTEEN

FOOD AND DRINK

I t takes a good deal of courage, and an intimate, frank occasion as well, to broach the question: 'What is "French civilization"?' Every French child hears those two words so often, is so bred up on them, that they become part of the data of his thinking. Teachers who themselves are far too sure of the assumption to analyse it, train him to believe that French civilization is the best on earth. His belief becomes more than unquestioned; it is unconscious. But if one is on such friendly terms with an intelligent Frenchman that one can ask for a definition, he will begin, in a state of immense surprise, to set his wits to examining what he really means by 'la civilisation française'. He will cite many sources of national pride, while honestly admitting that they may face rivals, or draw from alien origins. There is the Latin or classic way of thought—but after all France learned logic from Rome; the conception of democracy, but there Greece and Britain were before France; a glorious military past—pause—are we so certain, nowadays, that victory and power are linked with civilization? A history dramatized by the lives of many saints, heroes, and wise men, as well as plenty of fools and of the singularly wicked. Then the Frenchman will turn to the arts, and will pick, out of the endless array of manifestations of the national genius, two matters of which nobody can be so blackly ignorant that he (or even she) can be unaware of French achievement. One is medieval church architecture. 'Where is another Chartres?' says

the Frenchman unanswerably. 'And where else can you find so highly developed the pleasures of the table? French cookery, French wine, are not only unsurpassed; they are supreme.'

And so they are. Connoisseurs may put forward rivals in the art of cookery, China, for instance, or little Denmark. The former has achieved cooking of extraordinary subtlety; in the latter meat and fish of perfect quality are treated as they deserve. But taking the whole field, the combination of good raw material and honest, imaginative cuisine, and France still bears the palm.

Within her borders, as any Frenchman will tell you, the standard of cookery varies immensely. Every region has its specialities, but there are three which are generally outstanding. They are Normandy, Burgundy, and the south-west. And it happens that two of these are also the homes of the most famous wines in the world, the vintages of Burgundy and Bordeaux.

So if you visit the river-country you will find yourself in a gastronomical paradise. You will begin your day with the classic *petit déjeuner* of *croissants*, or new bread, with coffee. It may be said here that only an idiot, or worse, demands breakfast foods in southern France such as bacon or grapefruit, drink such as tea. If by chance a big hotel can produce them they will not be well prepared, and he will pay for them through the nose. We go to foreign lands to enjoy their good

Produce is rich in both quality and variety in the village markets of Three Rivers' country.

179

food, not to whimper for the meals of home. This warning note applies to all meals; but it is probably needless; the nitwits who merit it would never come to such a country.

The main meal of the day is *déjeuner*, luncheon. On Sundays it is more than a meal, it is a feast. A sensible person always arranges to have Sunday *déjeuner* in his hotel or a good restaurant. Dinner is much the same as lunch. At both soup is served, or hors-d'oeuvres, at least one meat course, and one separate vegetable course, and a dessert of pastry, fruit, or cheese. Besides the basic three meals, people drop into the *pâtisseries* to eat delicious cakes and sip coffee any time in the day; and the whole population gathers in the cafés to drink a glass before dinner and Sunday luncheon.

Motorists and walkers will find that their hotel will put up a picnic lunch for them; it is called *déjeuner en panier*. Or they may think it more amusing to shop for their own picnic. A bought lunch does not turn out any cheaper than the hotel parcel, unless it is confined to bread, an egg, tomatoes and cheese. But every woman will enjoy buying it and talking to the market-women, those humorous and polite merchants. The street markets are always fun, and always a delight to the eye. Bread is better bought early, for the bakers sometimes run out before midday. The charcuterie shops contain superb *pâtés*, from *foie gras* itself to much simpler and cheaper cooked meats. *Jambon d'York*—York ham—is perhaps the best of all, delicately cured and cut in wafer slices.

The food of the south-west is locally produced, and therein lies its great virtue. Nothing is imported, nothing is stale. The lettuces are straight out of the soil, the apricots off the tree. You eat the fruits of the earth in their season. In May and June there are trout, small and fine. Later the duller river fish succeed them, of course far inferior to trout, and strangely seeming to have more bones, perhaps because their anatomy is unfamiliar. In August the hotels of the Great Causses offer game, especially thrushes, flavoured with thyme and the aromatic herbs on which they feed. Gourmets travel hundreds of kilometres to lunch at famous restaurants of the Tarn causses in the game-season. And if you say that you would like another dish, since the British do not eat song-birds, the waiter will plainly think you sentimental, affected, or just demented.

The great local delicacies are truffles and cèpes, and various conserved meats. Truffles are all, and more than all, that they are cracked up to be; a truffled and an untruffled *pâté* are poles apart. Cèpes are a species of yellow toadstool, the beef-steak toadstool, which grows in the woods. They are eaten fresh or pickled, and have a slippery richness, but I think they do not compare with the ordinary wild mushroom of the pastures—though, of course, this is a matter of taste. The potted livers, goose and duck, are marvellous. They should only be eaten in small quantities and as a rare treat, for they are rich beyond belief. The same is true of the 'confits', the preserves of goose and duck. They may be consumed hot or cold, but in my opinion are better hot, as this lightens them somewhat. In either state they have the texture, and about the weight, of deliciously-flavoured alabaster. These regional luxuries are things the traveller ought to order once or twice, just to taste what food can be really like. Ordinarily he should take the menu of the day. Naturally the cook makes his *plat du jour* of the best the morning market has to offer, and it is nearly always better to trust him and take what he has provided. Besides it means extra trouble for him to cook the dishes which are named on the *à la carte* list. So it is but fair that they have to be dearly bought.

Cookery in Périgord is done with lard or walnut oil, further south with olive oil, and everywhere with garlic. Those who do not like garlic can ask for it to be left out; but it must be said that the best cooks use it with discretion, almost imperceptibly.

French cookery, and especially that of the south, is good because it is done in small quantities, with endless patience and attention to detail. That is why it is so rarely first-class in large restaurants. The traveller will find himself astonished at the meals he will eat in little inns, and tiny cafés—if luck guides him. There is no intrinsic connection between price and quality, either. I lived for a month in a village farm-hotel, with only one bedroom, where I ate the same food as the family of proprietors. The food was better than that of the London Ritz; but then Madame Delpeyrat cooked it slowly, in three iron pots, over a handful of wood fire on an open hearth.

Wine is a subject which a woman will always approach with trepidation. British wine-lovers, too, are trained to prefer dry wines; and it must be said at once that the wine of this region is usually sweet. But it is very good. No need to dwell on the great clarets, on the vineyards whose gates bear their lovely names, Château Yquem, Château Margaux, Haut Brion, and the rest of the roll-call second only to that of the Côte d'Or of Burgundy. All the hotels have some bottles of those names in their cellars, and the traveller can order them at will. The best-known vineyards are those of the Gironde, outside our country. All the same, the rivers can boast some that compare with all but the greatest. St-Emilion stands on its hill-top, besieged with vineyards tended like flower-gardens. Its red wines are excellent. Bergerac has been a wine-city for centuries. Near to it is Monbazillac, where a fine castle houses the 'crus' of sweet and perfumed white wine. Cahors exported its heady red wine to imperial Rome. There is a red sandstone valley between Rodez and Conques where a delicious wine is pressed from the 'pineau', the grape which is rarely cultivated outside Burgundy.

This is a country where everybody, rich or poor, grows grapes. There is hardly a house in village or country which has not a vine trained above its door, or a corner of land devoted to stocks and trellises. In the gorges, the vineyards are pitched so steeply that gatherers may have to hitch themselves to a stake by a rope in order to balance while they work. Most of the wine is grown in such small quantities that it is not sent away; it is grown for the people to drink locally. But that does not mean that it is poor stuff, just the contrary. A population to which wine is as natural a part of daily fare as bread, whose very babies of two years old are already drinking wine and water, 'eau rougie', at dinner, is a population of connoisseurs. The hotel-keeper offers, as *vin ordinaire*, the wine he grows himself to drink himself; he is not likely to ruin his custom by offering

An eye-catching and mouth-watering display in a *boucherie/charcuterie* in Uzerche.

bad wine. Some of the local wines, the 'little hillside wines' as they are called, might be famous if they were heavy enough to travel; they are delicate and fine.

The traveller need not fear that if he takes the *vin ordinaire* of the menu he will meet that awful bitter red ink for which the hotels of the non-wine-growing provinces charge so dearly. But this does not mean that he should sojourn in the heart of wine-culture and refrain from tasting the best. He should make a ceremony of drinking some of the great wines; the host of his hotel will advise him as to the best vintage in his cellar, and tell him the right wine to drink with the meal he has ordered.

Above all, we must realize that eating here is both a pleasure and a serious art. Meals are impossible to accelerate; one does

181

not hurry ritual. The average time of a restaurant meal is a couple of hours, from entry to departure. And why not? *Déjeuner* precedes the siesta, and business will not begin again till two-thirty at the earliest. The longest repasts are sometimes the most enjoyable. For instance, nothing is more typical than the midday dinner at the inn of any little town on market-day. The proprietors are in from all the country round. They have been standing and conversing about their produce with possible buyers for three hours. This is the truce in the campaign. They crowd in, mostly men and a few women. The men all wear their best berets, the big ones, worn pulled over one eye. They sit at the long tables on benches as close as they can squeeze. The courses arrive very slowly, for the maids of the inn have to do six women's work each on this occasion of the 'foire'. But how good is the food, and how huge the helpings, when they come! The conversation is mostly in the patois, and roars incomprehensibly like the sea. But the farmer opposite you, full of curiosity and courtesy, has long found out that you are not merely a stranger from the north of France, but a foreigner from overseas. He will tell you kindly about local matters, about the crops, about the weather, and as the bottles of red wine empty and are renewed, about what he thinks of the government and the world situation, and finally about life and the world to come. It is immensely instructive, and the greatest fun.

Dinner fills the evening from seven-thirty to nine o'clock. The hotels do not have sitting-rooms, apart from the restaurant. But they all have 'terrasses', where the guests sit and drink their coffee and liqueurs. The host and his wife, in the hospitable way of the country, come round and sit for a little while with each party. Now is the time, in the cool darkness, to find out what would be the best thing to do next day. Now is the time to learn, if one is interested without being nosey-parkerish, the character of this town. Then we go for a stroll, to see the moonlight on the castle walls; to listen to the ripple of the river lapping on the piers of the bridge. And so to bed.

Left: The church and rooftops of the wine town of St-Emilion.

CHAPTER SEVENTEEN

ENVOI

Traveller, I have come to the end of what I have to tell you. I have described this country as it is seen by a stranger, so that I have tried to choose these aspects that will interest a novice like myself. In the later chapters I have written some explanation of the nature of the region and its history, as it has made the present way of life of the people. Of course, these comments are slight, but they are of a sort not usually included in guide-books, and may be helpful to those who fail to read the rather inaccessible regional literature. I have reported conversations that seem to me to throw light on their subjects; in all cases they are authentic. And I have used some French words, not out of affectation, but deliberately, because they may be useful to some who are not especially fluent in the language.

The fairy-tales often begin with the Youngest Son of three, who sets out to seek his fortune. He does a kindness to an old woman by the roadside, and she offers him three wishes. If he chooses wisely, as the Youngest Son always does, he will conquer the giant, outwit the witch, and marry the Princess.

The three wishes of this book are the Dordogne, the Lot, and the Tarn, three rivers. The Dordogne has the Lascaux caves, the castles on its banks, the abbeys of Carennac and Souillac and Beaulieu. The Lot has the Pont Valentré and Bonaguil, the gorges and the abbey of Conques. The Tarn has the gorges, the high causses, the cathedral of Albi and the cloister of Moissac.

The Dordogne is a romantic river. The Lot is a magical river. The Tarn is a breath-taking river. Oh, happy Traveller, you have the choice of three.

The tree-lined banks of the Lot between Entraygues and Vieillevie.

CHAPTER EIGHTEEN

A GUIDE FOR THE MODERN TRAVELLER

In this guide I suggest, chapter by chapter, how the areas covered in Freda White's text can be combined to create a series of tours easily possible within two weeks.

In each case I have advised the most direct, and in most cases the quickest, route to the target area in order to allow the maximum amount of time to explore it. In many cases a more enjoyable, but much slower, journey can be made by avoiding the motorways and N roads and using the roads marked in yellow or white on the Michelin maps.

CHAPTER TWO
Northern Approaches

Chapter two provides a complete tour which could keep you well occupied for a couple of weeks. If you are particularly energetic this region could be combined with either the lower Dordogne, from where a different return route could be taken along the A10, or with Martel, Collonges and Turenne in the middle Dordogne.

The most direct route to this region from Paris is along the A10 Autoroute to Orléans and then the A71 to Salbris. From here the N20 leads to Limoges and Uzerche.

At Uzerche, the Hôtel Robert Tessier nestles beside the bridge over the River Vézère. The accommodation is modest,

but the hotel is attractive and comfortable, and it has a good restaurant.

At Brantôme is the Grand Hôtel Moderne et Chabrol. It is in an attractive setting beside the river, which many of the bedroom balconies and the restaurant overlook. The cuisine is stylish and imaginative. A particularly satisfying dish there is the terrine of cod studded with scallops and black mushrooms and served with a shellfish sauce.

Le Moulin de l'Abbaye is a very comfortable hotel set in an old mill beside the stone bridge near the abbey of Brantôme. A terrace and garden overlook the weir; the location and atmosphere are idyllic.

The Hôtel les Griffons in Bourdeilles looked equally enticing. It too overlooks the river close to the medieval bridge. The menu contained a good selection of regional specialities.

Ségur-le-Château is a small village with considerable charm which is worth including in your itinerary. It is a few kilometres to the north-west of Arnac Pompadour. Hidden away in a quiet valley, the village consists of a collection of curious turreted houses dating from the Middle Ages. The River Auvézère runs through the centre and an ancient watermill still grinds wheat beside the old stone bridge.

Near here is Coussac-Bonneval, a quiet unassuming village with a fourteenth-century château. There is an attractive old inn, the Hôtel des Voyageurs, which offers quite simple but

The Château de la Treyne, on the banks of the Dordogne to the west of Souillac, is now an atmospheric and luxurious hotel.

comfortable accommodation. Some of the bedrooms have french windows which open onto a small garden with views of the château. The restaurant has a good atmosphere and is popular with local people, doubtless because of a menu which includes dishes like *fricassée de cèpes a l'ail* and home-made *grattons de canard*.

Menus in this region tend to feature two ingredients which have much in common: the walnut and the truffle. Walnut oil is used to create a distinctive salad dressing, and the nut itself is crumbled over a green salad, sometimes with nuggets of Roquefort cheese, to create a refreshingly different flavour. Walnut bread is also a popular item in many *boulangeries*; it makes an ideal accompaniment to the cheese course and is delicious with the local honey for breakfast.

The truffle is a rather more exotic, and expensive, item on the menu. A celebrated extravagance is a large black truffle baked inside a brioche crust with a slab of *foie gras*; this is a speciality at the Hôtel l'Esplanade in Domme. Small slivers of truffle can be used more modestly to speckle a *pâté de foie gras*; and small pieces are used to give a uniquely subtle flavour to a creamy omelette. It is also an essential ingredient in sauce Périgueux, a lightly thickened combination of truffle slices, shallots, cognac, white wine and stock.

CHAPTER THREE
The Lower Dordogne

Chapter three provides a tour which will be particularly appealing to wine lovers. The vineyards of St-Emilion, Fronsac and Pomerol include some of the greatest names in red wines, and the more easterly wine-growing areas of Castillon and Bergerac produce wines of excellent value.

The Bergerac wine route is particularly enjoyable. You will find it clearly signposted from the D933 after crossing the bridge towards Marmande. Quiet country lanes meander through the best of the vineyards as well as many of the places mentioned by FW, such as the Château de Monbazillac and St-Michel-de-Montaigne. Do not miss the endearing little fourteenth-century château at Gageac, and that of Montpeyroux, set on a wooded hill.

The most direct route to the western limit of this region is to follow the A10 Autoroute from Paris. It is an attractive road and seldom crowded once the Loire valley has been left behind. If you leave at Exit 30, just to the north of Bordeaux, only a short drive along the D670 to Libourne remains.

The Hostellerie de la Plaisance in St-Emilion is highly recommended. It is set on a natural terrace above the rust-brown tiled rooftops of the medieval town, and has a wonderful outlook. It has only twelve rooms, so advance booking is advisable.

In the wine village of Saussignac is a pleasant, unpretentious hotel with a good restaurant, called the Relais de Saussignac.

Unless you intend to spend a great deal of time touring the vineyards you could extend your travels a little further afield to fill a two-week holiday. An ideal combination would be the tour of the bastides described in Chapter four.

An excellent wine, to be found on many lists in this area but quite uncommon outside France, is Pécharmant, a full-bodied red from the north-east of Bergerac. The sweet white Monbazillac is another famous wine of the region; lightly chilled, it is the perfect companion to a slice of *foie gras*.

CHAPTER FOUR
The Middle Dordogne

This region could easily fill a two-week holiday. Indeed, for those who like to laze a little, and with the river such a temptation to do so, it might be too much.

Although it is a relatively small area, there is a tangle of small lanes leading away from the meandering river to explore. There are also many picturesque villages and dramatically sited châteaux to visit.

The most direct route to this area from Paris is to go to Uzerche (see under Chapter two above) and then continue south along the N20 through Brive-la-Gaillarde to Souillac.

This part of the Dordogne can suffer from being *too* popular, particularly with English visitors, and in the summer months the riverside roads and small villages can become crowded. This region of the Dordogne has also become rather 'gentrified', with old farmhouses and manors ruthlessly renovated and many of the villages and towns possessing the atmosphere of a resort—albeit a stylish one. Out of season, however, it is a delight.

The Hôtel l'Esplanade in Domme is set on the edge of the steep hill from which one can survey the River Dordogne. Many of the rooms have river views and the sunrise is worth setting your alarm clock to see.

The restaurant has a Michelin rosette, and the food is indeed excellent. Feuilleté de *cèpes à la sauce périgueux* is one of the specialities: pieces of the meaty wild fungi sautéed, enfolded in feather-light pastry and served in a truffle-flavoured sauce.

The village has a lively country market on Wednesdays, held in the square beside the old market hall. Ducks and geese, bred primarily for their fattened livers, are a dominant feature of the cuisine in this region. Indeed the main street of Domme is lined with shops selling the numerous regional specialities which are based on their produce.

A block of *foie gras* is the king of the menu here. A less costly but very delicious product is *délice*, or *pâté de foie gras*, in which the liver is combined with a rich smooth pâté.

Grattons d'oie and *de canard* are also pâtés, made in a similar way to pork *rillettes*: the shredded meat of slowly roasted duck or goose is combined with the fat produced in cooking.

Boneless duck breasts are served as *magrets de canard*, often lightly sautéed and served with a variety of sauces. The legs of geese and duck are cooked and preserved in their own fat to produce *confits d'oie* or *de canard*. These are quickly grilled or roasted to produce a crisp golden skin with soft flesh inside.

Cou d'oie or *de canard* is a superb dish in which the duck or

A quiet corner in the small, fortified village of Loubressac near Autoire.

goose neck is filled with well-seasoned chopped meat and studded with pieces of *foie gras*. It can be served cold like a pâté, sometimes hot with sauce Périgueux or sliced thinly and sautéed as part of a *salade tiède*.

Another hotel worth recommending is the Hôtel du Pont de l'Ouysse. It is set in a charming country house in a peaceful spot beside the small river. The rooms are stylishly decorated and furnished and the cuisine is of a high standard.

Nearby is the Château de la Treyne mentioned by FW. It is now a hotel in a dreamily romantic setting high on the banks of the Dordogne and surrounded by a wooded park. It is hard to imagine a more pleasurable and evocative place to stay. It is magnificently furnished and decorated, and the comfort and service border on the luxurious.

On warm summer evenings dinner is served on a terrace overlooking the river; on other occasions in the superb Louis XIII drawing-room with a log fire flickering in the monumental fireplace and the tables lit by silver candelabra.

A few kilometres upstream, in the medieval village of Gluges, is the Hôtel les Falaises. This is a warm, friendly, family-run hotel with comfortable rooms and a good restaurant.

To the north of Monpazier is Montferrand-du-Périgord, an enchanting little medieval village. It is virtually a single street, lined with ancient houses, climbing steeply from the valley of the River Couze. At the top of the hill is a covered market and a château with a terrace from which there are splendid views of the valley.

Near Autoire is Loubressac, an attractive small fortified village set on a dominant hilltop. It has a château, streets of old houses decked with flowers, a great deal of charm and fine views.

A good place to stay in Collonges-la-Rouge is the Hostellerie Relais St Jacques de Compostelle. It occupies one of the distinctive red stone buildings in the centre of the village. The accommodation is modest but comfortable, and the restaurant provided a very enjoyable meal with *rillettes d'oie*, followed by *quenelles de brochet* and *lapereaux à la moutarde*.

I wonder whether FW would approve of the rather rigorous renovation to which her favourite place, Martel, was being subjected during my visit. It is, I am sure, necessary for reasons of preservation, but somehow it leaves a small town like Martel rather different from the place it was before.

CHAPTER FIVE
The Upper Dordogne

Chapter five can easily provide a full two weeks' touring, although a very satisfying fortnight could be spent in the Auvergne alone. It is also worth considering combining the Auvergne with the Tarn, since the drive from St-Flour to Millau or Mende is both easy and enjoyable.

The most direct route to this region is to take the road to Salbris (see under Chapter two above) and from there the D944 to Bourges and the N144 to Montluçon and Clermont-Ferrand.

In Besse-en-Chandesse is the Hostellerie du Beffroi, one of the Logis et Auberges de France network. At this nice old-fashioned hotel the cuisine was correspondingly homely and unpretentious. The *pâté de foie d'oie* was accompanied by hunks of country bread, a brick of hand-moulded yellow butter and an earthenware crock of crunchy gherkins.

Orcival is a small village to the north of le Mont-Dore and well worth adding to your itinerary. It is set in a lovely wooded valley and possesses one of the finest Romanesque churches in the Auvergne style. Nearby is the thirteenth- to sixteenth-century Château de Cordès, surrounded by landscaped gardens.

Salers is one of the most picturesque and unusual villages in France, its cobbled streets lined with ancient turreted houses and entered by fortified gateways, all built of a sombre grey stone. It also has a wonderful setting on the edge of a high plateau overlooking a deep valley.

One hotel worthy of recommendation is the Hostellerie de la Maronne. An elegant nineteenth-century country house in a peaceful setting down in the valley, it is close to le Theil on the road to St-Martin-Valmeroux. It also has a heated swimming pool, making it an ideal place to linger for a while.

The cuisine of this region has a number of quite unique dishes. *Pounti* is a cross between a soufflé and a savoury bread pudding, made with chopped ham, eggs, cream and various green vegetables. It is sometimes studded with prunes—*pounti aux pruneaux*. *Truffade* or *aligot* is a similarly filling dish made with freshly made cheese and puréed potatoes. *Aligot* is in fact the name for a pressed curd cheese which keeps only for a short time.

The region is renowned for its cheeses. Fourme d'Ambert and Bleu d'Auvergne, both blue cheeses, Cantal, a firm cheese with a nutty flavour, Salers, similar but harder with a stronger taste, and the creamy St-Nectaire are widely available. In addition to the *vin du pays* of the Côtes d'Auvergne, the VDQS wines of neighbouring St-Pourçain-sur-Sioule are worth looking out for.

------CHAPTER SIX------
The Lot

Chapters six and seven could be combined for a fairly energetic two-week tour. Alternatively the River Lot from Villeneuve-sur-Lot to Cahors could be combined with Albi and Moissac. Another variation would be to combine the Lot between Cahors and Figeac with the region around Cordes described in Chapter nine, or with the Rouergue uplands.

In the medieval hilltop village of Pujols is the Hôtel des Chênes. Its adjoining restaurant, la Toque Blanche, has been awarded a Michelin star. Near Montcabrier and just six kilometres from the Château de Bonaguil is an unusual hotel, le Relais de la Dolce. It is set deep in the woods and consists of a series of luxurious single-storey chalets. A short walk along a footpath leads to an atmospheric restaurant set in an ancient Quercynois farmhouse.

A breathtaking view of the château can be had by taking a small road a kilometre or so to the south. It leads east through woods up on to the hillside overlooking the castle and valley.

At Puy l'Evêque there is a simple but comfortable hotel, the Bellevue. Aptly named, it is set atop the steeply stacked village with impressive views of the Lot from its bedroom balconies and the restaurant.

A regional speciality, *tourtière*, is served here. It is the ultimate apple tart, in which a pastry base is covered with apple purée spiked with rum and then piled high with pinnacles of paper-thin pastry baked brown and dusted with cinnamon and nutmeg.

There is also a wonderful view of the River Lot from the old town of Luzech, set in a tight loop in the river's course. A small track leads from the town centre to the summit of steep conical hill known as l'Impernal. The sweeping views of the winding river and its vineyard-patterned banks extend for miles.

At St-Cirq-Lapopie is the Hôtel de la Pélissaria. It is quite enchanting. Set in a fifteenth-century house at the foot of the village, it has been sensitively, and very tastefully, restored and decorated. The rooms descend in a series of levels with bedrooms on the ground floor. Some have french windows which open onto a small garden with superb views of the village and the Lot curving below a sheer cliff. There are only six rooms and dinner is served in a charming dining room with easy chairs and a piano in one corner – François Matuchet, the *patron*, is a singer of some repute.

Near here on the road to Cabrerets is the Hôtel Pescalerie, delightfully situated in a sixteenth-century manor house on the banks of the Lot.

The deep-red wines of Cahors were once more popular in Britain than those from Bordeaux. The best wines come from the lower Lot valley between Fumel and Cahors. Near Parnac is the *cave coopérative* of the Côtes d'Olt, where the local wines can be tasted and bought.

The small round goats' cheeses called *cabécous* go well with Cahors wines. They are often sprinkled with herbs, flashed

under the grill and served on a bed of salad leaves dressed with walnut oil.

CHAPTER SEVEN

The Upper Lot

If your intention is to follow the course of the Lot, then Chapter seven provides a route which, discounting extended stays, would take only a few days.

The region beyond Mende fits more neatly with a tour of the Tarn. The drive from the source of the Lot, near le Bleymard, over Mont Lozère to le Pont-de-Montvert is exhilarating, with dramatic and extensive views all along the way.

Between Decazeville and St-Geniez d'Olt the Lot runs through a beautiful and unspoiled region which would be worth exploring more fully. This could be made into a neat and interest-packed round trip by combining it with the Rouergue uplands, perhaps using Figeac as a starting point.

The most direct route to Figeac is to follow the route to Brive-la-Gaillarde (see under Chapter four) and then continue south-east along the N140.

Estaing is one of the prettiest riverside villages in France. The simple but pleasant hotel, Aux Armes d'Estaing, faces the river close to the old stone bridge. The menu here contains a good selection of regional dishes such as *cou d'oie farci* and *tripou*. The latter is a fat round sausage made from tripe and served braised in a sauce. Unlike the rather resilient *andouillettes* found in other regions, *tripou* has a quite soft and tender texture. An interesting cheese to look out for is Tomme Blanche; it is like a small, thick Brie but with a firm texture and tangy flavour.

There are some interesting wines in this region. Vineyards are to be found on the steep hillsides around Estaing and Entraygues, which both have their own *appellations*. To the south-west the wines of Marcillac are similar in character to Beaujolais, but made from the Mansoi grape instead of the

Gamay. They can be tasted and bought at the *coopérative* near Valady on the N140 or from the individual makers who advertise along the roadside.

Near here, set in a lovely wooded valley, is the ancient bastide of Villecomtal, with a well-preserved fortified gateway and old houses. A few kilometres to the south is the pretty little village of Muret-le-Château, with the remains of a castle set on a spur of rock above the houses and near by a grotto and waterfall.

To the west of St-Geniez d'Olt is the particularly pretty small village of Ste-Eulalie d'Olt. It is set on the banks of the Lot and surrounded by peaceful meadows. There are many fine old houses from the sixteenth and seventeenth centuries along its narrow streets and a lovely fifteenth-century château. It is popular with anglers, and there are good places to swim in the

Above: An old village house next to the château in Ste-Eulalie d'Olt, in the upper valley of the Lot.

Opposite: Looking down to the Lot over the rooftops of St-Cirq-Lapopie.

Opposite: The main square and arcades of the bastide of Sauveterre-de-Rouergue.

river. It is also a convenient place from which to travel up into the Monts d'Aubrac.

The old town of St-Côme d'Olt has a delightful setting on the Lot and a fine old stone bridge. Within the ring of houses which marks the site of the old walls there remain a small château and numerous ancient houses, together with a fortified gateway.

CHAPTER EIGHT
Rouerge Uplands

The three towns described in this chapter could easily be combined with the tour outlined in the previous chapter. Indeed visits to Rodez and Villefranche would make an enjoyable change from the other, more rural, attractions of the region and provide alternative interest on days when the weather is poor.

The Hôtel Ste-Foy, in Conques, is in the centre of the village, just across the steep, narrow main street from the imposing abbey after which it is named. It is very comfortable but the rooms tend to be rather small. On summer evenings, dinner is served outside on a delightful patio.

From the D901, just south of Conques, a small road leads up to the Site du Bancarel, from where there is a wonderful view of the village and its spectacular setting.

Villefranche-de-Rouergue is a particularly attractive old town and a tempting place to shop for a picnic, with excellent *charcuteries* and *pâtisseries* offering local specialities.

FW does not mention Sauveterre-de-Rouergue. It would be a pity to miss this very attractive and well-preserved bastide which is nearly as good as Monpazier. It is near Naucelle on the D997, about 20km south-west of Rodez.

It was founded in 1281 by Guillaume de Mâcon, the Seneschal of Rouergue. In the centre of its network of tiny streets is a broad square, lined by tunnel-like stone arcades and many beautiful old houses. The fourteenth-century collegiate church contains choir stalls and a retable dating from the sixteenth and seventeenth centuries. There are numerous small shops, including a good *charcuterie*.

A few kilometres to the south-east is the Château de Castelpers, an atmospheric and unusual place to stay. It dates from the fifteenth century and is a curious mixture of architectural styles. The château overlooks a lovely park shaded by ancient towering trees, and there is a trout river rippling through the grounds. It is in the midst of an especially attractive region known as the 'country of a hundred valleys'.

Many of the bedrooms have four-poster beds, and the dining-room is very unusual. It is a magnificent room with a lofty barrel-vaulted ceiling and a massive carved wooden fireplace. The château is filled with beautiful antique furniture and *objets d'art*.

A delicious regional speciality is *caille à la ségalaise*, quail stuffed with *foie gras*. The cheese board includes local products such as Taurinol and Laguiole.

There are two châteaux nearby worth visiting: the Renaissance Château de Taurines and the twelfth-century Château du Bosc, one of the childhood homes of Toulouse-Lautrec, which contains many mementoes of the painter's life.

CHAPTER NINE
The Tarn

The places described in this chapter can provide more than enough interest for a two-week tour. Indeed if you want to enjoy the Tarn to the full, perhaps go walking, canoeing or just swimming and sunbathing on its banks, it might be more practical to leave Najac, Cordes, Penne, Albi and Moissac for another occasion. For those actively inclined there are several places in this region where you can hire mountain bikes.

The quickest route to the Tarn gorges is to take the A6 Autoroute from Paris to Lyon and then the A47 to St-Etienne. From here the N88 leads south-west to Mende.

Above: The Tarn gorges near the Cirque des Baumes.

Opposite: The village of le Rozier, at the junction of the Tarn and Jonte gorges.

If at Lyon you continue along the A7 to Bollène and follow the D994 west to Pont St-Esprit, you would be able to travel through the gorges of the Ardèche to Ruoms and Villefort, crossing the Col des Tribes from the east down to le Bleymard.

Albi and Moissac are in fact some distance from the Tarn gorges and could perhaps more easily be visited in conjunction with a tour based on the Lot valley or the Rouergue uplands.

One of the most appealing places to stay in the Tarn gorges is the Château de la Caze—if only for one night. It is the perfect dream castle, with turrets and towers, flagged floors, great stone staircases and windows that seem like small tunnels in the massive walls. It is set beside the silvery Tarn and the sheer cliffs of the gorge rise up on each side.

Dinner here was excellent. The presentation and style are clearly influenced by *nouvelle cuisine*, but the roots are firmly traditional: a combination which has earned a Michelin star. On warm summer evenings dinner is served on the terrace overlooking the river.

Lower down the gorges, at le Rozier, is the Grand Hôtel Muse et Rozier. This hotel is aggressively modern in design but very comfortable. It is set on the river bank, and lawns reach down to the water's edge, where you can watch big brown trout basking in the clear sparkling water. The swimming is superb, and canoes are also available.

At the other end of the scale, further down-stream opposite the bridge at les Vignes, is the small family Hôtel Gévaudan. Although simple, it is comfortable with a warm and friendly atmosphere. Good traditional French cuisine, such as roast quail and *lapereau à la moutarde*, is served in the restaurant, which has a shaded terrace overlooking the river.

There is a particularly good view of the Tarn gorges from le Roc des Hourtous. It can be found by taking the small road from les Vignes which climbs up on to the Causse Méjean. At the hamlet of Rieisse a small unmade road leads out to the edge of the gorge.

Another quite different, but very enjoyable, little hotel is the Hôtel du Midi in St-Jean-du-Bruel. It has a good restaurant with a terrace overlooking a small river. The specialities here include *confit de canard aux cèpes de bois* and *filet de sandre en papillote*. This hotel tends to be very popular and it is advisable to book during the summer months.

The Grand Hôtel du Parc at Florac is a nice old-fashioned sort of hotel of a type which, sadly, is beginning to disappear in France – spacious rooms with lofty ceilings, massive oak furniture, huge beds with fat mattresses and good unpretentious food at reasonable prices.

The Hôtel Rennaissance in Meyrueis is another with a similar atmosphere of faded grandeur. It is furnished with antiques and the restaurant offers a variety of regional specialities.

On the outskirts of Meyrueis on a wooded hillside is the Château d'Ayres, a comfortable hotel set in what was once a Benedictine monastery dating from the twelfth century.

There is also the Hôtel du Pont at Ambialet, a member of the Logis et Auberges de France chain. Although quite simple, it was comfortable. My room had a view of the river and the hilltop church. Dinner was enjoyable, if not outstanding, and the menu offered a number of regional dishes.

An excellent hotel is to be found in the village of Salles-Curan. The Hostellerie de Levézou is set in a fifteenth-century château, once the summer residence of the Bishops of Rodez. It has an attractive and atmospheric restaurant where the cuisine has earned a Michelin star with dishes like *riz d'agneau aux poireaux frits*, lambs' sweetbreads with leeks, and *feuilleté d'escargots à la fondue de tomates*, snails in pastry with a tomato purée.

A speciality of the causses which is worth looking out for is *pouteilles*, a robust, slow-cooked stew of pigs' trotters, beef and potatoes.

FW describes la Couvertoirade as emptying fast. If you visit early or late in the year this impression still prevails. In the summer months, however, it is a popular place for visitors; there are several small shops and craft workshops, and an audio-visual presentation which describes the history of the village is given in one of the old buildings .

Najac has two good hotels, the Oustal de Barry, which overlooks the village square, and the Hôtel Bel Rive, situated down in the valley beside the River Aveyron. A speciality here is *l'astet najaçoise*, fillet of pork stuffed with parsley, garlic and butter and baked in its own juices. The wines in this region are those of Gaillac. They are predominantly red, but there is also a good dry white called Gaillac Perlé.

Cordes is particularly well served with hotels, but it is an extremely popular village and it is advisable to book in advance during the peak season. The Hôtel le Grand Ecuyer deserves special mention. It is set in a listed historic building on the steeply sloping main street close to the fortified east gate. The house was once the hunting residence of Raymond VII, the Count of Toulouse. The interior is richly decorated and furnished with fine antiques; many of the bedrooms have

four-poster beds. The restaurant is renowned and chef Yves Thurie's menu is a pleasure to ponder.

To the south of Bruniquel, on the southern edge of the forest of the Grésigne, are two villages of interest in addition to those described by FW. Puycelci is a fortified hilltop town which dominates the valley of the Vère. Inside its tangle of narrow streets are numerous houses dating from the fourteenth and fifteenth centuries and a good Gothic church.

A short drive to the south-east is Castelnau de Montmiral, a bastide built in the thirteenth century. There are remains of its ramparts and gateways, picturesque old streets and a very pretty restored square surrounded by arcades and timber-framed houses. The Gothic church contains a Byzantine cross studded with precious stones.

MICHAEL BUSSELLE

Above: Stone arcades and old timbered houses surround the small square in the bastide of Castlenau-de-Montmiral.

Right: A view of the Tarn gorges from the Roc des Hourtous on the Causse Méjean.

PRACTICAL ADVICE

Opening times

This is the place for a few general remarks on the opening times of châteaux, museums and caves given in the notes to the text. Hours of opening are generally ten o'clock to twelve o'clock and two to five. In July and August these may be extended by an hour or two at both ends, and the most popular sites may even stay open during the sacred hours of lunchtime. It is wise to arrive at least an hour before closing, in case there are only guided tours. Some of the more celebrated prehistoric sites set a daily limit on the number of visitors in July and August, when it is advisable to buy tickets early in the day. The details of such arrangements, given in the notes, were as accurate as possible and up-to-date when this book went to press; however no guide-book is infallible, and opening times are always subject to change. The only way to be absolutely sure is to check with the local Syndicat d'Initiative or Office de Tourisme.

Churches are normally open during the day. This is not always so, however, and you may have to hunt for the key. The house or farm next door, the Mairie, the priest's house (*le presbytère*) or the nearest café are the places to try. In larger churches you may have to pay to visit the treasure, cloister, choir or crypt, any or all of which may be shut at lunchtime.

Maps

The standard maps are the Michelin 1:200,000 (yellow) series, clear, reliable and adequate for most purposes. The *Michelin Motoring Atlas of France* (Paul Hamlyn), covering the whole of France at this scale, is both practical and very good value. The IGN 1:100,000 (green) series, with contours and twice as much detail, is excellent for walkers and cyclists. Walkers are now well catered for in France, with a network of 30,000 kilometres of *sentiers de grande randonnée* (long distance footpaths, known as GRs), each with its own *Topo-Guide*, a small paperback guide containing maps and other information. The address to write to for information about these is given in the 'Addresses' section. Town plans are nearly always available free of charge from the local Syndicat d'Initiative or Office de Tourisme.

Syndicats d'Initiative and Offices de Tourisme

Wherever you may be in France, these are by far the most important and reliable source of practical local information. There is one in every town and many villages, and they are always well signposted. Go there for information on places to visit and opening times, hotels, restaurants and local specialities, festivals and special events. Bear in mind, however, that Syndicats d'Initiative are themselves not immune to lunchtime closing, and that the smaller ones may close altogether in winter, when their functions are taken over by the local Mairie.

As there are so many Syndicats d'Initiative and Offices de Tourisme it is not possible to list them all here; their details are available, if you need them in advance, from the Comité Departemental de Tourisme for each *département*, addresses of which are given below.

Addresses

Comités Départementaux de Tourisme:

Aveyron
33 avenue Victor Hugo, 12000 Rodez. tel: 65 68 11 43.
Cantal and Auvergne
19 rue de Parc, B.P. 113, 03204 Vichy Cedex. tel: 70 98 71 94.
Corrèze
quai Baluze, 19000 Tulle. tel: 55 26 46 88.
Dordogne
16 rue Wilson, 24009 Périgueux Cedex. tel: 53 53 44 35.
Limousin
boulevard de Fleurus, 87000 Limoges. tel: 55 34 46 87.
Lot
107 quai Cavaignac, B.P. 79, 46002 Cahors. tel: 65 35 07 09.
Lozère and Gorges du Tarn
place Urbain V, 48000 Mende. tel: 66 65 34 55.
Tarn
4 rue A. Malraux, 81000 Albi, tel: 63 41 02 44.

Loisirs-acceuil centres at the above addresses will be able to give information on caving, canoeing, cycling, camping, horseriding, fishing, walking, etc. in each area. The following addresses are of national organizations which may also be useful:

French Government Tourist Office
178 Piccadilly
London W1
tel: 01 491 7622 (administration and urgent enquiries)
or 01 499 6911 (recorded information)

Comité National des Sentiers de Grande Randonnée
92 rue de Clignancourt
75883 Paris Cedex 18
tel. 12 59 60 40

BIBLIOGRAPHY

A visit to any good bookshop or library will reveal the number of books now available to anyone wanting to read up on this part of France. This is a small selection. Asterisks indicate books included by Freda White in her original bibliography.

Richard Barber *The Companion Guide to South-West France* (Collins 1977)

James Bentley *A Guide to the Dordogne* (Penguin 1986)

James Bentley *Life and Food in the Dordogne* (Weidenfeld & Nicolson 1986)

James Bentley and Charlie Waite *Languedoc* (George Philip 1987)

Stephen Brook and Charlie Waite *The Dordogne* (George Philip 1986)

Jean Carrière and Philippe Joutard *Les Cévennes* (Autrement Editions 1988; French text)

*J.-J Escande *Histoire du Périgord* (Laffitte Reprints 1980; French text)

Fiona Fennell *Travels in the Dordogne* (Merehurst Press 1987)

*Jean Fourgous *A Travers le Lot* (Imprimerie Tardy Quercy 1980; French text)

France on Backroads (Pan 1986)

*Froissart *Chronicles* (Everyman)

Rob Hunter *Walking in France* (Oxford Illustrated Press 1982)

Logis et Auberges de France (published annually; French text)

Helen Martin *Le Lot* (Columbus Books 1988)

Claude Michelet and Anne-Marie Cocula *Le Périgord Noir* (Autrement Editions 1988; French text)

Michelin Green Guides:
Auvergne (1986; French text)
Berry Limousin (1987; French text)
Dordogne: Périgord-Quercy (1987; English text)
Gorges du Tarn: Cévennes-Bas Languedoc (1986; French text)
Pyrénées Roussillon Albigeois (1986; French text)

Jean Roques *Guide du Tarn* (Collection Rives du Temps 1981)

Les Routiers Guide to France (Macdonald Orbis; published annually)

M. Ruspoli *The Caves of Lascaux* (Thames & Hudson 1987)

Andrew Sanger *Exploring Rural France* (Christopher Helm 1988)

*Jean Secret *Le Périgord: Châteaux, manoirs et gentilhommières* (Tallandier 1966)

*Robert Louis Stevenson *Travels with a Donkey in the Cévennes* (Dent)

*Katharine Woods *The Other Château Country* (Bodley Head 1931)

INDEX

—ACKNOWLEDGEMENTS—

Many French people helped me to write this book, giving me kindness and information. So many that I cannot name them all here. I owe, however, an especial debt of gratitude to M. Géraud-Lavergne and M. Jean Secret of Périgueux, and to M. Henri de Chalup of Brive, for their generosity in sharing their great learning with a novice.

My thanks are due to Messrs. Jonathan Cape and the Society of Authors for permission to quote a verse of A. E. Housman's poetry. I am grateful, too, to Mr. Bernard Palmer for his beautiful drawing of the map.

Freda White, 1952